Beauty Industry

Dive into a complex and dynamic study of the beauty industry through this compelling volume that examines the intersection of gender, media, and everyday life. This book provides a multifaceted look at how beauty practices and perceptions are shaped and perpetuated today. This book is a must-read for anyone interested in understanding how beauty today is constructed, consumed, and contested, offering critical insights into the forces that shape our perceptions of self and others.

—***Anita Dremel*, PhD, Associate Professor,**
Department of Sociology, Faculty of Humanities and Social Sciences,
Josip Juraj Strossmayer University of Osijek

Beauty Industry: Gender, Media and Everyday Life is a timely and authoritative contribution to contemporary academic and cultural discourse centered on the beauty industry's impact on our social lives. Rather than defaulting to an easy criticism of the much-maligned industry, this work unpacks the nuances of a field that can at once empower and oppress, holding a delicate balance between constructive critique and celebration. This work, places focus on the complex ways in which identity, media, capitalism, and history intersect and shape the beauty rituals of our everyday lives. The diverse perspectives offered in this edited volume provide vital reflections on the power and impact of the beauty industry in all its manifestations across history, cultures, representations, and practices. A range of rigorous research methods and conceptual frameworks converge to provide a much-needed contemporary update on beauty industry scholarship.

Central to the premise of the volume is a focus on interdisciplinary and intersectional representation that reflects the contemporary cultural context. The collection of authors here illuminates the spaces of the beauty industry that have previously been ignored or underserved in research and cultural discourse demonstrating the ways in which beauty as a practice can transgress and shape our individual and collective ideologies. This edited volume will be significant for scholars, students, as well as industry practitioners looking for meticulously researched frameworks, histories, and material studies. This is an invaluable compendium for our complex post-beauty, late capitalist social context.

—***Vanessa Gerrie*, Massey University, New Zealand**

From makeup, skin care, shampoo to soap, our everyday lives are impacted by the beauty industry. As Dr. Martina Topic noted in her Foreword, "beauty standards and expectations are intertwined with capitalism and gender," but also with race, age, class, and consumerism. This book is essential reading for anyone interested in looking critically at beauty and its impact on society. The interdisciplinary approach used by the editors, themselves representing sociological, cultural, and communication perspectives, allows diverse scholars an opportunity to voice their views on the topic, opening new debates and raising thought-provoking research questions. The book is a fresh and innovative look at beauty for an uncertain, challenging time.

—***Karla K. Gower*, PhD Director,**
Plank Center for Leadership in Public Relations.
Behringer Distinguished Professor, The University of Alabama

WOMEN, ECONOMY AND LABOUR RELATIONS

Series Editor: Martina Topić, The University of Alabama, USA

This series aims to publish monographs and edited collections that tackle the position of women in the economy as well as explore labour relations. By labour relations, it means studying human relations in work in its broadest sense and analysing how labour relations affect social inequality with particular reference to women. In terms of social inequality, this series particularly welcomes analyses of women and class and broader analyses of labour relations. The series will publish perspectives from around the world, and thus the series fits into the understanding of labour relations through both work relations in a Western sense and non-Western forms of labour. The series is also interested in studies of the position of women in worker's unions, the stance on women's affairs within workers' unions and the position of women and women's affairs in labour movements. Both historical and contemporary perspectives are welcome. Studies in industrial and economic sociology are particularly welcome.

The book series aims to publish books from a variety of perspectives, e.g. the series will equally accept both theoretical and empirical perspectives. Also, the book series will accept case study perspectives on women working in various industries. We would particularly like to hear from authors who research the position of women in working-class jobs, e.g. factory workers, supermarket workers, etc. Studies on women in feminised industries (e.g. nursing, teaching, PR) and masculine industries (construction, business, finance) are equally welcome. This book series's main aim is to deconstruct women's position in the economy and explore labour relations from a feminist perspective. All feminist perspectives are welcome, which includes liberal feminist perspectives, as well as analyses of the position of women from radical and socialist feminist positions. In the case of the latter, we particularly welcome proposals that tackle the economic system and inequalities with special reference to the position of women. The proposed books should particularly focus on analysing structural problems that bring about inequality, the distinctiveness of women's contributions to the economy, work conditions and masculinities in organisations and wider societies and differences between men and women. Besides, books that tackle economic systems and link this to the position of women are also welcome.

Beauty Industry: Gender, Media and Everyday Life

EDITED BY

MARIJA GEIGER ZEMAN

Institute of Social Sciences Ivo Pilar, Croatia

MICHAL CHMIEL

Royal Holloway, University of London, UK

AND

MIRELA HOLY

VERN' University, Croatia

emerald
PUBLISHING

United Kingdom – North America – Japan – India – Malaysia – China

Emerald Publishing Limited
Emerald Publishing, Floor 5, Northspring, 21-23 Wellington Street, Leeds LS1 4DL

First edition 2025

British Library Cataloguing in Publication Data
A catalogue record for this book is available from the British Library

ISBN: 978-1-83608-941-4 (Print)
ISBN: 978-1-83608-940-7 (Online)
ISBN: 978-1-83608-942-1 (Epub)

Printed and bound by CPI Group (UK) Ltd, Croydon, CR0 4YY

Contents

List of Figure and Tables

Figure

Tables

About the Editors

Marija Geiger Zeman (PhD) is a Senior Research Scientist in Sociology at the Institute of Social Sciences Ivo Pilar in Zagreb (Croatia). Geiger Zeman is the author of many papers and conference presentations focused on gender issues, body issues, ageing issues and media representations. Her empirical work is based on qualitative methodology. In 2010, Geiger Zeman received Annual Science Award by the Croatian Parliament in the field of social sciences.

Mirela Holy (PhD) is a Professor of Ethnology and Comparative Literature. She works at the VERN' University in Zagreb as Head of three graduate studies and one undergraduate study. She has published six books and many articles about environment, human rights and communication. She received Miko Tripalo award for outstanding contribution to the society democratisation and promotion of human rights in 2012.

Michal Chmiel (PhD) is a Senior Lecturer (Associate Professor) in Psychology. He is a former Public Relations practitioner and now researcher and educator. Formerly a BA (Hons) Public Relations Course Leader at London College of Communication (UAL), he is currently a BSc (Hons) Programme Director for Environment and Social Change at Royal Holloway, University of London. Michal's research interests revolve around the role of the impact of Brand PR on attitudes of audiences, with particular focus on the co-creational influence of PR on women's gender portrayal. He has also researched into the mechanism of sharing fake news as well as PR education in the United Kingdom. Michal is a Senior Fellow of the Higher Education Academy and a member of European Public Relations Education and Research Association and Chartered Institute of Public Relations.

About the Contributors

Jacek Barlik, PhD (habil.), is an Assistant Professor at the Faculty of Journalism, Information and Book Science of the University of Warsaw, Poland, where he has been working full time since 2014. He is also a communication and public relations practitioner with over 30 years of experience advising Polish and international corporations, government agencies, public institutions and NGOs. He has authored articles, chapters, papers and two books on public relations, communication strategies, awareness campaigns, crisis communication, social media, sales and persuasion. He was a Fulbright scholar at the University of Maryland at College Park (USA).

Melissa Beattie was awarded a PhD in Theatre, Film and TV Studies from Aberystwyth University and has published several papers relating to television, audience research and identity. She is currently an Assistant Professor of Liberal Arts at Al Akhawayn University in Ifrane, Morocco, and is under contract with Lexington for a book on fictitious countries and Palgrave for a book on Canadian crime dramas. She has previously worked at universities in the United States, Korea, Pakistan, Armenia, Ethiopia and Cambodia.

Nikolina Borčić is an Assistant Professor at the Faculty of Political Science, University of Zagreb. She holds a BA in German and Russian languages and literature from the University of Zagreb. She earned two PhDs: one in Linguistics, focusing on conceptual metaphors and gender in political interviews, and another in Communication Studies, exploring argumentation and non-verbal communication in political performances. Her research focuses on the media portrayal of public figures, examining how public speeches and media discourse shape political and public image in various fields and contexts. In addition to her work on political communication and the image creation of celebrities, she teaches courses and corporate communication, celebrity image management and media language. Borčić has extensive experience in delivering international lectures and contributing to interdisciplinary fields of communication and media studies.

Anne-Mette Hermans is an Assistant Professor in Beauty, Health and Wellbeing at Tranzo, the scientific center for care and wellbeing at Tilburg University. She received her PhD from King's College London in 2019. Her research is largely qualitative in nature and focuses on (consumerist) notions of the malleability of (women's) bodies. Hermans' expertise lies in beauty practices, mainly cosmetic procedures. Her book *Discourses of Perfection*, which explores the normalisation of cosmetic procedures, was published by Routledge in 2021. Hermans is the co-founder and chairwoman of the Cosmetic Procedures Expertise Group. This interdisciplinary group aims to monitor, research and improve the medical cosmetic industry in the Netherlands.

Ioannis Kostopoulos is a Reader in Digital Marketing and the Head of the Digital Marketing and Retailing research group at Liverpool Business School, Liverpool John Moores University. He holds a PhD from Athens University of Economics and Business. Prior to his current position, he has taught Marketing and PR at several universities in the United Kingdom, Greece and Italy and has participated in many consulting and research projects. From 2015 to 2018, he led the very successful Journalism and PR subject group at Leeds Beckett University. He is a member of the Academy of Marketing Science, the European Marketing Academy and the Economic Chamber of Greece. He has more than 60 publications, including articles in peer-reviewed journals such as the *Journal of Travel Research*, *Journal of Business Research*, *European Management Review*, *Journal of Strategic Marketing*, *Journal of Marketing Theory and Practice* and *International Journal of Innovation Management*. In 2017, he published his first book on Marketing Communications with Palgrave. He has presented his work in more than 28 international academic conferences. His research interests are digital marketing and transformation, consumer behaviour, services marketing and public relations.

Petra Krpan, Postdoctoral Assistant, earned her Bachelor's and Master's degrees at the University of Zagreb, Faculty of Textile Technology, and her PhD at the University of Zagreb, Faculty of Humanities and Social Sciences. Dr. Krpan has been teaching at the university for 12 years and currently works as a Postdoctoral Assistant at the Department for Fashion and Textile Design, where she teaches the following courses: Fashion Theory I, Fashion Theory II, Ethnology of Textiles, Sociology of Fashion, New Media and Fashion and Performance and Fashion. Her first book, published in 2022, researched contemporary Croatian fashion photography from the 1990s to the 2020s and gave an overview of the most influential photographers in Croatia during the period of 30 years. Dr. Krpan's scientific and research interests include fashion theory, photography, cinema and performance studies.

Val Meneau is currently a Research Associate at the University of Vienna, Austria. They completed their PhD with distinction in Dance Studies at the University of Salzburg, Austria, with a dissertation entitled DanceSport's Economy of Desire – a Dispositive Analysis of the Heteronormative Gender Binary in Latin Competitive Dancing, for which they have received a scholarship from the Austrian Academy of Sciences and two awards, from the Austrian Ministry of Education, Science and Research and the University of Salzburg. They have held positions at the Institute of Sociology in Graz and the Institute of Dance Studies in Salzburg and have presented on body and sexual politics in DanceSport at many conferences in gender, queer and critical dance studies. Val has worked with the Austrian Task Force on the adaptation of heteronormative competition regulations to include same-sex couples and is committed to scholarly outreach within the community.

Rebeka Mesarić Žabčić (PhD) is a Senior Research Scientist in Geography and Demography at the Institute of Social Sciences Ivo Pilar in Zagreb (Croatia). She is the author of many articles and conference presentations about return migrations, women's experiences of migrations and entrepreneurial experiences of returning migrant women in Croatia.

Rebecca Nash is a Senior Teaching Fellow based in the Faculty of Social Sciences at the University of Southampton. She received her PhD from Southampton in 2017. Her research interests revolve around beauty and body modification practices, with a current focus on non-surgical cosmetic procedures as an increasingly normalised route to altering appearances. She is also interested in the complexities of writing about cosmetic procedures, recently writing a short article on the topic for the *Sociological Review Magazine* (2022). Rebecca is tentatively stepping back into active research alongside her role as an Academic Developer.

Lea Pešec is an Early-Stage Researcher in Cultural Studies and a doctoral candidate at the University of Graz. Currently, Lea is working on her PhD dissertation on the topic of exploring drag performers' online and offline identities in the contemporary US-American context. She has completed the joint MA degree in English and American studies with a focus on cultural studies at the University of Graz and the University of Bamberg, as well as BA degrees in Sociology and English Language and Literature from the University of Zadar. Lea is also an affiliated student with the *Aging in Data* project and a board member of the *Austria's Young Americanists* network. In terms of research, Lea has an interest in age and ageing studies, gender and queer studies, and digitalisation.

Dominika Sobiesiak, MA, is a graduate of the Faculty of Journalism, Information and Book Science (University of Warsaw, Poland). She completed her BA at the Stefan Cardinal Wyszyński University in Warsaw in 2020. In September 2024, she obtained her Master's thesis under the supervision of Dr. Barlik.

Martina Topić is a Behavioural Sociologist and a mass communication scholar. Currently, she is an Associate Professor in Public Relations Leadership at the University of Alabama, College of Communication and Information Sciences, Department of Advertising and PR, USA (10/2023-). Previously, she worked at Leeds Beckett University, UK, where she held roles such as Graduate Teaching Assistant, Lecturer in Public Relations, Senior Lecturer in Public Relations and Reader at Leeds Business School (2014–2023). She is the Editor-in-Chief of the *Corporate Communications: An International Journal* and *Northern Lights* journals and the Editor-in-Chief of the book series, *Women, Economics and the Labour Relations* (Emerald). Since 2021, she has been leading the EUPERA research network, Women in PR (previously a research project, 2018–2021). She is an author of *Corporate Social Responsibility and Environmental Affairs in the British Press: An Ecofeminist Critique of Neoliberalism* (Routledge, 2021) and

Workplace Culture in Mass Communication Industries (Routledge, 2023). She is a member of the American Sociological Association, British Sociological Association and EUPRERA. She is the author and lead of the Comms Women advocacy initiative (https://www.commswomen.uk/).

Foreword: Celebrating Interdisciplinarity

Martina Topić

Many years ago, when I first started to research ecofeminism and use this framework in my media research (Topić, 2021), one colleague asked me, "But you always see things differently and use these unconventional frameworks, how do you come up with these ideas?" My answer was interdisciplinary education because I hold BA degrees in Journalism and Political Science, a PG Diploma in Global Media, a PhD in Sociology and a PhD in Marketing, Communications and Public Relations, which means that I have looked into journalism and media practice from both sociological and media perspectives, and upon stumbling upon ecofeminism (which came from works of sociologists), I immediately saw an opportunity to apply that framework to media research. However, interdisciplinarity is not just important for doing different research and seeing things differently. It is also important because it fosters cross-cultural collaborations, enhances knowledge and builds international collaborations. The latter is incredibly important because cross-disciplinary collaborations enable younger authors to access publication opportunities. We all know it is not easy to get a start in academic publishing and edited books, particularly interdisciplinary ones widen participation among younger scholars who can start their publishing careers by answering calls for chapters, which is how I also started. But since there are not so many calls for chapters, it is important that books are open to interdisciplinarity and collaborations are available to all.

Beauty and beauty industries have been a subject of academic inquiry for decades, and it would be fair to say that studying beauty is an interdisciplinary area because scholars from many fields have studied the beauty phenomenon and the beauty industry. In 1990, Naomi Wolf published her famous book, *The Beauty Myth*, criticising images of beauty and how these images and portrayals are imposed on women and used against them if uncompliant with expectations on appearance (Wolf, 1990). However, the debate has evolved since the 1990s and now also encompasses studying the beauty industry in the context of capitalism as well as gender, and how beauty standards and expectations are intertwined with (and perpetuated by) capitalism and gender debate.

The current book, *Beauty Industry: Gender, Media and Everyday Life*, co-edited by Dr. Marija Geiger Zeman, Dr. Mirela Holy and Dr. Michal Chmiel provides an interdisciplinary account of beauty, thus giving a space for diverse voices who provide their perspective on beauty and the beauty industry, as well as beauty culture. As such, the book provides insights into the beauty industry from gender, media and everyday life perspectives, and it also opens a space for writing about resistance to beauty and social norms, looking into issues such as race, age, class, consumerism, etc. By doing this, the book serves both as a collection of contemporary works that study beauty in depth, but it can also be used as a textbook because of its richness of topics and the depth the author's chapters provide. The book is interdisciplinary in the true sense of the word, not just in chapters accepted for publication and perspectives they offer but also in the editors' background because the editors come from the sociological background (Geiger Zeman), ethnology and cultural studies (Holy) and psychology of communication and behaviour (Chmiel). In a true sense of their distinctive perspectives, the authors also start the book with an innovative approach of offering two introduction studies, one looking at beauty from a sociological and cultural perspective (Geiger Zeman and Holy) and one looking from a communication perspective (Chmiel). With this, editors give two different views of beauty and the beauty industry and provide their reading of the issue, which is compelling and novel.

Beauty Industry: Gender, Media and Everyday Life provides valuable insights into beauty – a concept (and an industry) stubbornly rooted in patriarchy – from an interdisciplinary perspective, answering also a question on what the beauty debate is in the 21st century. It will be an essential reader for anyone interested in this important phenomenon. In addition to that, the Emerald book series – *Women, Economy and the Labour Relations* – which I authored and now edit is generally rooted in interdisciplinarity and supporting original research. So far, two books have been published, one on women and capitalist expectations on diets and one on ecofeminism with further titles being focused on the ecofeminist perspective of workplace relations and women's housework in the 21st century. This beauty-focused book, *Beauty Industry: Gender, Media and Everyday Life*, complements the series and provides and celebrates interdisciplinarity of scholarly inquiry, and since the beauty industry is inherently linked to women, the book also celebrates interdisciplinarity of women's studies.

References

Topić, M. (2021). *Corporate social responsibility and environmental affairs in the British press: An ecofeminist critique of neoliberalism*. Routledge.

Wolf, N. (1990). *The beauty myth: How images of beauty are used against women*. Perennial (Harper Collins Books).

Introduction One

Marija Geiger Zeman[a] *and Mirela Holy*[b]

[a]Institute of Social Sciences Ivo Pilar, Croatia
[b]VERN' University, Croatia

Abstract

In the introductory chapter key terms, authors and studies that dealt with topics related to beauty standards, the beauty industry and gender are presented. Beauty and beautification are important topics in feminist theory, therefore distinctions between second-wave feminist and postfeminist understandings of beautification and beauty products are emphasised. The beauty market is no longer exclusively marked as a feminine domain, which is shown by the growing number of men of different sexual orientations who use grooming products. It also highlights the importance of beauty products, particularly make up products in LGBTQ+ culture. In conclusion, all chapters are presented.

Keywords: Beauty standards; beauty industry; beauty advertising; celebrities; gender; feminism; LGBTQ+; everyday life; beautification; interdisciplinarity

1. Beauty as Cultural Ideal(s)

For centuries, beauty has been the subject of theoretical discussions 'in a range of fields from art theory to philosophy' and the initiator of concrete practices to realise the culturally defined ideal (Black, 2004, p. 6). Beauty standards are dynamic social constructs that should be researched cross-culturally and intersectionally (race, ethnicity, class, gender, age, etc.), considering they are not universal and trans-historical phenomena (Kuipers, 2015). According to Jha (2016, p. 13), beauty is 'structural inequality' and 'an analytical category to examine the intersectionality of gender relations', nationalism, (post)colonialism and colourism (Jha, 2016, p. x). Concerning the attribution of increasing importance to physical appearance in society, which has been pointed out by social scientists since the 1970s (Anderson et al., 2010), 'corporeal beauty is central to the ways in which people evaluate and judge others, as well as themselves' (Hua, 2013, as cited in Holla, 2018, p. 8). In the late modern age, the importance of physical appearance is no longer reserved

Beauty Industry, 1–13

doi:10.1108/978-1-83608-940-720251003

exclusively for celebrities and fashion models (Anderson et al., 2010; Howson, 2011). In more and more sectors of society, physical appearance is given importance or 'privileged positions' (Holla, 2018, p. 9), therefore 'beauty functions as a form of human capital' (Holla, 2018, p. 8); 'aesthetic capital' (Anderson et al., 2010, p. 564; Foster & Baker, 2022; Holla, 2018, p. 8; Kuipers, 2015, p. 38) or 'symbolic capital' (Kuipers, 2015, p. 38). Western mainstream beauty standards are very limiting and exclusionary because they glorify a thin body, fair complexion and youth (Jones, 2008; Kuipers, 2015). Jha (2016, p. 8) points out that beauty corporations, media and entertainment industries produce and institutionalise 'Eurocentric, white beauty norms'. Some critics emphasise that despite 'the democratic and inclusive potential of social media platforms' (Foster & Baker, 2022, p. 2) online beauty representations of the most followed social media celebrities 'generally reflect rather than challenge Western standards of beauty' (Pham, 2015, as cited in Foster & Baker, 2022, p. 2) thus maintaining 'existing norms and social privileges surrounding appearance and its symbolic significance online' (Foster & Baker, 2022, p. 2).

2. Selling Beauty

Anderson et al. (2010, p. 564) point out that 'beauty is accomplished', so one of the most common and widespread ways of everyday aesthetic labour, the goal of which is to achieve a desirable and 'prestigious' physical appearance, is the purchase and use of beauty industry products (Kuipers, 2015, p. 38). Beauty is a highly profitable industry (Jones, 2010, p. 1) and a continuously growing market (McKinsey and Company, 2023). In parallel with the economic analysis of the beauty industry as a global business (Jones, 2010) and a profitable sector (Turcu & Brancu, 2023), the academic focus is shifted to other aspects of the beauty industry that include interactions, institutions, layered systems of meaning, discourses, representations, complex power relationships, and the ideologies that the beauty industry produces, maintains and supports. For a deeper understanding of the complexity and multi-layered nature of the beauty industry, it is necessary to connect the economic component, primarily oriented towards profitability, with historical, social, environmental and cultural aspects. In this context, interdisciplinary approaches and the linking of different theoretical positions make it possible to ask new questions, find new research niches and create innovative methodologies.

Black (2004, p. 20) points out that 'the beauty industry is not a historically recent phenomenon'. Archaeological findings and historical materials confirm the use of various preparations for beautification and care (Jones, 2010). In addition to beautification, these beauty preparations were associated with marking social status, ritual functions and cultural beliefs (Black, 2004; Jones, 2010; Kuipers, 2015; Tungate, 2011). Throughout history, the role and meaning of beautification preparations have changed (Schaffer, 2006). The roots of the modern beauty industry go back to the 19th century, but only during the 1920s and 1930s did the beauty industry become expansive, mass and commercial (Black, 2004; Jones, 2010; Manko, 2021). The development of the beauty product market in the first-half of the 20th century was marked by many changes: the marginalisation of female entrepreneurs who distributed their beauty products locally (see Manko, 2021; Tungate, 2011); the entry of men into the beauty industry and the synergistic connection of the beauty industry with other industries 'such as advertisers, retailers, manufacturers and magazine editors' (Black, 2004, p. 33), whereby Black (2004) especially emphasises the connection of cosmetics with visual cultures of cinematography and fashion.

Beyond the glossy pages of magazines and the gleaming storefronts of cosmetics retailers lies a multifaceted ecosystem where marketing, media, labour and societal norms intersect to define and dictate our notions of beauty and physical attractiveness. The beauty industry relies on the commodification of people, especially women, because, for the beauty industry, people selected on principles of beauty or attractive/striking appearance are products (Ages, 2024).

3. Feminism, Femininity and (Everyday) Beauty Practices

After the Second World War in Western culture, beauty products 'had become part of a culture of femininity' (Black, 2004, p. 35), more precisely conventional femininity (see Manko, 2021), because the meaning of applying make-up products during the 1950s was 'in general disassociated from' sexual work and 'loose morals' (Black, 2004, p. 35). During the 1960s and 1970s, systematic criticisms of the capitalist beauty industry and patriarchal beauty culture based on 'the hegemony of white beauty' (Black, 2004, p. 37), sexism and ageism (Sontag, 1972) were articulated. Radical feminists emphasised the beauty-fashion industry complex as a lever of male patriarchal exploitation (Jeffreys, 2005). Feminists called on women to reject the male-constructed 'world of beauty' and return to the 'natural body' (Holliday et al., 2019, p. 32). Zeisler (2008) points out that feminist ideas of liberation and criticism of femininity in the late 1960s influenced women and their consumerist choices related to purchasing beauty products. In order to prevent a decline in sales of beauty products in the late 1960s, advertisers appropriated the language of women's emancipation, liberation and empowerment (Zeisler, 2008, pp. 58–60; see also Geiger Zeman & Zeman, 2015). Black (2004, p. 39) emphasises the flexibility of the capitalist economy, which, by commodifying emancipatory values, neutralises their political potential and turns them into commodities and advertising slogans – 'the "liberated woman" became an advertising type, and the rejection of make-up among feminists was reinterpreted in the industry as the "natural look."' A new niche of beauty products for a 'natural look' or makeup-free look has appeared on the market (Zeisler, 2008, p. 60). For decades, advertising campaigns have unabashedly exploited gender stereotypes to sell products, perpetuating harmful ideals and reinforcing oppressive gender norms and double standards (Wolf, 2002). Beauty markets produce and consume 'feminine beauty, sexuality, and youthfulness' (Jha, 2016, p. 2). Bordo (2003) pointed to the destructive influence of idealised media images of 'beauty' on women and their self-image and body image (see also Holliday et al., 2019; Mills et al., 2017; Wolf, 2002). In recent decades, the focus of attention has been on beauty brands and advertising campaigns which change the traditional gender images, challenge traditional gender roles and promote more inclusive representations of beauty; for example, (celebrity) beauty brand Fenty Beauty engaging 'the all-embracing' approach, redefined the ideals of beauty and addressed women who were ignored by the beauty industry (Fetto, 2020). Although the beauty industry has adopted the language of empowerment and inclusiveness, Qiao and Wang (2019, p. 35) emphasise that instead of challenging gender stereotypes, femvertising under the guise of empowerment strengthens them. According to Black (2004, p. 39), since the second wave of feminist analysis, 'it has not been possible to understand the beauty industry without reference to politics'. 'The discourse of choice' has been taken over not only by the beauty industry but also by consumers, and the debates created on polarisation 'victimisation and self-invention'/'prison of beauty and the play of make-up' (Peiss, 1998, as cited in Black, 2004, p. 39; see also Bartky, 1998; Elias et al., 2017) shaped both second wave feminist theories and postfeminist understandings of femininity, body, beautification, and consumerism (Geiger Zeman & Zeman, 2015; Gill, 2012; Grdešić, 2013; Tasker & Negra, 2007). While second wave feminists emphasised the patriarchal oppressiveness of beautification practices and their destructive influence on women's self-confidence (Jeffreys, 2005), post-feminist authors affirm the concepts of '"agency," "choice" and "empowerment"' (Jeffreys, 2005, p. 5) and insisted that beauty products are fully compatible with feminism (Lehrman, 1997, as cited in Jeffreys, 2005, pp. 1, 2; also see Geiger Zeman & Zeman, 2019, p. 79). Postfeminism produces 'new femininities' (Gill & Scharff, 2011, p. 2) that resonate with neoliberalism and 'with the hyper-aestheticization of everyday life' (Postrel, 2003, as cited in Tasker & Negra, 2007, p. 7). Apart from the fact that postfeminist subjects are focussed on 'luxury life-styling', 'pleasure and self-expression' (Postrel, 2003, as cited in Tasker & Negra, 2007, p. 7), they are preoccupied with the body, physical appearance and 'self-policing narcissistic gaze' (Gill, 2012, p. 258). According to Elias et al. (2017, p. 5), the feminist debate on beauty as a key feminist issue 'stuck in an impasse between polarised positions' (for example, oppression versus playfulness, agency versus cultural dominance, resistance versus obedience) therefore it is necessary to ask new questions and build new 'theoretical avenues'. Elias et al. (2017, p. 5) introduce fresh perspectives and situate debates about beauty in the context of neoliberalism.

'Why do people use make-up?' asked Plante (2016, p. 167) in an article in which, among other things, she deals with her daily beautification rituals. One of the answers to this seemingly simple but actually very complex question is given by symbolic interactionists, more specifically Goffman in his study *The Presentation of Self in Everyday Life* (1956), in which he explains the dramaturgical model of the self and how individuals, like actors, create their character and manage it (Goffman, 1956; see also Blackman, 2008; Geiger Zeman & Zeman, 2019; McCabe et al., 2020). Everyday beautification practices such as applying make-up products are an important part of 'inventing a story for myself' and for others (Plante, 2016, p. 165), but the other meanings and aspects of that mundane ritual are not exhausted there. For Plante (2016, p. 166), it is about 'face work' and 'act' that is simultaneously conformist and creative. Everyday 'face work' shows how, like the body, our face is a location where they meet and intersect individually and socially (Gimlin, 2002). Research that deals with the lived experiences of women points to complex and ambivalent relationships between women and dominant ideologies of beauty and 'the varying degree of female autonomy within given social frameworks' (Geiger Zeman & Zeman, 2019, p. 80) and/or 'a gendered social order' (Davis, 1995, p. 5). According to McCabe et al. (2020, p. 660), 'for women, the core meaning of putting on makeup is connecting internal and external self, inner, and outer beauty... Women's makeup practices not only reproduce discourses of beauty but also transform the self'. Everyday 'face work' or 'make-up rituals' are 'reflexive practices' by which women enhance their body, transform their self and carve their identity (McCabe et al., 2020, p. 662).

4. New Beauty Realities

In the new millennium, the beauty industry adopts and appropriates new (economic, cultural, gendered) realities, discourses, ideas and ways of communicating (Tungate, 2011). Even though 'male beautification practices have a long and significant history' (Hermans, 2021, p. 139), in Western culture, make-up products are marked as a gendered practice reserved primarily for women. However, today's beauty industry and products should be understood more gender-complexly. Virakul (2022, p. 3) points out that previous research has mainly focussed on make-up products and their daily use by women, while the experiences of cis-men and trans-persons have been marginalised (see also Foster & Baker, 2022). In recent decades, make-up collections and products of well-known cosmetic brands have shown that the 'male-grooming business is exploding' from feminine and drag/queer domains and entering the mainstream (Jacobs, 2019). Harrison (2008, p. 56) points out that in recent decades, 'the concept of masculinity is undergoing significant social change as many men re-evaluate their appearance, re-position themselves as consumers of fashion and style products, and ultimately re-construct their idea of what it is to be male'. Consumerism and media (especially social media) are important for understanding transformations of traditional concepts of masculinity and for understanding men's interest in beautification and grooming practices (Edwards, 2003; Hermans, 2021; Zeman & Geiger Zeman, 2012). In the 1980s, 'masculinity was more extensively transformed by economic and commercial forces' (Beynon, 2002, p. 98). Also, new visual representations of men and male bodies, which are similar to the sexual objectification of women, appeared in the media (Beynon, 2002; Edwards, 2003; Zeman & Geiger Zeman, 2012). Style magazines for men and advertisers created a new type of masculinity – the 'new man' (or 'the new man-as-narcissist') (Beynon, 2002, p. 102) who is preoccupied with his physical appearance, health, fitness, clothes and grooming that includes the use of skin care products and toiletries (Beynon, 2002, pp. 124–125). Mark Simpson, a British columnist, 'coined the term "metrosexual"' in 1994, but the term became visible in the public space at the beginning of the new millennium (Harrison, 2008, p. 55). According to Simpson (cited in Harrison, 2008, p. 55; see also Gough et al., 2014, p. 110), a 'typical metrosexual' is a young, gay/straight/bisexual man who lives in or near an urban area and has money for fashion and beauty products and several services related to the body (e.g. grooming, fitness, etc.). Coad (2008, as cited in Hall et al., 2012, p. 210) points out that the 'marketing of high profile sports celebrities', especially David Beckham, is 'responsible for encouraging heterosexual men to "engage in practices stereotypically associated with femininity and homosexuality, such as care for appearance and latest fashion trends"' (Hall et al., 2012, p. 210). Although the term has become 'passé' (Harrison, 2008, p. 55), it is important to highlight it because 'metrosexuality' 'challenges traditional notions of gender and sexuality' and transcends 'constrictive bipolar categorisations masculine/feminine and hetero/homo' (Coad, 2008, as cited in Hall et al., 2012, p. 210). Care for appearances and beautification practices have become part of many men's daily routines and rituals (Harrison, 2008). In the last few years, many make-up brands have advertised, offered and sold gender-neutral beauty products and beauty products intended exclusively for men (for example, Boy de CHANEL, Charlotte Tilbury, etc.) (Geiger Zeman & Holy, 2023). The entry of men into formerly exclusively defined feminine areas does not mean greater inclusivity because 'conventional notions of masculinity are still influential' (Gough et al., 2014, p. 113). Research with 'metrosexual men' and 'men on weight loss programmes' conducted by Gough et al. (2014, p. 106) shows the following: heterosexual men engaged in so-called feminised practices are very 'careful not to appear too soft, effeminate or gay' (p. 110); men try hard to '"masculinise" potentially feminising appearance-related practices' (p. 113); men associate the use of make-up with health and practicality (for example, covering skin problems, protection from the sun) and 'heterosexual appeal and success' (p. 115). Also, by confirming their heterosexual status, men distance themselves from gay orientation (Gough et al., 2014). Byrne and Milestone (2023, p. 148) researched the experiences and knowledge of men about skincare practices and skin care products and came to interesting findings: (1) age is a key factor that affects the purchase and use of skin care products, more precisely 'younger men are much more open to engaging in caring for their skin and buying skin care products'; (2) 'men do not discuss their skincare practices with other people'. Byrne and Milestone (2023, p. 148) conclude that the purchase of skincare products for men is a 'private, invisible form of consumption', and the use of skincare products is 'a "back-stage" (Goffman, 1959) activity'. Despite cultural and social pressure on men to take care of and improve their appearance in late modernity, 'strong societal expectations around "appropriate masculinity"' still exist (Byrne & Milestone, 2023, p. 148).

Coetzee et al. (2023, p. 2) highlight research results that show that 'gay men place a higher value on image, appearance and fashion consumption' than heterosexual men, so 'consumption of grooming and fashion products is higher within the LGBTQ community as opposed to the heterosexual community'. Nudson (2021) recalls the critical role of 'makeup as a tool for queer resistance'.

Furthermore, while for feminists' makeup was a form of conforming to the patriarchal system, for members of the queer community, it was historically an important element in challenging the system and its gender binary/heteronormative standards (Nudson, 2021). At the same time, 'markers of makeup and clothing also helped LGBTQ people recognise each other and create (relatively) safe havens' (Nudson, 2021). In addition to the activist importance for the LGBTQIA+ community, researching the meaning of make-up and its role in (de)constructing, maintaining and performing gender identities is important for understanding recent phenomena such as 'post-queer and postfeminist intersections' (Chen & Kanai, 2022, p. 101) visible in the 'production of femininity by...gay male beauty influencers' (Chen & Kanai, 2022, p. 98), the use of consumer culture by 'the queer male beauty influencers' in order to make 'queer outsider' experiences available to the public through the use of beauty products (Taylor, 2024, p. 195), 'queer immaterial labour' of LGBTQ-Identified YouTubers (Homant & Sender, 2019, p. 5386), the dynamics and practices of beauty community on YouTube (García-Rapp & Roca-Cuberes, 2017), etc.

5. Beauty Through Interdisciplinary Lenses

Each chapter in this book thematises some of the many facets of the beauty industry related to one or more anchor themes – gender, media and/or everyday life, to critically question the beauty system and the cultural, social, political and economic relations that shape it. The book is also intended to create space for different voices, opening up new research areas and asking some familiar and new questions related to the reality of the beauty industry and beauty culture in which we live and participate in various ways every day through conforming to and/or resistance to sociocultural norms, ideologies, discourses regarding gender, race, age, class, consumerism, advertising, media, (post)feminism, appearance, etc. Rebecca Nash and Anne-Mette Hermans explore new phenomena in the recent beauty environment. These non-surgical aesthetic procedures are increasingly popular and have more and more consumers. For many people, non-surgical interventions have become part of their daily beauty routine, and their normalisation opens up space for important questions about, on the one hand, beauty trends and gendered pressures related to physical appearance and, on the other hand, the '"de-medicalisation" of non-surgical procedures' (Nash & Hermans, p. 23 in this publication) which encourages debates on the regulation of the cosmetic surgery sector, the qualification and certification of persons who perform non-surgical aesthetic procedures. In their research, Nash and Hermans focus on practitioners, ensuring their professional experiences and client relationships are visible through their voices. Martina Topić and Ioannis Kostopoulos inaugurate a new approach to thinking and analysing 'environmental costs of vanity' (Topić & Kostopoulos, p. 43 in this publication). Innovatively connecting the themes of environmentalism, ecofeminism and consumerism, for these authors, the beauty industry is defined as a 'vanity industry' (Topić & Kostopoulos, p. 43 in this publication). The focus of online quantitative research conducted in the United Kingdom is the use of mirrors as a cosmetic item that signifies vanity and the influence of personal characteristics on shopping and environmentally (un)conscious behaviour. In addition to theoretical contributions to further research on gender, beauty products consumerism and environmentalism, Topić and Kostopoulos point to interesting connections between gender, personal values and environmental attitudes that have the potential to be a significant input in creating environmentally sensitive campaigns and promote environmentally friendly consumerist behaviours.

Michael Chmiel introduces the issues of responsible communication and responsible advertising into the discussion, which takes on new meanings in the context of the 'post-truth communication landscape' (Chmiel, p. 69 in this publication). Chmiel examines and critically questions the dynamic relationships between the beauty industry, marketing and science. In order to ensure the credibility of their products and convince customers to buy them, the beauty industry and advertisers often refer to science in their persuasion strategies. Chmiel points out that the beauty industry contributes to disseminating fake news and pseudo-facts with this way of communicating for sales. Using the social psychological methodology, Chmiel suggests instructions for responsible communication and affirms marketing based on truthful claims, appealing to the importance of developing and practising 'corporate epistemological responsibility' as an important aspect of corporate social responsibility (Lamy & Beyneix, 2022, as cited in Chmiel, p. 69 in this publication).

Lea Pešec points to the ageist aspects of the beauty industry, which engages and reinforces dominant cultural narratives about ageing and socially constructed ideals of beauty based on youth and youthful appearance. Anti-ageing products and anti-ageing ads further reinforce fears of ageing and negative perceptions of ageing and produce unrealistic expectations that negatively affect individual perceptions and expectations about ageing. Pešec contributes to discussions about media representations of ageing, 'the gendered nature of ageing portrayals' (Pešec, p. 87 in this publication), meanings of anti-ageing beauty products and the status of age and ageing in a wider social context.

Petra Krpan shows how beauty is an inseparable part of the fashion system. Through the medium of fashion photography, the beauty-fashion complex defined and represented what was considered 'beautiful' and 'in fashion' at a certain time in Western culture (Krpan, p. 105 in this publication). Krpan presents an interesting and rich analysis of changes in beauty and representational practices in fashion photography and cinematography, where the backbone of the analytical procedure is the distinction of 'clothed body' (Calefato, 2004, as cited in Krpan, p. 105 in this publication) and the 'covered body' (Krpan & Simončič, 2024, as cited in Krpan, p. 105 in this publication). From the 1920s to the present, fashion photography in each decade represented different beauty and body standards that functioned as representations of desirable and conventional femininity. Krpan points out that contemporary fashion and fashion photography soften conventional ideas about femininity and masculinity by representing human bodies in new and innovative ways. Beauty salons (Black, 2004; Kerner Furman, 1997), hairdressing and barber shops are forms of beauty entrepreneurship and places where different relationships intersect (e.g. client–employee) and social categories such as gender, race, class, ethnicity, age, etc. Analysing the British comedy Desmond's (Channel 4, 1989–1994), Melissa Beattie shows the importance and significant role of the barbershop in Black communities in the UK and the US. The focus of the analysis is the daily life of the migrant family Ambrose, who owns a barbershop, which, in addition to providing grooming services for community members, is also a key place of gathering, support, networking, identity preservation, cultural expression and negotiation of social and cultural norms. For Beattie (p. 123 in this publication), the barbershop in the TV series is an interesting representation of the beauty industry 'as a sociocultural institution' (or 'social club' as one of the characters in the TV series mentioned) (Beattie, p. 123 in this publication) for the Afro-Caribbean community in the United Kingdom, where 'characterisation, dialogue and music' are particularly prominent. This work represents an important contribution to discussions about racial and ethical issues related to the beauty industry as well as the beauty culture of minority communities. Jacek Barlik and Dominika Sobiesiak contribute to research on the perception and reception of drag culture in Poland. Using several methods, the authors develop an interesting analysis that is focussed on several relevant topics: the perception of 'RuPaul's Drag Race', a globally famous TV show in Poland, the contribution of this popular show in strengthening and promoting tolerance towards diversity and the LGBTQ+ community, opinions about the meanings of beauty and beautification techniques practised by RuPaul and the participants of the show. Polish fans primarily perceive the show as entertainment, not as education about tolerating diversity. Drag aesthetics is connected with the art of beautifying, challenging and deconstructing dominant concepts of beauty and standards of feminine beauty, where self-acceptance, self-expression and freedom come to the fore. The research participants were introduced to 'original beautification methods' (Barlik & Sobiesiak, p. 143 in this publication) that drag queens practice when constructing their original and creative appearance. Nikolina Borčić points out the different and contradictory meanings attributed to red lipstick, from marking status and gender identity to complex political connotations, especially if the lipstick is analysed from a feminist perspective. For Borčić, red lipstick on the lips conveys a symbolic self-presentational message, so the author positions her analysis in media communication. By analysing media texts published on Croatian portals, Borčić determines that red lipstick functions as a communication tool that signifies 'authority, rebellion, sensuality, and professionalism' (Borčić, p. 163 in this publication). Positioning the research findings in a wider social context, it is evident that media representations of red lipstick indicate dynamic relations of gender and power in society.

Make-up products have long been coded as crucial to achieving (conventional) femininity in Western culture. Val Meneau points out the gender neutrality of make-up products and application practices. Using an autoethnographic approach, Meneau describes their 'make-up journey' as an essential part of becoming aware of one's own non-binary identity and articulates several important questions related to different dance contexts and their relationship to gender non-binary. Meneau's new non-binary identity as a former male competitor of LatinDance sport brings them into challenging situations in which the strict heteronormative and discriminatory rules that define the competitive DanceSport scene are challenged and negotiated. On the other hand, raving and (queer) clubbing open space for experimentation and exploration of make-up skills. Meneau shows how make-up products' functions, meanings and roles are complex and need to be understood differently, respecting the contexts in which these meanings are produced. The perspective of everyday life provides a new dimension in understanding the complex relationships between gender, media and the beauty industry. Marija Geiger Zeman, Mirela Holy and Rebeka Mesarić Žabčić start from the sociological connection of everyday life and popular culture (Waskul & Vannini, 2016, as cited in Geiger Zeman et al., p. 204 in this publication). From this point of view, the daily practice of beautification connects beauty industry products, the purchase and consumption of beauty products and their daily use. The analysis focusses on the beauty video shot by Kate Moss for Vogue's beauty series (Vogue's Beauty Secrets). The video about the daily beauty routine of a well-known supermodel is a sociologically interesting text imbued with layers of meaning that, viewed from a gender, class and racial perspective, point to dynamic relations between postfeminism and neoliberalism, on the one hand, and micro and macro levels, on the other.

The goal of this book was not to condemn or exonerate the beauty industry but to provoke interdisciplinary debates and foster new research questions about its unquestionable impact on gender identities, gender performances, media culture, and everyday lives. By illuminating the complexities and contradictions that define the beauty industry, we aim to empower readers to navigate the terrain where beauty, gender, media and everyday life are intertwined in the context of late capitalism and the neoliberal environment with greater discernment and understanding.

References

Ages, A. (2024, April 25). Femininity, hyper-commodified: Consumerism, social media, and beauty standards. *Perspectives Journal.* https://perspectivesjournal.ca/femininity-hyper-commodified/

Anderson, T., Grunert, C., Katz, A., & Lovascio, S. (2010). Aesthetic capital: A research review on beauty perks and penalties. *Sociology Compass*, *4*(8), 564–575. https://doi.org/10.1111/j.1751-9020.2010.00312.x

Bartky, S. L. (1998). Foucault, femininity, and the modernization of patriarchal power. In R. Weitz (Ed.), *The politics of women's bodies. Sexuality, appearance and behavior* (pp. 25–45). Oxford University Press.

Beynon, J. (2002). *Masculinities and culture*. Open University Press.

Black, P. (2004). *The beauty industry: Gender, culture, pleasure*. Routledge.

Blackman, L. (2008). *The body. The key concepts*. Berg.

Bordo, S. (2003). *Unbearable weight. Feminism, western culture, and the body*. University of California Press.

Byrne, A., & Milestone, K. (2023). 'He wouldn't be seen using it. . . ' Men's use of male grooming products as a form of invisible consumption. *Journal of Consumer Culture*, *23*(1), 146–167.

Chen, S. X., & Kanai, A. (2022). Authenticity, uniqueness and talent: Gay male beauty influencers in post-queer, postfeminist Instagram beauty culture. *European Journal of Cultural Studies*, *25*(1), 97–116. https://doi.org/10.1177/1367549421988966

Coetzee, C., de Villiers, M. V., & Chuchu, T. (2023). LGBTQ consumers' engagement and attitudes toward online brand communities within the cosmetics industry. *Global Business Review*, 1–18. https://doi.org/10.1177/09721509221141198

Davis, K. (1995). *Reshaping the female body*. Routledge.

Edwards, T. (2003). Sex, booze and fags: Masculinity, style and men's magazines. In B. Benwell (Ed.), *Masculinity and men's lifestyle magazines* (pp. 132–146). Blackwell Publishing.

Elias, A., Gill, R., & Scharff, C. (2017). Aesthetic labour: Beauty politics in neoliberalism. In A. Elias, R. Gill, & C. Scharff (Eds.), *Aesthetic labour. Rethinking beauty politics in neoliberalism* (pp. 3–49). Palgrave Macmillan.

Fetto, F. (2020, April 6). How fenty beauty changed the state of play in the industry. *Vogue*. https://www.vogue.co.uk/beauty/article/rihanna-fenty-beauty-diversity

Foster, J., & Baker, J. (2022). Muscles, makeup, and femboys: Analyzing TikTok's "Radical" masculinities. *Social Media + Society*, *8*(3), 1–14. https://doi.org/10.1177/20563051221126040

García-Rapp, F., & Roca-Cuberes, C. (2017). Being an online celebrity: Norms and expectations of YouTube's beauty community. *First Monday*, *22*(7). https://doi.org/10.5210/fm.v22i7.7788. https://firstmonday.org/ojs/index.php/fm/article/view/7788/6331

Geiger Zeman, M., & Holy, M. (2023, September 14–15). The right to makeup: Masculinities, creative industries and redefining beauty practice [media creative industries]. In *2nd International Scientific Conference Creative Future Insights*, September 14–15, 2023, VERN' University, Zagreb, Croatia.

Geiger Zeman, M., & Zeman, Z. (2015). Potrošački snovi chic djevojaka: rodno lice konzumerizma. *Narodna Umjetnost*, *52*(2), 105–137. https://doi.org/10.15176/vol52no206

Geiger Zeman, M., & Zeman, Z. (2019). "Zašto bih izgledala mlađe?": žene, starenje i svakodnevne prakse upravljanja tijelom. *Narodna Umjetnost*, *56*(2), 75–99. https://doi.org/10.15176/vol56no204

Gill, R. (2012). *Gender and the media*. Polity.

Gill, R., & Scharff, C. (2011). Introduction. In R. Gill & C. Scharff (Eds.), *New feminities: Postfeminism, neoliberalism and subjectivity* (pp. 1–17). Palgrave Macmillan.

Gimlin, D. L. (2002). *Body work. Beauty and self-image in american culture*. University of California Press.

Goffman, E. (1956). *The presentation of self in everyday life*. University of Edinburgh/Social Sciences Research Centre.

Gough, B., Hall, M., & Seymour-Smith, S. (2014). Straight guys do wear make-up: Contemporary masculinities and investment in appearance. In S. Roberts (Ed.), *Debating modern masculinities: Change, continuity, crisis?* (pp. 106–124). Palgrave Macmillan.

Grdešić, M. (2013). Cosmopolitika. Kulturalni studiji, feminizam i ženski časopisi. Disput.

Hall, M., Gough, B., & Seymour-Smith, S. (2012). "I'm METRO, NOT gay!": A discursive analysis of men's accounts of makeup use on YouTube. *The Journal of Men's Studies*, *20*(3), 209–226. https://doi.org/10.3149/jms.2003.209

Harrison, C. (2008). Real men do wear mascara: Advertising discourse and masculine identity. *Critical Discourse Studies*, *5*(1), 55–74. https://doi.org/10.1080/17405900701768638

Hermans, A.-M. (2021). *Discourses of perfection. Representing cosmetic procedures and beauty products in UK lifestyle magazines*. Routledge.

Holla, S. M. (2018). *Beauty, work, self: How fashion models experience their aesthetic labor*. Thesis, fully internal. Universiteit van Amsterdam. https://dare.uva.nl/search?identifier=9930b516-1efb-4250-bec9-b8ad5fdd4970

Holliday, R., Jones, M., & Bell, D. (2019). *Beautyscapes: Mapping cosmetic surgery tourism*. Manchester University Press.

Homant, E., & Sender, K. (2019). Queer immaterial labor in beauty videos by LGBTQ-identified YouTubers. *International Journal of Communication*, *13*, 5386–5404. https://ijoc.org/index.php/ijoc/article/viewFile/10572/2853

Howson, A. (2011). *The body in society. An introduction*. Polity.

Jacobs, B. (2019, February 8). Is men's make-up going mainstream? *BBC Culture*. https://www.bbc.com/culture/article/20190206-is-mens-make-up-going-mainstream

Jeffreys, S. (2005). *Beauty and misogyny. Harmful cultural practices in the west*. Routledge.

Jha, M. R. (2016). *The global beauty industry: Colorism, racism, and the national body*. Routledge.

Jones, M. (2008). *Skintight. An anatomy of cosmetic surgery*. Berg.

Jones, G. (2010). *Beauty imagined. A history of the global beauty industry*. Oxford University Press.

Kerner Furman, F. (1997). *Facing the mirror. Older women and beauty shop culture*. Routledge.

Kuipers, G. (2015). Beauty and distinction? The evaluation of appearance and cultural capital in five European countries. *Poetics*, *53*, 38–51. http://doi.org/10.1016/j.poetic.2015.10.001

Manko, K. (2021). *Ding Dong! Avon calling!: The women and men of Avon products, incorporated*. Oxford University Press.

McCabe, M., de Waal Malefyt, T., & Fabri, A. (2020). Women, makeup, and authenticity: Negotiating embodiment and discourses of beauty. *Journal of Consumer Culture*, *20*(4), 656–677. https://doi.org/10.1177/1469540517736558

McKinsey and Company. (2023, May 22). The beauty market in 2023: A special state of fashion report. https://www.mckinsey.com/industries/retail/our-insights/the-beauty-market-in-2023-a-special-state-of-fashion-report#/

Mills, J. S., Shannon, A., & Hogue, J. (2017). Beauty, body image, and the media. In M. P. Levine (Ed.), *Perception of beauty*. InTech. https://doi.org/10.5772/intechopen.68944. https://www.intechopen.com/chapters/55388

Nudson, R. (2021, July 14). On makeup as a tool for queer resistance. *Literary Hub*. https://lithub.com/on-makeup-as-a-tool-for-queer-resistance/

Plante, R. F. (2016). Putting on makeup. In D. D. Waskul & P. Vannini (Eds.), *Popular culture as everyday life* (pp. 165–174). Routledge.

Qiao, F., & Wang, Y. (2019). The myths of beauty, age, and marriage: Femvertising by masstige cosmetic brands in the Chinese market. *Social Semiotics*, *32*, 35–57. https://doi.org/10.1080/10350330.2019.1682279

Schaffer, S. (2006). Reading our lips: The history of lipstick regulation in western seats of power [2006 Third Year Paper]. *Digital Access to Scholarship at Harvard (DASH)*. https://dash.harvard.edu/handle/1/10018966

Sontag, S. (1972, September 23). The double standard of aging. *Saturday Review of the Society*. http://www.unz.com/print/SaturdayRev-1972sep23-00029

Tasker, Y., & Negra, D. (2007). Introduction: Feminist politics and postfeminist culture. In Y. Tasker & D. Negra (Eds.), *Interrogating postfeminism. Gender and the Politics of popular culture* (pp. 1–25). Duke University Press.

Taylor, A. S. (2024). Consuming queerness: Jeffree Star and the paradox of profit and pleasure in the queer male beauty influencer. *Celebrity Studies*, *15*(2), 193–208. https://doi.org/10.1080/19392397.2024.2341598

Tungate, M. (2011). *Branded beauty. How marketing changed the way we look*. Kogan Page Limited.

Turcu, O., & Brancu, C. (2023). The impact of the beauty industry on the economic growth at the European Union level. *Proceedings of the International Conference on Business Excellence*, *17*(1), 468–474. https://doi.org/10.2478/picbe-2023-0045

Virakul, S. (2022). Makeup: A genderless form of artistic expression explored by content creators and their followers. *Journal of Student Research*, *11*(3), 1–16.

Wolf, N. (2002). *The beauty myth. How images of beauty are used against women*. HarperCollins Publishers Inc.

Zeisler, A. (2008). *Feminism and pop culture*. Seal Studies.

Zeman, Z., & Geiger Zeman, M. (2012). "Brže bolje u formu:" - mitologija ljepote, komercijalizacija i discipliniranje tijela. *Metodicki Ogledi*, *19*(1), 59–75.

Introduction Two

Michal Chmiel

Royal Holloway, University of London, UK

Abstract

This chapter introduces several industry challenges that beauty brands face in relation to consumers' needs. The arrival of new stakeholders, such as celebrities who are beauty brand owners, and the rising expectation of consumers to demonstrate the efficacy of beauty products are discussed. The current definition of beauty is briefly contrasted against its historical development and explained in terms of a psychological mechanism based on building knowledge that comes from various sources. The conclusion proposes an approach that uses evidence from different levels of analysis, including micro-level (psychological), to create sustainable communication and to appreciate the interests of various stakeholders.

Keywords: Celebrities; evidence; efficacy; consumer psychology; responsible marketing; multidisciplinarity

Beauty industry is becoming a crowded place. In addition to the existing, usual set of stakeholders (i.e. producers of cosmetics, experts, influencers and consumers), new players have come to the field. More and more celebrities are attempting to establish themselves as entrepreneurs, who want to capitalise on their knowledge of the needs of their followers and relationships with marketers of brands, for whom they had previously provided endorsements. At the same time, a shift in the expectations of consumers can be observed. Closer examination of marketing communication of major beauty brands suggests that users are no longer persuaded by products offering good value-for-money and recommendations of celebrity endorsers – using a product that a famous movie star or footballer is using may no longer be enough. Beauty brands also need to be sustainable, ethical and offer personalised experience (Infosys, 2024). But perhaps the biggest change has not been caught by professional reports, but brands' owners are aware of it: beauty products need to work! As simplistic as this assertion might appear, the

Beauty Industry, 15–19

Published under exclusive licence by Emerald Publishing Limited
doi:10.1108/978-1-83608-940-720251008

need for evidencing the efficacy of cosmetics has become more visible, especially in in-store product communication. Using the marketing terminology, the experience of the first moment of truth, i.e. the time a consumer decides to choose one product over another (based on brand's promise) should be reaffirmed when a consumer uses the product and decides to continue using it. The necessity to understand the reasons behind the decisions of consumers makes some branches of science particularly well positioned to get involved. Especially, when one wants to understand how the efficiency of products is evaluated and what type of evidence is used by consumers. Indeed, the practical relationship between marketers of beauty products and consumers as recipients of brand communication makes beauty industry business highly psychological. In the post-truth environment, where opinions and personal anxieties matter more than rational facts (Laybats & Tredinnick, 2016), approaches that have had a long focus on the formation of attitudes and individual experience appear as a natural ally. Psychology, a discipline that explains the behaviour of individuals (especially social psychology) and pertains to establish links between various contexts of human interaction (e.g. Sutton & Douglas, 2019), seems well-positioned to understand the relationship between beauty brands and consumers.

Although Plato held that beauty is an objective quality, a quick look at the current definition of beauty in Merriam-Webster dictionary points to its subjective and perceptual character: 'the quality or group of qualities in a person or thing that gives pleasure to the senses or the mind' (Merriam-Webster, n.d.); but is it possible to define any of these qualities? Another definition from the Oxford Dictionary gives a few more details: 'a combination of qualities, such as shape, colour, or form, that pleases the aesthetic senses, especially the sight' (Oxford Dictionary, n.d.). The lack of semantic clarity about the defining components of beauty does not suggest definitional problems but instead hints that the meaning of beauty undergoes a constant reformulation as a function of the debate between consumers, brands, influencers and (much less frequently) experts. Similarities exist between the lacking semantic clarity of beauty and how marketers of beauty brands outline the basic principles of their trade. For example, the authors of Cosmetics Marketing see beauty as a historically fluid social construct with definitions existing within social values and politics, and components used to define perception of gender, race or class (Karchin & Horvath, 2023).

On the one hand, certain characteristics associated with beauty have remained stable. For example, the title of an Ancient Egyptian manuscript cited by Stewart (2020), 'The beginning of the book on how to make the old young', suggests that the thrive for youth as a feature of beauty has been a prominent concern throughout history. In fact, this has been present within marketing communication since the birth of the modern beauty industry in the 20th century. For example, *Elizabeth Arden*'s print ad from 1936 promised a 'Farewell to Age' and enticed consumers to 'Grow young alone with me [Elizabeth Arden], the best is yet to be'. And the incentive of youthfulness was still used by beauty industry in 2013 (e.g. Forever. Youth Liberator by *Yves Saint Laurent*). These references seem reasonable as recent scientific evidences that ageing may be a form of illness; for example, a prominent geroscientists, and the head of Harvard Medical School, has proposed a mechanism that considers ageing as a disease whereby failures of transmission of information on a cellular level are the underlying cause of ageing (Sinclair & LaPlante, 2019; Brenner, 2023 for critique).

On the other hand, the beauty industry in the third decade of the 21st century seemed to focus more upon the recipient of beauty ('Beauty is for everyone' by *Dove*), the provider of beauty ('No one does beauty like we do' by *Lookfantastic*) or the inclusivity of beauty ('40 Shades. 40 Powers' by *Lancome*), rather than explicitly stating what the characteristics of a beautiful person are. Allusions to youthfulness have been slowly disappearing from marketing communication and replaced with a more holistic understanding of the concept as an interplay between physical and psychological experience. Several beauty brands seem to have embraced that trend. For example, *Unilever's* luxury brand *Murad* links lack of stress and wellbeing with beauty, and *Dr Barbara Sturm* recommends meditating or spending time with family as a part of an anti-inflammatory lifestyle. These marketing strategies of beauty brands resonate well with the 2023 McKinsey report on beauty industry findings that suggests beauty and wellness as convergent because consumers want to simultaneously look and feel good (McKinsey & Company, 2023) .

One aspect of the public debate regarding the meaning of beauty has remained constant: the mechanism that explains consumer psychology. Albert Bandura's (1986) social cognitive theory proposes that human behaviour can be explained as a knowledge acquisition process that involves imitating behaviours of other people. Three sources of knowledge that are used to form judgements about the external world include information and the behaviour of other people, the environment and one's own beliefs and attitudes. Beauty brands of today exploit that mechanism on an amplified scale: they give sample product to increase behavioural feedback (word of mouth), seek endorsement from celebrities and influencers to provide stimulus for imitation (influencer marketing) and communicate their values to increase alignment with consumers (social purpose) or turn to science for evidence about the effectiveness of their products. However, not all sources of information have equal value and credibility, which leads to perceptions of consumers being turbo-charged with pseudoscience and distorted by users of social networks.

To tackle the post-truth consumer challenges brand marketers have been facing, Swaminathan et al. (2020) proposed hyperconnectivity as a defining feature of the current consumer–brand relationship. They considered constant accessibility and abundance of information as factors that should change traditional approaches to marketing. Among other newly acquired functions, brands have become cultural icons, tools of identity expression and self-expression. At the same time, creating content to maintain relevance and occupying shortened attention spans of consumers has led to creating large quantities of content that are not possible to process by modern – especially young – consumers.

The information challenge that has emerged is not only about the quantity of content but also about its quality. The beauty industry as a creator of persuasive communication aims primarily to change attitudes towards marketed brands, as well as creating changes in a myriad of aspects of individual lives of consumers. This – we argue – should come with a considerable realisation of responsibility for the well-being of consumers. In our view, responsible marketing communication should include the responsibility of marketers for content they are creating and disseminating. That could mean accounting for characteristics of marketing content that includes, but is not limited to, truthfulness. More specifically, its impact on a full spectrum of issues identified in the United Nations Sustainable Development goals should be explicitly acknowledged. It seems that content created for promotional purposes by the beauty industry has a considerable potential for changing (sometimes negatively) at least several important areas included in the UN framework: gender equality, good health and wellbeing, and responsible production and consumption. For example, until recently the implications of objectification of women in promotional communication had not been fully acknowledged by practitioners, partly because of the view that advertising (and promotional communication) only mirrored gender representations already found in society (e.g. Chmiel, 2024). Many advertisements used to include simplified representations of gender in order – supposedly – to respond to explicit needs of their consumers. Positively, a few major advertisers have already decided to change what gender images they had promoted and to assume greater responsibility for their marketing communication, despite evident financial success of former marketing communication strategies (e.g. Lynx/Axe). However, following the COVID-19 pandemic, companies were understandably weakened, and some shareholders voiced their criticism of putting purpose before profit; thus, companies started making changes to their social agenda. For example, Unilever's CEO Hein Schumacher said that he would stop 'force fitting' brand purpose on the entire portfolio of the company's brands (Carroll, 2023).

But perhaps beyond arguing about the applicability of one particular scientific discipline to help consumers make better decisions, or marketers to act and communicate responsibly, as with any other complex task, multiple points of view and voices are needed. As much as consumers expect marketing communication to be more inclusive, the same can be said about the desired outcome of scientific discussions. In general, problems and tasks should be tackled from different perspectives, especially as plethora of scientific evidence suggests that single-perspective methods lead to obscure and biassed solutions. With this volume in particular, it is hoped that by including evidence from various disciplines, a more comprehensive understanding of the beauty industry and its contemporary challenges has been achieved. Whether the collection of chapters serves as evidence to make well-informed decisions by marketers, or merely as a starting point for a discussion, the goal of the editors has been achieved. The beauty industry – as an applied sphere, where various individual and institutional needs meet and collide – should benefit from a multidisciplinary scientific approach.

References

Bandura, A., & National Inst of Mental Health. (1986). *Social foundations of thought and action: A social cognitive theory*. Prentice-Hall, Inc.

Brenner, C. (2023). A science-based review of the world's best-selling book on aging. *Archives of Gerontology and Geriatrics, 104*, 104825. https://doi.org/10.1016/j.archger.2022.104825

Carroll, N. (2023, October 26). Unilever CEO: We will stop 'force fitting' purpose to our brands. *Marketing Week*. https://www.marketingweek.com/unilever-ceo-stop-force-fitting-purpose-brands/

Chmiel, M. (2024). Societal impact of brand public relations on gender equality: Evidence for a mediation-type mechanism. *Corporate Communications: An International Journal, 29*(6), 796–817. https://doi.org/10.1108/CCIJ-04-2024-0059

Infosys. (2024, February 29). Beauty and the beast of consumer expectations. https://www.infosys.com/iki/perspectives/beauty-beast-consumer-expectations.html

Karchin, L., & Horvath, D. (2023). *Cosmetics marketing: Strategy and innovation in the beauty industry*. Bloomsbury Visual Arts.

Laybats, C., & Tredinnick, L. (2016). Post truth, information, and emotion. *Business Information Review, 33*(4), 204–206. https://doi.org/10.1177/0266382116680741

McKinsey & Company. (2023, May). The state of fashion: Beauty report. https://www.mckinsey.com/industries/retail/our-insights/the-beauty-market-in-2023-a-special-state-of-fashion-report. Accessed on June 5, 2023.

Merriam-Webster. (n.d.). Citation. *Merriam-Webster.com dictionary*. https://www.merriam-webster.com/dictionary/beauty. Accessed on May 31, 2024.

Oxford Dictionary. (n.d.). Citation. *oxforddictionaries.com*. https://en.oxforddictionaries.com/definition/beauty. Accessed on May 31, 2024.

Sinclair, D. A., & LaPlante, M., D. (2019). *Lifespan: Why we age—And why we don't have to*. Simon & Schuster.

Stewart, S. (2020). *Painted faces: A colourful history of cosmetics*. Amberley Publishing.

Sutton, R., & Douglas, K. (2019). *Social psychology* (2nd ed.). Bloomsbury Academic.

Swaminathan, V., Sorescu, A., Steenkamp, J.-B. E. M., O'Guinn, T. C. G., & Schmitt, B. (2020). Branding in a hyperconnected world: Refocusing theories and rethinking boundaries. *Journal of Marketing, 84*(2), 24–46. https://doi.org/10.1177/0022242919899905

Chapter 1

Cosmetic Entrepreneurs: Exploring Beliefs and Experiences of Practitioners Administering Non-surgical Aesthetic Procedures in the UK

Rebecca Nash[a] *and Anne-Mette Hermans*[b]

[a]University of Southampton, UK
[b]Tilburg University, The Netherlands

Abstract

Cosmetic surgery has long been a controversial pinnacle of invasive aesthetic labour, but in recent years, the cosmetic landscape has diversified and expanded. Minimally invasive, non-permanent cosmetic 'tweakments' like injectable dermal fillers are increasingly embedded amongst, and advertised as, 'everyday' beauty practices. This normalization has been enabled by the accessibility of these procedures, both in terms of lower costs and locations where they are offered. In many cases, non-surgical procedures have migrated beyond medical locales and, in the UK, can be administered by a range of aesthetic practitioners across diverse spatialities, including beauty salons and spas. In light of discussions surrounding the legitimacy and scope of their business models in a sector where there currently exists little regulation, this chapter will focus on everyday cosmetic entrepreneurship(s) by aesthetic practitioners who offer non-surgical procedures. The vantage point of practitioners is key to exploring an increasingly saturated medico-cosmetic industry in the UK, and such perspectives have rarely been the focus in scholarly work, where motives and desires of cosmetic consumers have taken precedence. Using semi-structured interviews with practitioners focussing on their role(s) within these medico-cosmetic servicescapes, we situate non-surgical, often discreetly transformative, interventions firmly within everyday (gendered) routinized body projects.

Beauty Industry, 21–42

Published under exclusive licence by Emerald Publishing Limited
doi:10.1108/978-1-83608-940-720251011

Keywords: Cosmetic enhancement technologies; non-surgical cosmetic procedures; cosmetic entrepreneurship; emotional labour; beauty; aesthetic medicine

1. Introduction

Medical aesthetic procedures have grown in global popularity in recent decades. In 2023, approximately 35 million procedures were undertaken worldwide, of which 19.2 million were non-surgical (ISAPS, 2024). Non-surgical 'tweakments' like minimally invasive injectables botulinum toxin and hyaluronic acid dermal fillers have contributed to an expansive, diversified and normalized medico-cosmetic servicescape (Berkowitz, 2017; Dowrick & Holliday, 2022). Faces, especially, can be sculpted more cheaply, non-permanently, and with less downtime. The normalization of aesthetic procedures is not new (cf. Heyes, 2007) but accelerated from the mid-2000s, as reality television shows like *Extreme Makeover* and *The Swan* broadcast surgical cosmetic 'transformations', and thereby domesticated them (Heyes, 2007; Jones, 2008b). These examples of traditional media were complemented by the growth and diversification of digital spaces across the 2010s; transforming how medical aesthetic treatments were seen, sold, and consumed. How we invest in, and subsequently present our bodies – or perceive others' appearances – has become an inescapable facet of an all-encompassing cosmetic gaze – the idea that bodies are awaiting improvement via technological intervention (Wegenstein, 2012). Indeed, Hermans and colleagues (2022) found a significant relationship between the use of highly visual social media (e.g. Instagram and Snapchat) and young adults' aesthetic surgery intentions and acceptance. There have been arguments for understanding medical aesthetic procedures as intersubjective processes; mediated through networked relationships between human (and non-human) actors (Jones, 2008a; Pitts-Taylor, 2009). With traditional media like television and magazines usurped by omnipresent visual platforms like Instagram and TikTok, as well as apps focussed on beautification, intensification of corporeal surveillance has contributed to the ongoing boom in non-surgical aesthetic procedures (Elias & Gill, 2018).

Affordability and availability have further aided normalization of such treatments. No longer just in the preserve of surgeons offering costly cosmetic surgical interventions; cheaper, less invasive alternatives are focussed on treating and/or preventing ageing, enhancing features, and 'balancing' facial profiles where there may be (perceived) asymmetry. Arguably, the expansion of non-surgical interventions has resulted in their increased integration into everyday 'mundane' aesthetic routines (Cook & Dwyer, 2017, p. 888). Signifying a considerable socio-technical shift, procedures have moved beyond medicine both spatially and professionally, dispersing on to the high-street and even into domestic premises (e.g. home-run clinics or 'Botox parties') (Dowrick & Holliday, 2022, p. 3). This has not only (re)ignited debates about (gendered) pressures to alter appearances that reflect both pervasive and temporary aesthetic trends (Nuffield Council on Bioethics, 2017) but also arguments about who is qualified to administer treatments, and where these can be performed (Department of Health and Social Care, 2013, 2023). In the UK, governments have been reluctant to regulate the cosmetic surgical sector comprehensively and consistently, and this 'incoherent, diverse approach' (Latham & McHale, 2020, p. 2) is reflected even more starkly in the practice of non-surgical procedures. There are training pathways to non-surgical aesthetics for not only those in medicine and healthcare professions but also those who have no previous experience in administering treatments involving medical materials and devices, like beauticians. Zargaran et al. (2023, p. 152) profiled practitioners in the UK and found that, although they had different profiles, most had (some) medical background, as displayed in Table 1.1. In addition, unlike the male-dominated cosmetic surgery landscape, there has been an increased uptake in the industry by female practitioners (DHSC, 2023; Morton, 2015). This presents a shifting relational dynamic, from (overwhelmingly) female bodies operated on by (overwhelmingly) male surgeons to female bodies treated by (increasingly) female aesthetic practitioners. The 'de-medicalization' of non-surgical procedures distinguishes them from surgical procedures and provides a clear illustration of the perpetually fraught entanglement of medicine with beauty.

A reckoning with the societal implications of entwining medicine and beauty has heightened calls for rethinking how aesthetic medicine is ethically and commercially approached (Atiyeh et al., 2020; da Prato et al., 2024; Edmonds, 2013). Craddock et al. (2022) explored the prospect for sector-wide adoption of corporate social responsibility (CSR) across the aesthetic procedure industry to lessen harms to body image. They found that those they interviewed held (medical) ethical views about their duty of care to client-patients but expressed little intrinsic reflection of broader societal harms. Furthermore, in line with Hermans (2022), the question of how the aesthetics industry aligns itself with medicine 'oscillates' depending on the priorities – medical or business – of the context. Non-surgical aesthetic procedures are situated in a highly competitive business environment. In turning attention to how practitioners attract, treat and retain client-patients within this crowded industry, they must adopt numerous strategies. Looking to scholarly work about other aesthetic professionals – such as beauty therapists and hairdressers – to explore entrepreneurial activity is useful here.

Sharma and Black's (2001) exploratory research, and Black's (2004) extensive ethnographic research in beauty salons, delve into beauty therapists' everyday

Table 1.1. Professional Profiles of Aesthetic Practitioners.

(Medical) Professions	Number	Relative Percentage (%)
Doctors, dentists, nurses	2,510	69
Aestheticians	470	13
Dental nurses	310	8
Allied healthcare professionals	307	8
Pharmacists	30	1
Total	3,667	100

Source: From Zargaran et al. (2023).

experiences of body work and emotional labour. These earlier works on the purposes, pleasures and pressures of the beauty industry as sites of gendered corporeal (re)invigoration can be viewed as a precursor to the study of aesthetic clinics offering non-surgical treatments. Entrepreneurship within aesthetic settings requires ongoing investment in the (professional) self, premises, technologies, modes of promotion and growing clientele (Black, 2004, p. 127). Drawing upon Hochschild's (1983) theory of emotional labour, strategies to build rapport, empathy and trust with an aim to physically (and psychologically) improve wellbeing of clients are a business necessity (Sharma & Black, 2001). Similar studies have explored hairdressing, particularly as a form of temporally ongoing body work where repeat clientele are important, and as a result the hairdresser often adopts additional roles like confidant (Hanson, 2019; Harness et al., 2021). Repeat custom is a significant way that non-surgical aesthetic interventions differ from surgical interventions. Undergoing a surgical procedure is usually a time-limited relationship; ending once the operation and post-operative check is complete. Non-surgical interventions, however, are typically ongoing due to their non-permanence. Looking more specifically at aesthetic clinics offering non-surgical interventions, Morton's (2015) study into anti-ageing modifications, and the medico-cosmetic spatialities within which such body work occurs, highlights the complex entwinement of medicine and beauty. Morton (2015) demonstrates the significant role of practitioners as the literal and figurative holders of not only aesthetic technologies to remedy embodied anxieties but also of spaces where such anxieties can be verbally disentangled. Extending beyond a transactional process of 'just' performing body work, the relationship between aesthetic practitioner and client-patient, therefore, reflects an ongoing intersubjective dynamic aimed at maintaining a disciplined aesthetic.

Considering the above, this chapter will explore cosmetic entrepreneurship(s) from the vantage point of aesthetic practitioners. We specifically focus on how practitioners navigate a saturated commercial field, how they create and promote their aesthetic 'brands', and lastly how they manage relationships with their clientele. Much literature on aesthetic procedures has focussed on motives, desires and experiences of patients (cf. Bonell et al., 2022; Davis, 1995; Gimlin, 2000). Fewer accounts have taken into consideration those who administer the treatments, and their experiences of occupational labour. Therefore, the research question addressed here is 'how do UK-based aesthetic practitioners construct cosmetic entrepreneurship(s) in a saturated medico-commercial field?' We argue that aesthetic practitioners traverse a market landscape at an uncomfortable nexus of medicine and beauty to curate a reputable aesthetic 'brand', comprising a balance of (medical) professionalism and commercialism. They also assume multiple, intersecting roles in their everyday client-patient interactions: acting as an expert/educator, confidant/therapist and corporeal (re)maker. This study presents a view of entrepreneurial experiences of practitioners, adding to understandings of non-surgical procedures as medically (un)tethered, normalized, and embedded into everyday aesthetic routines.

2. Methodology

Participants were recruited to the study through several means, comprising active and passive strategies which were reflected upon throughout, as we constantly evaluated our sampling strategies and adopted new strategies when recruitment was slow (Negrin et al., 2022). Existing practitioner contacts were emailed, and targeted communications were sent to individuals and organizations (i.e., the Joint Council for Cosmetic Practitioners). An online recruitment poster was created and posted on social media sites (e.g., Instagram, Facebook and LinkedIn). The aim of the sampling method was to attract practitioners from different professional backgrounds. Between February and April 2024, 10 participants were recruited to the study, presenting a mixed group of practitioners as detailed in Table 1.2. Practitioner experience in the aesthetics industry varied from 2 years practicing to 18 years. There was a reasonably even gender split of women ($n = 6$) and men ($n = 4$). Whilst the sample was relatively small, for this research, the data held high information power as the study's aim and sample were specific, and the quality of dialogue was good (Malterud et al., 2016).

Interviews were conducted both online and offline, and lasted between 45 minutes and 1 hour. The questions explored autobiographical details about the participants' professional backgrounds, their perceptions of the wider commercial field in the UK, their day-to-day experiences of operating and promoting their services, and how they built and maintained relationships with their clientele.

Table 1.2. Interview Participant Information.

Id	Name	Current Role	Professional Background
1.	Melissa	CEO of aesthetic training company	Non-medic (previously: Sportsperson)
2.	Oscar	Ear, nose and throat surgeon Owner of aesthetics company (sole) Medical director of aesthetics company (regional premises)	Ear nose and throat surgeon
3.	Emma	Owner of aesthetics company (sole)	Nurse
4.	Simon	Aesthetic doctor	General practitioner
5.	Lisa	Prescribing nurse injector at beauty studio	Nurse
6.	Ramona	Owner of aesthetics company (sole)	Dentist
7.	Amber	Aesthetic nurse at aesthetic surgery clinic	Nurse
8.	Jennifer	Owner of aesthetics company (sole)	Nurse
9.	Adrian	Aesthetic doctor	General practitioner
10.	Amir	Owner of aesthetics company (sole)	Nurse

Once the interviews were conducted, they were transcribed verbatim by the researchers and two student-assistants, and pseudonyms were assigned to ensure data confidentiality. Reflexive thematic analysis was conducted (Braun & Clarke, 2006, 2022) using NVivo, and was done so inductively, as the study was exploratory. For the first three transcripts, both authors generated initial codes. These were compared and discussed, and initial themes were identified together. Subsequent transcripts were assigned to be coded independently, with review and finalization of the themes completed in collaboration, checking for consistency and coherence against the data, as per Braun and Clarke's (2006) protocol.

3. Results

Based on our analyses, three main themes were identified. Firstly, participants described how they navigated the non-surgical commercial field in the UK, highlighting advantages and disadvantages pertaining to normalization of treatments. Secondly, participants shared how they established themselves as cosmetic entrepreneurs. This theme encompasses an exploration of investment(s) in the 'professional' practitioner regarding their training, treatments and premises, and the 'public' practitioner with reference to profile-raising and modes of promotion. Thirdly, participants described the varied role(s) they adopt within their commercial premises related to client-patient relationship management.

3.1 An Uncomfortable Medico-Commercial Axis: Navigating the Non-surgical Commercial Field in the UK

It is useful here to understand how aesthetic practitioners perceived the broader commercial field in the UK to contextualize how they navigated the market in their own practice. The participants were unified in expressing concern about how 'diluted' the industry had become, both ethically regarding client-patient safety and also in respect to marketing:

> [Obviously] with TikTok, I don't agree with some of it, because it's not taking aesthetic treatment serious, but then again the whole industry is changing in the way it markets and stuff, and it's not the serious approach. (Melissa)

The increasingly casualized approach to marketing aesthetic procedures is matched by 'everyday' visibility of aesthetic premises. It is now commonplace in the UK to find multiple aesthetic clinics within close geographical proximity; with Emma quipping that their prevalence on highstreets was comparable to the commonness of 'hairdressers and coffee shops'. Increased availability of non-surgical procedures was felt to have contributed to destigmatizing and normalizing treatments; feeding into routinization, with Lisa stating: 'I've got some of my girls booked in for Botox every 3–4 months until 2025, because it's their maintenance'. The role of non-surgical aesthetic treatments to attenuate corporeal anxieties and contribute to mental wellbeing has been noted with reference to the beauty salon (Black, 2004; Sharma & Black, 2001) and in relation to clinics focussed on attending to skin, specifically (Morton, 2015; Straughan, 2010). Furthermore, normalization of procedures was welcomed as evidence that client-patients were increasingly turning to ways that they could improve or preserve their skin health:

> I think 'well, why would you not look after your skin?' People look after their hair, people wear nice clothes, people go to the gym, people try to eat healthy [. . .] then why would you not look after your skin as well? (Emma)

Subsuming non-surgical interventions as aligned with 'everyday' health pursuits like a balanced diet and attending the gym highlights their 'mundanity' (Cook & Dwyer, 2017, pp. 895–896). The proliferation of 'professional' clinical premises to address skin concerns using enhanced (medical) technologies is key to more immediate, effective and transformative modifications. The effects such treatments could have on mental wellbeing was noted as a particular positive:

> I'll get a text saying 'oh my gosh, my husband said that he doesn't know what's happened but I look fresh', or 'I went to see a friend today and she said that my skin is glowing'. I love hearing the confidence. (Lisa)

Everyday enhancements to the lives of client-patients were considered a positive impact that non-surgical treatments enabled. Corporeal anxieties can be assuaged, noticeable to others, and thereby enhancing psychological benefits like increased confidence.

However, not all practitioners were welcoming of changes regarding increased normalization of non-surgical procedures. In particular, there was unease about younger people engaging in 'anti-ageing' treatments and procedures to augment parts of their faces, such as cheeks and lips. This was attributed in large part to representations across social media, which were discussed as a particularly problematic aspect of the commercial field:

> [. . .] because of the Instagram generation, everybody's constantly looking at pictures of themselves. Everyone looking at pictures of other people who've had treatment like celebrities and yeah, social media is very much I think the root of what's caused this massive expansion. (Oscar)

Increased commercialization driven by intensification of highly visual social media like Instagram and TikTok is reminiscent of Elias and Gill's (2018, p. 75) argument that casual technologization of aesthetics has the potential to render procedures 'culturally intelligible as normal'. Apps that alter appearances fed into the characterization of social media as 'fake', with Melissa elaborating: 'social media has created monsters in people. Perfection, like filters and things. When younger clients come, they'll show a picture and say "I want to look like this" . . . but we can't make them look like that'. Aspirations to actively obtain an appearance reminiscent of a digitally altered image brings to mind Gimlin's (2010, p. 64) surgical 'other', who is characterized by a 'willingness to sacrifice a "natural" or authentic look in favour of an obviously enhanced, "artificial" one'. Desires to emulate such an aesthetic was of concern to practitioners, in part due to the potential for 'unnatural'-looking outcomes. Here, Simon reflects on a 'distorted' aesthetic as driven by a desire for social media 'clout': 'particularly women felt that they wanted to sort of fit in with this kind of overfilled or distorted lip, or that there was some sort of reward for it. They were rewarded with likes and followers by Instagram'. Broadly, though, concern was in relation to practitioners who performed excessive, or poor-quality treatments. Non-surgical treatments' largely unregulated status in the UK meant that worry was expressed by participants about 'unscrupulous' practitioners from a plethora of professional backgrounds.

Discussion of practitioners' competencies conveyed a clear divide between medics and non-medics practicing non-surgical aesthetics. Notably, participants mentioned how easy it was to set oneself up as a practitioner with minimal or no training, which attracted humoured (and horrified) responses:

> [One] of my patients was saying this woman who owns the cleaning company, who cleans her house is now doing Botox, and I was like, 'well, should I clean the toilet and then inject your face with Botox?' (Emma)

The experience of 'qualified' aesthetic practitioners operating alongside 'un(der) qualified' practitioners raised concerns regarding accountability, including by the sole non-medic participant, Melissa. She blamed lax insurers for opening the 'floodgates' to non-medics and critiqued the lack of regulation: 'I always refer to it as the "wild, wild west" this industry. You can do whatever you want. Who's going to come for you? The Botox police? [laughs]'. Largely though, participation of un(der) qualified practitioners was met with alarm regarding safety of clientele, especially if complications occurred:

> Very sadly, what sometimes happens is those patients don't get any fix to their problem by the clinic that did the procedure in the first place, because the practitioners are inexperienced and don't know how to fix the problems. (Oscar)

Where anyone could administer treatments, poorly trained practitioners were felt not to be equipped to deal with complications. There was a sense that un(der) qualified practitioners were driven largely by financial gain at the expense of safety and a 'good' aesthetic outcome, illustrated here by a scenario where a prospective client–patient had been turned away by Oscar because the procedure was not felt to be suitable:

> But the really sad thing is, they'll then go off to find the same treatment somewhere else with someone who's not an ethical injector and will happily go and treat them for a couple of £100 in their pocket and then come back to the NHS. Or to us when they have a complication. (Oscar)

Destigmatization of non-surgical aesthetic treatments presents a wealth of opportunity for those who set themselves up as cosmetic entrepreneurs. However, becoming increasingly untethered from medical exclusivity has seen the commercial field in the UK become a vast, unregulated aesthetic servicescape where practitioners of varying qualifications and competencies operate alongside each other. Against this backdrop, participants in this study engaged in a variety of everyday entrepreneurships. Related to this, the next section will explore how aesthetic practitioners construct their 'brands', with emphases on investments in training, premises, profiles, and promotion.

3.2 Cosmetic Entrepreneurship: Curating a Reputable 'Brand'

Most of the participants were sole practitioners who ran their own clinics and necessarily engaged in a range of cosmetic entrepreneurship(s) to build, grow and sustain their businesses. Throughout the interviews, it became clear that entrepreneurship was not necessarily something that came 'naturally' to all practitioners. Adrian for example, who had come from a background as a General Practitioner working in the British National Health Service, emphasized that learning how to run a business was sometimes a shock; business and medicine did not immediately make for the most comfortable pairing:

> I remember one of my senior colleagues once telling me doctors make really bad businessmen, and I think she was right because we think of things quite differently. We think of things as we put the patient first, which is obviously great, but sometimes you need to think of the business as well and like how does that operate? (Adrian)

Adrian went on to discuss turning to other experts in different sectors to help with aspects like accounting and business management. This assistance eased some of the commercial pressure, and avoided what he characterized as a 'hero mentality' among medics to burden themselves with every task. For others, however, 'entrepreneur' was a label that they actively shirked:

> Entrepreneur, meaning like a kind of businessman... No, I'm not. I mean, look at where I am, I mean. It's very basic. I mean, you don't see the kind of chandeliers and the kind of Harley Street type thing. I'm very far away from Harley Street. And it's on purpose. (Simon)

Simon equated 'entrepreneur' with a negative perception of other practitioners in the industry who present a 'flashy' exterior (Atiyeh et al., 2020, p. 1365). However, with aesthetic medicine being provided by private practitioners in pursuit of profit (Adams, 2013), there is inevitable – even if 'reluctant' – entrepreneurship in their practice. Where most participants had migrated from medical backgrounds, the ethos underpinning medical care followed them into running commercial businesses. There was often a steep learning curve regarding not only business practice but navigating a different occupational identity.

For the participants, ensuring they 'got it right' regarding investments in training, treatments and premises was important. There was substantial financial cost in setting-up:

> [I]t's not cheap to set up - that was a really big factor. Each training course was a minimum of £1000, and it was broken down - generally - into individual courses. So, you'd do your foundation Botox, and then lip filler was a separate course, then advanced filler was a separate course. (Lisa)

Further to training, some practitioners decided to obtain external accreditation, getting registered either with the Care Quality Commission, or Save Face – a prominent, government-approved organization in the UK that campaigns for safer aesthetic procedures. Craddock et al. (2022) note the current self-regulatory nature of the industry, where the reputation of a premises and/or practitioner can be enhanced by adherence to voluntary professional standards. Training and qualifications were markers of credibility, safety and trust. Whilst investment in training was a key consideration for cosmetic entrepreneurs, so too was deciding what procedures to offer. The aesthetic clinic has been considered a site of 'innovative' medico-cosmetic technologies (Morton, 2015, p. 1052) with some practitioners indicating a keen interest in new interventions, becoming what we could consider a 'beauty pioneer':

> Last year I introduced Polynucleotides in the clinic. It's been the biggest boom ever. Everyone loves Polynucleotides, and at the beginning, no one knew about Polynucleotides. Because I'm a faculty member I got access to the products maybe a little bit earlier. I got involved in some studies and I just talked about it with a passion that I still talk today. (Ramona)

Whereas investments in novel aesthetic technologies was key to some, others took a more cautious approach. They were committed to 'staple' treatments with well-proven clinical results and reluctant to offer emerging treatments:

> We only do treatments that have pretty much guaranteed results and longevity. They last a decent length of time and with minimal complications. Things like botulinum toxin and fillers. (Oscar)

Demonstrable results and a mastery regarding administering treatments was also important to other practitioners:

> [Whilst] a lot of my colleagues were jumping on the bandwagon of doing this, doing that, I just really wanted to master and be good at what I was interested in before offering X, Y, Z. So, at times I wonder, am I a little bit behind the curve with offering certain treatments? (Lisa)

For Lisa, reluctance to jump on a treatment 'bandwagon' was accompanied by anxiety of falling behind with popular aesthetic trends. Other practitioners were more critical of this aspect of the medico-commercial field, particularly pertaining to the influence of pharmaceutical companies on selling new treatments, with Amir stating that, 'some people are very easily led by the manufacturer sales pitch on these sorts of things. It's very easy to be taken in by that, and you have to be really critical about it'.

In addition to appropriate training and treatment-offerings, participants indicated that investing in a reputable setting was a priority for building client-patient trust, safety and comfort. Prior to incoming legislative changes that require aesthetic practitioners to obtain a premises licence (DHSC, 2023), establishing a reputable clinic environment has not been mandatory. This was an ongoing source of chagrin for some: 'If you're doing a house, or the backroom in a salon on a side street, that's clearly vastly different from doing it in the private wing at the NHS hospital' (Oscar). Emphasizing spatial respectability was an important element of cosmetic entrepreneurship, and it was echoed by other participants: 'If a client comes into [clinic], it's like a medical centre. They can see a PPE wall, they can see their safety, they can see professional staff' (Melissa). Again, here, there is a commitment to cultivating an environment that reassures the client-patient that their (medical) safety is taken seriously. Lisa, however, was operating out of a room based within a beauty salon, and felt she had to compensate in other ways to enhance her credibility with prospective client-patients: 'I try and make sure that I give off a very professional, medical trust for someone, and where I work in a beauty salon I think that is confusing at times and conflicting for [client-patients]'. Lisa was conscious that her setting was not one that represented her professional background as a nurse. So, whilst she emphasized that she was lucky because she had lower overheads and attracted custom from those who came to the salon for other beauty treatments, she felt she had to emphasize her expertise to ensure she was trustworthy. Morton (2015, p. 1051) highlights that aesthetic spatialities present a 'hybrid space, with cosmetic and medical function'. There was a balance to be struck in how practitioners presented their aesthetic spatialities, oscillating between those that reflected traditional clinical locales, and those where other ways of highlighting (medical) professionalism were employed to ensure client-patient trust was met.

Having focussed on key elements of cosmetic entrepreneurship regarding investment in training, treatments and premises, there were also a small number of participants who revelled in raising their profiles within the industry. This included partnerships, sponsorships or being invited into the role of 'Key Opinion

Leader' for aesthetic brands and organizations; being nominated for awards; and contributing comments to media articles about (non-surgical) beauty treatments. On the other hand, there were those who cast a more critical view of the industry. Simon saw 'greed' as prevalent, as well as the influence of pharmaceutical companies:

> I do not want to be identified with any brand. Because... Just because I don't want to be. So, that's my position. I mean, other practitioners are very happy to and I know a lot of them and some of them are very credible and very, very knowledgeable, very good. But they've decided that, you know... It's all about the bucks.

Whilst there were different approaches to investment in the cosmetic entrepreneur's professional self, premises, and profile, effective modes of promotion to attract clientele were key. Whilst almost all participants mentioned attracting a lot of their clientele through word of mouth, a majority utilized social media. The shift from static, often clinically branded webpages of aesthetic surgeons to more personable social media presence reflect changes in digital technologies over recent years, and also the increased normalization of aesthetic procedures, and how they are promoted (Camp & Mills, 2012; Hermans, 2023). It was noted by participants who had entered the aesthetics industry in the past few years how intrinsic social media, particularly Instagram, had been to promote their businesses. Lisa invested heavily in her social media presence, estimating that around 80 percent of her clients came from Instagram:

> I probably pay about £200 just in apps and subscriptions just to make sure my Instagram is as good as it can be, there's a lot of money, time, effort put into that... if you lose that, I mean I wouldn't know what to do if I lost my Instagram page.

Several participants asserted using their social media in a capacity to 'educate' the public. Keeping things informative on social media posts heightened practitioners' visibility, as well as treatment visibility, and emphasized their knowledge and professionalism. Ramona asserted that education was a key part of her promotional identity, stating her output was 'always educational, my social platforms. You won't see me selling anything. It's all educational'. Additionally, methods of promotion in an age of social media presented multiple opportunities for aesthetic practitioners to showcase their skills, personalities, and broader perceptions of the industry. Producing personable and engaging content was of particular importance to Adrian, who had cultivated a significant social media presence that was distinctive and memorable:

> I will see a trend on TikTok or something and I make it medical [...] and people were like, 'Oh yeah, I saw a girl do that with makeup. He's doing it with like dermal filler, what?' [laughs] I'm

> like, you know, actually that's absolutely fine. And people find that cool and different and interesting.

Curating a reputable brand meant that practitioners had to invest carefully in training, treatments, premises, their individual profiles, and promotion. They had to navigate costly initial outlay, and particularly for those who were newer to the industry, a number of strategies that carefully balanced (medical) professionalism and commercialism were used to distinguish them in a saturated medico-commercial field. This meant investment in curating a personable, knowledgeable 'external' face, using their respective social media for engaging and educating prospective client-patients. Within the clinic, much like the entrepreneurships that surround the clinic, the practitioner adopted multiple roles when it came to their relationships with client-patients.

3.3 The Wearer of Many Hats: The Role(s) of the Cosmetic Entrepreneur Inside the Commercial Clinic

The relationship between practitioner and client-patient in non-surgical aesthetics is built on small, non-permanent tweaks. In this respect, we could argue that aesthetic practitioners aimed to become a corporeal (re)maker of their client-patient. Practitioners all indicated the importance of continuous custom, as Ramona stated during her interview, it is 'a lifelong relationship that I'm trying to build. It's not a quick in and out'. The practitioner, like other aesthetic occupations, adopted many roles within the clinic, combining body work with emotional labour to ensure client-patient satisfaction. Practitioners were unified in their approach to building positive relationships with their clientele from the first consultation, focussed on developing trust and empathy. Listening to client-patients' aesthetic expectations were the foundation for a collaborative, bespoke aesthetic plan:

> If I had to put it in one single word about the relationship with my clients, it's trust. I wouldn't do any procedure on anybody unless I had that understanding and that trust with them. And I'm prepared to do whatever it takes at that initial consultation stage to engage with them in a way that makes them truly understand that they can trust me. (Amir)

The importance of not rushing a consultation to build rapport and trust was key to establish the groundwork for any procedure, ensuring attentiveness in 'getting to know' their client–patients' desires, motivations, and expectations, without making assumptions as to why the individual had come to them:

> I give the mirror to the patient and say when you look in the mirror, what are the things that attract your eye, positive or negative? Because actually beauty for me could be very different

> to beauty to you [. . .] so it's quite important to not superimpose my idea of beauty on the patient. (Adrian)

Attentiveness in that initial consultation and taking the time to ensure there was an understanding between the practitioner and the client-patient was felt to be a fundamental stepping-stone to collaboratively working towards a desirable aesthetic outcome: 'It's about really developing those relationships, listening to what somebody wants and working out a plan together, so you're working collaboratively with somebody' (Emma).

This 'collaboration' involves emotional labour, as well as being entrusted to carry out body work that has more physical implications than other beauty treatments. Participants reflected that one of their roles was often 'confidant'. There were parallels drawn by participants between the types of relationships they built with their client–patients and those in other parts of the beauty industry. Routinized corporeal interventions – particularly with the same individual – meant development of a sometimes-enduring relationship: 'It's like when you go to your hairdressers, you just do all the small talk and the more small talk you do, the more of a friend you can develop from that small talk' (Amber). The development of friendships was noted by other participants. Elsewhere, the relationship-building elements of the aesthetic 'journey' was noted by Adrian as being part of his 'fun packaging' approach to aesthetics: '[Client-patients] come in, they like my personality, we chit chat and then they find the journey quite enjoyable'.

Emotional labour did not always end after the appointment, either. The relationship between practitioner and client-patient was not temporally or spatially bound. There were admissions that personal phones numbers were provided in case of any problems, and Ramona emphasized that, in many cases, she could envisage herself going to 'have dinner or coffee with [client-patients] because we have this sort of relationship'. In addition to confidant, there were multiple allusions – though somewhat facetiously – to the practitioner as a 'therapist', with Jennifer noting that 'there's a lot of times that it's like a therapy session, we'll just talk about things and you just build up that relationship from there'. It was felt that aesthetic spatialities could provide a 'safe' place to talk about potentially sensitive intricacies of their lives, and then formulating a plan to enable them to – aesthetically, at least – feel better. Emma reminisced about a client-patient who was in her 70s and had a stressful domestic life:

> I asked her after probably an hour how something made her feel, and she just started crying. And she was like 'seriously, I don't think anyone's asked me how I feel, and I didn't realise I was feeling this bad'. And you know, it's just allowing people to sit with those emotions, really, and then to think about 'how do we support that?'

Being trusted with information disclosed by client-patients was generally regarded as a positive aspect of the practitioners' role. As Solomon et al. (2004, p. 791) note in their ethnography of beauty salons, practitioners become 'natural helpers' regarding issues or crises outside (or sometimes related to) a client-patient's aesthetic desires.

In addition to their role as confidant/therapist, practitioners needed to carefully balance this with their role as expert/educator. Participants argued that part of the consultation was ensuring clear and transparent communication to educate client-patients, set expectations regarding cost, procedure suitability, and outcomes. Some mentioned that client–patients occasionally attended consultations with a preconceived idea of what they wanted, but it was the job of the practitioner to assess, educate and advise on what was most suitable:

> A lot of people will come in and say - and this is really common - they want their nasolabial folds filled, but actually when you look at their face, it's not those, it's their cheeks - it's the mid-face rejuvenation you need to work on first. Then you've got to explain why and the structure, and what drops and all of this sort of thing. When you explain that to them, they're quite receptive because long-term it's the better option. (Jennifer)

The practitioner positions themselves as an authority in facial anatomy and the effects of ageing and other impacts on skin health. They inform the client-patient of any misconceptions they may have about the site(s) of their aesthetic concern; spending time exacting a clinical eye over the client-patient and balancing their expertise with learning more about the client-patient's motivations:

> [We'll] have an hour consultation, I'll do a skin analysis, we'll do a PowerPoint presentation where I explain ageing, skin ageing, bone ageing and how the ageing process works, what types of treatments are available and they have also time to discuss what they want. So the first 5 minutes is for them. I want to listen. Why do they want to come and see me? Then I will go in and start explaining. (Ramona)

The consultation is integral for not only ensuring clear communication of the aesthetic area(s) of concern, and how the practitioner can help, but also *if* they are able to provide suitable treatments. In some cases, participants would turn client-patients away for a variety of reasons, e.g. the treatment requested was felt to be unnecessary, or not representative of the type of aesthetic outcome the practitioner was comfortable in creating. For the participants, part of building a reputable brand was saying 'no', often citing medical ethics:

> [Some] of the young ladies, they're not interested, they want to continue and that's fine by me, they just won't have their work done by me. I have a strong ethos that I'm not going to do anything out of my comfort zone for a patient. (Amber)

Becoming a corporeal (re)maker meant sometimes being selective about whom to treat. Drawing boundaries on what they would and would not do regarding aesthetic treatments was important to participants, even if it meant losing custom. The nature of the saturated medico-commercial field meant it would be likely that prospective clientele would find another practitioner. Participants had a sense of their own boundaries regarding what they were comfortable with.

Concluding, the aesthetic practitioner, much like those in other aesthetic occupations, wears multiple hats within (and outside) of their commercial clinic. To become a trusted corporeal (re)maker, they often perform the role of therapist/confidant, and expert/educator with their client/patients. The body work and emotion work of the aesthetic clinic is comparable to other aesthetic occupations, but it cannot be ignored that the types of aesthetic treatments provided in these spaces are more physically significant and risky than other beauty treatments. Cosmetic entrepreneurs, therefore, approach their responsibilities to client-patients with rigour, care and, fundamentally, (medical) professionalism, whereby deference to the desires of prospective client-patients must be carefully navigated, and the ethos and expertise of the practitioner retained.

4. Discussion

The aim of this research was to begin exploring the experiences of aesthetic practitioners and how they construct cosmetic entrepreneurship in a highly saturated medico-commercial field. Overarchingly, tensions between (medical) professionalism and commercialism recurred in practitioners' critiques of the broader non-surgical market, and their experiences of cosmetic entrepreneurship, and there are three key themes to be explored in the discussion. Firstly, practitioners had to navigate a medically (un)tethered aesthetic landscape. Whilst many praised the propensity for non-surgical treatments to heighten mental wellbeing, there were numerous concerns. Key amongst these were 'casual' and unrealistic representations of treatments across social media, and lax regulation resulting in proliferation of unscrupulous practitioners driven solely by financial gain as opposed to ethical duties to their clientele. The second theme builds on this in exploring how practitioners balanced (medical) professionalism and commercialism to curate a reputable aesthetic brand. This included investment in training and treatments, respectable spatialities, and the cultivation of a professional-yet-personable public profile. Thirdly, the 'balancing act' continues into the running of a commercial clinic, where the aesthetic practitioner assumes many roles in their everyday client-patient relationship management. This theme provides insights into practitioners' multifaceted occupational identities.

Multiple factors intersect to medically (un)tether non-surgical procedures and more firmly embed them into routinized aesthetic labour. Jones (2008a) highlights that sociotechnical processes interknit to mediate normalization and routinization of aesthetic procedures. Participants in this study emphasized that social media representations of procedures and outcomes, in combination with a saturated offline marketplace – spanning medical/non-medical professions and spatialities – have contributed to medical (un)tethering. Echoing Wegenstein's (2012) work on the cosmetic gaze, alongside Elias and Gill's (2018) assertion that apps for beautification intensify corporeal self-surveillance, there appeared to be consensus across practitioners that non-surgical treatments had become – for good and for bad – 'culturally intelligible as normal' (p. 75). Indeed, non-surgical procedures have become subsumed as part of holistic corporeal interventions (Morton, 2015; Straughan, 2010). Edmonds (2013, pp. 247–248) argued that it is not possible to totally '*dis*entangle aesthetics and health' particularly where – as is the case for non-surgical aesthetic procedures – the nexus is especially blurred. Hermans (2022) notes this in her work, arguing that different types of (medical) aesthetic products, treatments and procedures are constructed across a continuum, and are perceived differently by social actors: where some may deem non-surgical interventions as normative, others consider them not so.

Nonetheless, normalization and routinization of non-surgical treatments has arguably rendered them as 'unremarkable' (Cook & Dwyer, 2017; Dowrick & Holliday, 2022). However, banality of medico-cosmetic technologies does not mean they are without consequence. Medical (un)tethering was considered to have implications regarding 'unnatural' (thus undesirable) aesthetic outcomes, alongside the potential for complications with complex recourse, where the original practitioner may not have the expertise to remedy issues. Practitioners alluded to the vast aesthetic servicescape in the UK as disparate – there existed mixed quality of aesthetic practice, as well as scrupulous and unscrupulous practitioners. Gimlin's (2010) work on cosmetic surgical 'others' is useful here for understanding characterizations of both consumers and practitioners of non-surgical treatments. Similarly to the surgeons from Gimlin's (2010) study, most participants in the current research asserted being guided by (medical) ethical principles in duties of care to the client-patients; distinguishing themselves from practitioners who undermined such ethics by prioritizing financial recompense. Non-surgical aesthetic procedures have been regarded a 'golden goose' – and where regulation is lax and potential for lucrative business is high, 'ethical questions follow' (Atiyeh et al., 2020, p. 1367).

Despite incoming legislation (DSHC, 2023) and calls for the sector to engage with socially responsible commercial pursuit (Craddock et al., 2022; Da Prato et al., 2024; Nuffield Council on Bioethics, 2017), fragmentation of the industry and dispersion of services across professions and spatialities makes it difficult to comprehend at this stage how non-surgical aesthetic procedures may be (re) tethered to medicine. This was summed up by Melissa, as the industry being 'like wildfire now and it's not slowing down. No one's put off by regulations, everyone just says it won't happen'. Aesthetic practitioners, in curating their reputable brands, had to navigate the challenges of a medically (un)tethered commercial environment marred by incongruent (un)ethical practice, in order to present themselves with (medical) professionalism that was complemented by their success in commercial endeavour.

For practitioners in this study, creating a reputable brand comprised a number of strategies that struck a balance between (medical) professionalism and commercialism. Adams (2013) notes that the aesthetic surgical industry is a dominant example of a consumer-driven medical market, whereby practitioners must adopt entrepreneurial practices in order to attract (and retain) consumers.

This extends to non-surgical procedures as well, where market forces are arguably greater, given the saturation and diversification of the UK aesthetic servicescape. For participants in this study, much like with other aesthetic occupations, becoming a cosmetic entrepreneur entailed necessarily investing in training, treatment offerings and premises befitting their occupational identity and aspirations for their business (Black, 2004). Craddock et al. (2022) and Hermans (2022, 2023) note tensions in how the aesthetics industry balances (medical) ethics and the business priority to sell medico-cosmetic interventions. Participants in this study indicated that their priority was to foreground (medical) professionalism. Cosmetic entrepreneurship was not consistent across the sample we interviewed. This meant some actively eschewed entrepreneurial activities like adopting emerging aesthetic technologies, or working in partnership with aesthetic brands/manufacturers, whilst others revelled in these pursuits.

Nevertheless, significant in highlighting the balancing act between (medical) professionalism and commercialism was how practitioners marketed their aesthetic services, particularly their presence on social media. Hermans (2023) argued that tonality of aesthetic clinics' promotional content shared via social media oscillates between professional and commercial; formal and informal. The current study found similar results, with practitioners being keen to strike a balance between showcasing their work and educating their audience; but doing so in a personable way. For the practitioner, this cultivates a reputable public face, combining their expertise with facets of their personalities that has become a standard when promoting services online (Camp & Mills, 2012). Whilst participants in this study asserted that they used social media as an 'educational' tool as much as – or sometimes more than – a showcase of their work, Sullivan (2010, p. 409) notes in her overview of the ethics of marketing aesthetic surgery 'the purpose of advertising is to *persuade* people to do something, [original emphasis]. Therefore, even when 'education' is the stated aim of social media posts, it is still being posted by the practitioner on their business page, cultivating interest in their aesthetic practice.

Lastly, cosmetic entrepreneurs adopted several intersecting identities *within* the clinic. As outlined by scholarly work pertaining to other aesthetic occupations like beauty therapy and hairdressing, temporally ongoing body work necessitates building a positive relational dynamic that adapts to each individual (Black, 2004; Hanson, 2019; Harness et al., 2021; Sharma & Black, 2001). Participants in this study explained the intricacies of effective relationship management with their client-patients; emphasizing trust, compassion, compromise and collaboration as key. Hanson (2019, p. 151) found that within beauty salons, practitioners exerted commercialized empathetic listening, acting as a 'supportive confidant'. Practitioners frequently exert emotional labour (Hochschild, 1983) in their everyday interactions, and this is particularly pronounced in the aesthetic clinic where corporeal anxieties often gave way to larger conversations about general life stressors. Practitioners in this study explored aesthetic motives, concerns and desires with their client-patients, using their expertise combined with skills in emotional management to suggest appropriate routes forward; becoming 'natural helpers' (Solomon et al., 2004).

Though there is much congruence with other aesthetic occupations when considering the different tasks and role(s) one must adopt, aesthetic practitioners differ where there is entanglement between medicine and beauty. The proximity of the practitioner to (and under) the skin of the client-patient comes with a unique implication: the practitioner is a corporeal (re)maker in a way that even subtle tweaks can have a dramatic effect on appearance. Morton (2015, p. 1054) asserts that non-surgical body projects combined 'medicalized practices, technologies and corporeal knowledges' and this was certainly reiterated by the participants in this study. Relatedly, Pitts-Taylor (2009) highlights the importance of understanding aesthetic procedures as intersubjective processes where social, psychological and broader ontological contexts and complexities are understood to impact on experiences of becoming/being a client-patient. Whilst Pitts-Taylor (2009) was writing specifically about surgical procedures, it can be argued that when considering temporally ongoing non-surgical body work, intersubjectivities – particularly in the cultivation of a positive relationship between the practitioner and the client-patient – are a crucial aspect of cosmetic entrepreneurship.

5. Conclusion

This chapter has contributed to literature that explores the increased routinization of non-surgical procedures, and specifically provides insight into how aesthetic practitioners approach cosmetic entrepreneurship in the context of the UK's highly saturated medico-commercial market. This has implications for research that may explore further the intersubjective relational dynamics between aesthetic practitioners and their clientele, as well as delving further into practitioner experiences of cosmetic entrepreneurship. This chapter provides a broad exploration pertaining to several aspects worthy of further investigation. Finding that aesthetic entrepreneurship requires a delicate balancing act regarding (medical) professionalism and commercialism, the participants in this study were keen to emphasize their commitment to client-patient safety. This was often distinguished against 'unscrupulous' entrepreneurships of 'other' practitioners operating in the field. Within their respective spatialities, it was also the case that aesthetic practitioners assume many roles, including expert/educator, therapist/confidant and corporeal (re)maker. There was significant emotional labour involved in client-patient relationship management. Viewing this relational approach as similar to those within other aesthetic occupations like hairdressing and beauty therapy, there were also marked differences regarding physical and psychological proximity to corporeal anxieties. The cosmetic entrepreneur must deftly traverse a fragmented industry to establish themselves as reputable and personable practitioner who will simultaneously care for and aesthetically transform their clientele.

References

Adams, J. (2013). Medicalization and the market economy: Constructing cosmetic surgery as consumable health care. *Sociological Spectrum*, *33*(4), 374–389. https://doi.org/10.1080/02732173.2013.732895

Atiyeh, B. S., Rubeiz, M. T., & Hayek, S. N. (2020). Aesthetic/cosmetic surgery and ethical challenges. *Aesthetic Plastic Surgery*, *44*(4), 1364–1374. https://doi.org/10.1007/s00266-020-01821-z

Berkowitz, D. (2017). *Botox nation: Changing the face of America*. New York University Press.

Black, P. (2004). *The beauty industry: Gender, culture, pleasure*. Routledge.

Bonell, S., Austen, E., & Griffiths, S. (2022). Australian women's motivations for, and experiences of, cosmetic surgery: A qualitative investigation. *Body Image*, *41*, 128–139. https://doi.org/10.1016/j.bodyim.2022.02.010

Braun, V., & Clarke, V. (2006). Using thematic analysis in psychology. *Qualitative Research in Psychology*, *3*(2), 77–101. https://doi.org/10.1191/1478088706qp063oa

Braun, V., & Clarke, V. (2022). Conceptual and design thinking for thematic analysis. *Qualitative Psychology*, *9*(1), 3–26. https://doi.org/10.1037/qup0000196

Camp, S. M., & Mills, D. C. (2012). The marriage of plastic surgery and social media: A relationship to last a lifetime. *Aesthetic Surgery Journal*, *32*(3), 349–351. https://doi.org/10.1177/1090820X12439862

Cook, P. S., & Dwyer, A. (2017). No longer raising eyebrows: The contexts and domestication of Botox as a mundane medical and cultural artefact. *Journal of Consumer Culture*, *17*(3), 887–909. https://doi.org/10.1177/1469540516634414

Craddock, N., Spotswood, F., Rumsey, N., & Diedrichs, P. C. (2022). 'We should educate the public that cosmetic procedures are as safe as normal medicine': Understanding corporate social responsibility from the perspective of the cosmetic procedures industry. *Body Image*, *43*, 75–86. https://doi.org/10.1016/j.bodyim.2022.08.011

Da Prato, E. B., Cartier, H., Margara, A., Molina, B., Tateo, A., Grimolizzi, F., & Spagnolo, A. G. (2024). The ethical foundations of patient-centered care in aesthetic medicine. *Philosophy, Ethics, and Humanities in Medicine*, *19*(1), 1. https://doi.org/10.1186/s13010-024-00151-1

Davis, K. (1995). *Reshaping the female body: The dilemma of cosmetic surgery*. Routledge.

Department of Health and Social Care. (2023). The licensing of non-surgical cosmetic procedure in England. https://www.gov.uk/government/consultations/licensing-of-non-surgical-cosmetic-procedures/the-licensing-of-non-surgical-cosmetic-procedures-in-england. Accessed on December 12, 2023.

Department of Health and Social Care. (2013). Review of the regulation of cosmetic interventions. https://assets.publishing.service.gov.uk/media/5a7a25dee5274a319e77831c/Review_of_the_Regulation_of_Cosmetic_Interventions.pdf. Accessed on February 03, 2024.

Dowrick, A., & Holliday, R. (2022). Tweakments: Non-surgical beauty technologies and future directions for the sociology of the body. *Sociology Compass*, *16*(11), e13044. https://doi.org/10.1111/soc4.13044

Edmonds, A. (2013). Can medicine be aesthetic?: Disentangling beauty and health in elective surgeries. *Medical Anthropology Quarterly*, *27*(2), 233–252. https://doi.org/10.1111/maq.12025

Elias, A. S., & Gill, R. (2018). Beauty surveillance: The digital self-monitoring cultures of neoliberalism. *European Journal of Cultural Studies*, *21*(1), 59–77. https://doi.org/10.1177/1367549417705604

Gimlin, D. (2000). Cosmetic surgery: Beauty as commodity. *Qualitative Sociology*, *23*(1), 77–98. https://doi.org/10.1023/A:1005455600571

Gimlin, D. (2010). Imagining the other in cosmetic surgery. *Body and Society*, *16*(4), 57–76. https://doi.org/10.1177/1357034X10383881

Hanson, K. (2019). Beauty 'therapy': The emotional labor of commercialized listening in the salon industry. *International Journal of Listening*, *33*(3), 148–153. https://doi.org/10.1080/10904018.2019.1634572

Harness, O. M., Jamie, K., & McMurray, R. (2021). 'They've been with me the whole journey': Temporality, emotional labour and hairdressing work. *Work, Employment and Society*, *35*(6), 1073–1090. https://doi.org/10.1177/0950017020955081

Hermans, A.-M. (2022). Lifting, sculpting, and contouring: Implications of the blurred boundary between cosmetic procedures and 'other' beauty products/services. *Poetics*, *90*, 101610. https://doi.org/10.1016/j.poetic.2021.101610

Hermans, A.-M. (2023). *Watermelons, syringes, and regulation: Instagram marketing by cosmetic clinics in the UK and The Netherlands.* Aesthetic Plastic Surgery. https://doi.org/10.1007/s00266-023-03420-0

Hermans, A.-M., Boerman, S. C., & Veldhuis, J. (2022). Follow, filter, filler? Social media usage and cosmetic procedure intention, acceptance, and normalization among young adults. *Body Image*, *43*, 440–449. https://doi.org/10.1016/j.bodyim.2022.10.004

Heyes, C. J. (2007). Cosmetic surgery and the televisual makeover: A Foucauldian feminist reading. *Feminist Media Studies*, *7*(1), 17–32. https://doi.org/10.1080/14680770601103670

Hochschild, A. (1983). *The managed heart: Commercialization of human feeling*. University of California Press.

International Society of Aesthetic Plastic Surgery. (2024). ISAPS international survey on aesthetic/cosmetic procedures performed in 2023. https://www.isaps.org/media/rxnfqibn/isaps-global-survey_2023.pdf. Accessed on June 20, 2024.

Jones, M. (2008a). *Skintight: An anatomy of cosmetic surgery*. Berg.

Jones, M. (2008b). Media-bodies and screen-births: Cosmetic surgery reality television. *Continuum: Journal of Media & Cultural Studies*, *22*(4), 515-524. https://doi.org/10.1080/10304310802189998

Latham, M., & McHale, J. (2020). *The regulation of cosmetic procedures: Legal, ethical and practical challenges*. Routledge.

Malterud, K., Siersma, V. D., & Guassora, A. D. (2016). Sample size in qualitative interview studies: Guided by information power. *Qualitative Health Research*, *26*(13), 1753–1760. https://doi.org/10.1177/1049732315617444

Morton, K. (2015). Emerging geographies of disciplining the ageing body: Practising cosmetic technologies in the aesthetic clinic. *Gender, Place & Culture*, *22*(7), 1041–1057. https://doi.org/10.1080/0966369X.2014.939151

Negrin, K. A., Slaughter, S. E., Dahlke, S., & Olson, J. (2022). Successful recruitment to qualitative research: A critical reflection. *International Journal of Qualitative Methods*, *21*, 1–12. https://doi.org/10.1177/16094069221119576

Nuffield Council on Bioethics. (2017). Cosmetic procedures: Ethical issues. https://www.nuffieldbioethics.org/publications/cosmetic-procedures. Accessed on December 18, 2023.

Pitts-Taylor, V. (2009). Becoming/being a cosmetic surgery patient: Semantic instability and the intersubjective self. *Studies in Gender and Sexuality*, *10*, 119–128. https://doi.org/10.1080/15240650902979202

Sharma, U., & Black, P. (2001). Look good, feel better: Beauty therapy as emotional labour. *Sociology*, *35*(4), 913–931. https://doi.org/10.1017/S0038038501009130

Solomon, F., Linnan, L., Wasilewski, Y., Lee, A. M., Katz, M. L., & Yang, J. (2004). Observational study in ten beauty salons: Results informing development of the North Carolina beauty and health project. *Health Education & Behaviour*, *31*, 790–807. https://doi.org/10.1177/1090198104264176

Straughan, E. R. (2010). The salon as clinic: Problematising, treating, and caring for skin. *Social & Cultural Geography*, *11*(7), 647–661. https://doi.org/10.1080/14649365.2010.508563

Sullivan, D. A. (2010). Advertising cosmetic surgery. *AMA Journal of Ethics*, *12*(5), 407–411. https://doi.org/10.1001/virtualmentor.2010.12.5.mhst1-1005

Wegenstein, B. (2012). *The cosmetic gaze: Body modification and the construction of beauty*. MIT Press.

Zargaran, D., Zargaran, A., Terranova, T., Khaledi, H., Robinson, A., Davies, J., Weyrich, T., & Mosahebi, A. (2023). Profiling UK injectable aesthetic practitioners: A national cohort analysis. *Journal of Plastic, Reconstructive & Aesthetic Surgery*, *86*, 150–154. https://doi.org/10.1016/j.bjps.2023.06.057

Chapter 2

The Environmental Cost of Vanity: An Ecofeminist Analysis of the Beauty Industry, the Consumer Behaviour and Environmental Attitudes

Martina Topić[a] *and Ioannis Kostopoulos*[b]

[a]The University of Alabama, USA
[b]Liverpool John Moore University, UK

Abstract

This chapter analyzes environmental attitudes and consumer behaviour for mirrors. Purchasing mirrors is conceptualized as vanity and thus, the research explored to what extent showing a higher degree of vanity influences purchase behaviour and this was analyzed against other demographic characteristics such as gender, income, and education. An ecofeminist theory was taken as a starting point, exploring the historical ecofeminist claim that women are more likely to express pro-environmentalist attitudes. A national survey was conducted with a purchased sample of UK adults from a Smart Survey pollster. Results show marginal differences in environmental attitudes with women showing marginally more concern than men, not only confirming ecofeminist findings but also showing that environmentalism as a concern is becoming a universal concern. Vanity was found to be a predictor of anti-environmentalist views and vanity is linked to an increase in income and it negatively impacts the environmental attitudes of men. Social values such as tradition and security were found to be the biggest predictors for women and their environmental attitudes.

Keywords: Ecofeminism; women; beauty industry; mirrors; vanity; environmental attitudes; consumer behaviour; purchase behaviour

Beauty Industry, 43–67

Published under exclusive licence by Emerald Publishing Limited
doi:10.1108/978-1-83608-940-720251014

1. Introduction

Ecofeminist research has argued that, historically, women were more engaged with environmental activism than men due to the specific oppression that women face (Brownhill & Turner, 2020; Diani, 1989; Geiger Zeman & Holy, 2014; Giacomini, 2014; Godfrey, 2008; Goldstein, 2006; Holy, 2007, 2008; Kirk, 1998; Mann, 2011; McMahon, 1997; Poole & Harmon Zeigter, 1985; Salleh, 1984; Schahn & Holzer, 1990; Shapiro & Mahajan, 1986; Steger & Witt, 1989; Stoddart & Tindall, 2011; Topić, 2020, 2021; Topić et al., 2021). In addition to that, patriarchal oppression has historically imposed expectations on women regarding their appearance, which was always particularly visible in the prominence of the beauty industry, and an expectation imposed on women to look pretty and use beauty products to appear more appealing and youthful by often implementing unhealthy beauty routines (Faludi, 1991; Mellicker, 2016; Parkins, 2006; Wolf, 1991). Some authors also argued that women were historically pushed towards fashion, which was done by a male-dominated advertising industry in response to the threat of second-wave feminism (Tyner & Ogle, 2009).

At the same time, studies in consumerism and environmentalism gained prominence, particularly not only from a marketing and green marketing perspective but also from a general anti-consumerist perspective with some authors arguing that there is a saturation of media coverage of environmentalist affairs, but without substantial call for behaviour change, which might result with the public rejecting environmentalism, particularly since the conservative press is not in favour of the movement and often labels it as a white, middle-class movement consisting of privileged people who can afford to care for the environment (Topić, 2021). Economists and environmentalists have been indeed advocating for behaviour change in consumption and the way of living since the 18th century but the attention started to increase during the 1960s when Kenneth Boulding (1966) published an article warning about growing ecological problems, which increased attention of economists, environmentalists and sociologists towards the issue of consumerism (Calder, 1990; Ewen & Ewen, 1992; Krstić & Krstić, 2017; Trentmann, 2016; Wright & Nyberg, 2015).

Some critical authors warned that human civilzation is based on anthropocentric and liberal values that promote the view of humans as the only rightful right holders over the environment, which they can exploit as they wish (Krstić, 2018); a critique that echoes ecofeminism. In 1972, a study entitled *The Limits of Growth* was published calling the planet finite and warning that resources would run out (Meadows et al., 1972). The same authors also published an update in 2004 and argued that their prediction came to fruition sooner than originally predicted with the planet's population and exploitation of resources growing at unprecedented rates (Meadows et al., 2004).

With increased environmental activism and media coverage of climate change (Meadows et al., 2004), as well as increased prominence of the feminist movement such as the #metoo (Diaz, 2020), we asked a question to what extent do women still show more concern for the environment now that environmental affairs are on the public and media agenda and to what extent women buy beauty products, including vanity products such as mirrors and how this links with environmental attitudes. We were interested in understanding to what extent patriarchal expectations on personal appearance drive consumer behaviour and in that, we particularly looked at the beauty and mirrors industries by exploring consumer behaviour and environmental attitudes of women and men in the United Kingdom. The mirrors industry was valued at $3,245.27 million in 2022 with a projection to continue to grow to $5,032.4 million by 2031 (Industry Growth Report, 2023) with smart mirrors alone being valued at $4.42 billion in 2023 (Statista, 2023). The beauty industry was valued at $430 billion in 2022 (McKinsey, 2023) with an expectation to reach $580 billion by 2027 (McKinsey, 2023), thus showing relevance for the analysis of consumer behaviour in the context of environmental activism and climate change.

In the subsequent part of the chapter, we first explain the position of ecofeminism, which inspired our research, then we discuss the purchase behaviour and environmentalism and then we present the results of our UK survey on environmentalism and purchase behaviour in the context of mirrors to explore the concept of vanity, which is largely missing from scholarly exploration of purchase behaviour and environmentalism but should be considered if consumerism and environmental degradation are to be tackled.

2. Ecofeminism

Ecofeminism is a movement that links feminist and ecological struggles by arguing that there is a duality of oppression of women and nature, which stems from the ideology of hegemonic masculinity and patriarchy, both of which with links to capitalism (Đurđević & Marjanić, 2020; Gaard, 1997; Henderson, 1997; Ling, 2014; Mallory, 2012; Marjanić, 2020; Merchant, 1992; Radford Ruether, 2012; Sandiland, 1999; Stoddart & Tindall, 2011; VonWerlhof, 2013; Warren, n.d.). With this, ecofeminism presents itself as a movement and a critique that sits at the intersection of radical (the focus on patriarchy) and socialist (the focus on the opposition to capitalism) feminism (Topić, 2020). Despite numerous definitions, ecofeminism is often seen as an anti-hierarchical and anti-capitalist movement that works on a global scale, due to its focus also on the inequality between the West and the Global South (Bandyopadhyay, 1999; Fakier & Cock, 2018; Green Belt Movement, n.d.; Griffin, 2020; Holy, 2007; Jain, 1984; Moore, 2011; Mishra et al., 2021; Shiva & Bandyopadhyay, 1986; Topić, 2021). Ecofeminists argue that there is a dichotomy between how men and women are assigned role in societies with men being linked to culture and rationality whilst women are being linked with nature and irrationality, which then also results in a 'domestification' of women as emotional creatures who should stay at home and be tamed like the nature (Topić, 2021). Ecofeminism, in a nutshell, fights *-isms* (sexism, racism, and speciesism) and conflicts with all major ideologies (liberalism, conservativism, nationalism, fascism) as well as capitalism and patriarchy (Đurdjević & Marjanić, 2020, see also Brownhill & Turner, 2020; saed, 2017).

Because of the deep connection between women and nature, and the fact both experienced oppression, ecofeminists have mapped out a history of women's environmentalism and argued that historically, women were more likely to stand up for the environment and defend it (Brownhill & Turner, 2020, Giacomini, 2014; Salleh, 1984; Stoddart & Tindall, 2011, Topić, 2020, 2021; Topić et al., 2021). For example, the Chipko movement in India was led by women attempting to stop the destruction of forests whilst women in Kenya formed the Green Belt Movement and tried to fight the destruction of nature by planting millions of trees and founding training centres to educate people on ecological agriculture (Shiva & Bandyopadhyay, 1986; Jain, 1984; Bandyopadhyay, 1999; Moore, 2011; Mishra et al., 2021, Green Belt Movement, n.d; Holy, 2007). Ecofeminism has historically equally been interested in women who fight for the environment and basic survival such as women in Nigeria fighting with the slogan 'fish, not oil' as well as white- and blue-collar women from western cities who fight for workplace equality (Brownhill & Turner, 2020).

However, this does not mean that absolutely all women defend nature whilst absolutely all men seek to destroy it. Historically, many women showed negligence and hostile attitudes towards the environment and nature whilst many men actively campaigned for its preservation (Topić, 2021). In a study of shopping behaviour in the UK, Topić et al. (2021), using a quantitative method of a large national survey, showed that many women who come from a lower socio-demographic status demonstrate negative views of discounted food, the so-called yellow sticker food because of a perceived lack of agency in deciding to buy discounted food despite this food presenting a more environmentally friendly shopping. Not all women in this sample were anti-environmentalist per se but some were seen to show hostility due to a lack of purchasing power to make a conscious decision to shop in this way and because of a lack of identification with people with a higher purchasing power who can make these decisions. Leahy (2003) argued that some working-class people indeed see environmental movements as middle-class movements. As Hugo Blanco, a peasant leader from Peru wrote,

> 'At first sight, environmentalists or conservationists are nice, slightly crazy guys whose main purpose in life is to prevent the disappearance of blue whales or pandas. The common people have more important things to think about, for instance how to get their daily bread...' (Blanco, 1991, cited from Martínez-Alier, 1995, p. 97)

3. Consumerism, the Beauty Industry, and (the Lack of) Ecofeminist Analysis

The environmentalist movement generally has links with anti-consumerism (Roszak, 1992), which is also one of the pillars of the ecofeminist critique due to an ecofeminist position being that consumerism destroys the environment and is a Western way of life that is burdening the Global South, which is suffering disproportionate consequences of Western consumerism (Holy, 2007; Sandberg & Sandberg, 2010). Ecofeminist works have tackled the beauty industry by emphasizing the cruelty of animal testing for beauty products and recognizing that many women participate in this oppression, particularly Western ones who are also embedded in a liberal feminist paradigm often only, even if inadvertently, advocating for white middle-class women of the West fighting work equality and who are often complacent with environmental destruction including through the use of beauty products (Glazebrook, 2002; Warren, 2000). However, beyond these analyses of animal cruelty and the harm the beauty industry does to animals, who in ecofeminist view have the same right to the planet as humans, not much analysis has focussed on the beauty industry nor there are analyses of women's environmental views in the context of ecofeminism.

Consumerism equally comes from consuming endless goods and things but also from the negative effects of employment such as long hours, and the need for higher salaries (Mont, 2004; Sheth et al., 2011), and modern society is, generally, driven by consumerism (Topić et al., 2024). However, despite the rise of the environmentalist movement and the climate change debate, many consumers hold cynical attitudes towards green businesses and sustainable products and see them as greenwashing. In a study on personality predictors of consumerism and environmentalism, Hirsh and Dolderman (2007) argued that consumerism and environmentalism are seen as mutually exclusive constructs because consumerism emphasizes the accumulation and consumption of material sources whilst environmentalism argues for resource conservation and long-term sustainability. Whilst, normally, highly materialistic individuals are seen as selfish, possessive, and concerned with the accumulation of material possessions, environmentally concerned individuals are more likely to be motivated by compassion, social concern, and a broader self-concept, but authors of this study argue that consumerism and environmentalism can be predicted by the personality trait of agreeableness with consumerism being negatively associated with agreeableness whilst environmentalism was positively associated with both agreeableness and openness (Gifford & Nilsson, 2014; Schultz et al., 2005).

Studies on purchase behaviour have shown that consumers sometimes dislike sustainable options if they are discounted because of a perceived lack of power to decide to buy these products, as already mentioned above (Topić et al., 2021). Consumers also find organic products or sustainably packaged products too expensive, often also expressing views that they would shop more sustainably if they could afford it (Mitchell & Topić, 2019). Other studies also showed that cognitive factors such as knowledge about the environment have a limited influence on purchase behaviour whereas a significant influence comes from affective factors on making an environmentally conditioned purchase decision (Davis, 1993; Finger, 1994). In a recent study on consumer behaviour in the context of sustainability, Ryzomiliotis (2024) argued that perceived risk and security along with perceived privacy predict trust on e-commerce websites, which then predicts online purchase intention for sustainable products because consumer trust in sustainable products is also moderating this relationship.

When it comes to beauty products, Kim and Seock (2009) argued that health and environmental consciousness significantly influenced the importance placed on beauty products' attributes with those with a high level of health and environmental consciousness showing significantly more positivity in evaluating natural beauty products whereas those with lower health and environmental consciousness showed less willingness to pay extra for natural beauty products. Many studies, from the field of marketing in particular, look at the role of beauty influencers and vloggers on beauty purchase behaviour (Purnamaningsih et al., 2024; Xiao et al., 2024) but not many studies look at this issue with an ecofeminist lens and thus at a moderating gender influence and the influence of vanity as a variable that explains purchase behaviour and environmental attitudes (Jin & Ryu, 2020; Konstantopoulou et al., 2019).

Vanity has been studied in the context of marketing and purchase behaviour but again, not from an environmental/ecofeminist perspective and there are lots of studies studying vanity in the context of purchase behaviour with implications for marketers. For example, Durvasula and Lysonski (2008) argued that both gender and country have an impact on vanity perceptions with concern for physical appearance and professional achievement being higher in Eastern cultures compared to Western cultures. The authors analyzed vanity in the context of Eastern cultures and the Gen Y demographic and argued that vanity appeals can resonate well with Gen Y, particularly in China and India, and that marketers should use vanity appeals to sell products. Similarly, Wang and Waller (2006) analyzed consumer vanity in the United States and China looking at vanity constructs such as appearance concern, appearance perception, achievement concern, and achievement perception. Results have shown that Chinese respondents show more concern for professional achievement than American ones, but their achievement perception is lower than for American respondents. But, when it comes to personal appearance, in both countries' consumers showed similar levels of vanity in their self-perceptions at a national/cultural level with women in both countries showing slightly more concern with personal appearance. Authors, thus, concluded that marketers could develop appearance-based appeals for the US market and achievement-based appeals for the Chinese market to make the best use of vanity construct pertaining to two cultures. Furthermore, in an Indian study, similar to the Chinese one, consumers have shown a link between vanity and luxury consumption. Luxury consumers tend to be primarily motivated by achievement vanity and are likely to evaluate brands based on their price, fame, and ability to portray professional achievement, and consumers buy them to portray success and accomplishment (Sharda & Bhat, 2019).

4. Method

Looking at the beauty industry as a whole as a vanity industry, this chapter analyzes findings from a study on the British public's attitudes towards the beauty industry and the environment. In order to fulfil our research aims, we followed a positivistic research approach, and we carried out primary quantitative research with the use of a structured questionnaire. This method was chosen to ensure the results' generalizability to the overall population (Parasuraman et al., 2006). Moreover, quantitative research allows for the operationalization and measurement of variables, providing objective insights into phenomena. Additionally, quantitative research often yields replicable results, enhancing the reliability and validity of studies.

In collecting our data, we followed a probability sampling strategy and collected a random sample of UK consumers. The sample was stratified based on specific demographic variables (gender, age group) to ensure further representativeness. The sample was purchased from a Smart Survey pollster, which ensures a very low non-response bias (since respondents are getting paid for their participation). After discarding some questionnaires that had a lot of missing values, the size of our final sample was 513 UK consumers. The research instrument we used included quantitative scales (with Likert-type items) on the consumption of mirrors and consumers' attitudes towards the environment.

As discussed previously, we used mirrors' consumption as a variable that shows vanity and analyzed results against gender, education, and income. Our questionnaire, therefore, included questions about how much time people spend in front of a mirror, how much they spend on these products, etc. These questions were meant to unpick to what extent personal characteristics influence purchase and environmental behaviour and findings are contrasted and measured against other demographic characteristics such as gender, income, and education.

We tested the validity of our scales using Exploratory Factor Analysis (EFA) and their reliability by calculating the pertinent Cronbach coefficient. The results of these analyses indicate that all scales were indeed reliable and valid (Fornell & Larcker, 1981; Nunnally, 1978). In order to analyze the collected data, we employed a series of statistical analyses, including a *t*-test, Analysis of Variance (ANOVA), and multiple linear regression.

5. Results

5.1 Environmental Attitudes and Demographics

5.1.1 Gender

Initially, we ran a *t*-test analysis to explore potential differences in consumers' environmental attitudes depending on their gender. The results show that women marginally show more concern for environmental affairs, which goes in line with the ecofeminist view of environmentalism being fundamentally a woman's issue (Brownhill & Turner, 2020, Giacomini, 2014; Stoddart & Tindall, 2011; Salleh, 1984; Topić, 2020, 2021; Topić et al., 2021), however, since this difference is marginal, the findings suggest that environmentalism is becoming more of a universal value that no longer resides within women's sphere as it has been the case historically, at least when this sample is in stake (Tables 2.1 and 2.2).

5.1.2 Income

Consequently, we conducted Analysis of Variance (ANOVA) to determine whether consumers develop different environmental attitudes based on their income. The results of the analysis indicate that income doesn't influence attitudes towards the environment (Tables 2.3 and 2.4).

Table 2.1. Gender and Environmental Attitudes.

		i	**df**	**Sig. (2-Tailed)**
Environmentalism	Equal variances assumed	−1.802	511	0.072
	Equal variances not assumed	−1.819	476.201	0.070

Table 2.2. Group Statistics.

	Q2. What Is Your Gender?	***N***	**Mean**	**Std. Deviation**	**Std. Error Mean**
Environmentalism	Male	215	3.7810	0.75904	0.05177
	Female	298	3.9077	0.80479	0.04662

Table 2.3. Income and Environmental Attitudes.

	N	**Mean**	**Std. Deviation**	**Maximum**
a. 0–20K	107	3.9385	0.80440	5.00
b. 21K–35K	210	3.8460	0.80632	5.00
c. 36K–50K	120	3.8028	0.76757	5.00
d. 50K–100K	67	3.8197	0.75456	5.00
e. More than 100K	9	4.0093	0.71740	4.75
Total	513	3.8546	0.78768	5.00

Table 2.4. ANOVA.

	Sum of Squares	**df**	**Mean Square**	***F***	**Sig.**
Between groups	1.388	4	0.347	0.557	0.694
Within groups	316.276	508	0.623		
Total	317.664	512			

5.1.3 Education Level

Similarly, we employed ANOVA to examine if consumers develop different environmental attitudes based on their income. The results of the analysis indicate that income doesn't influence attitudes towards the environment (Tables 2.5 and 2.6). The results indicate that education influences positively people's environmental attitudes. The more educated someone is, the better attitudes he/she will develop towards the environment. The results are similar for men and women (Tables 2.5 and 2.6), thus showing that education has universal ability to sensitize people towards environmental protection, not just their life experiences.

Table 2.5. Education Level and Environmental Attitudes.

	N	**Mean**	**Std. Deviation**
Elementary school	10	3.7250	0.80224
GSCE	118	3.7500	0.82962
A levels	181	3.8389	0.81435
PG degree (MA, MSc, PG diploma)	191	3.9498	0.72476
PhD	13	3.7244	0.85214
Total	513	3.8546	0.78768

Table 2.6. ANOVA.

	Sum of Squares	**df**	**Mean Square**	***F***	**Sig.**
Between groups	3.456	4	0.864	1.397	0.234
Within groups	314.207	508	0.619		
Total	317.664	512			

5.2 Vanity and Demographic Characteristics

5.2.1 Gender

Contrary to the results regarding environmental attitudes, the results of the ANOVA analysis we employed didn't indicate any gender influence on vanity. For example, men and women answered similarly to questions regarding the time they spend in a front of reflective surface that is not a mirror (Tables 2.7 and 2.8).

5.2.2 Income

The results indicate that income is a significant factor of influence on vanity. It seems that the more money people earn, the higher their degree of vanity (Tables 2.9 and 2.10).

Table 2.7. Gender and Vanity.

	Q2. What is Your Gender?	*N*	Mean	Std. Deviation
Q6. How much time do you spend looking at your reflection in a reflective surface that is not a mirror?	Male	215	1.34	0.737
	Female	298	1.24	0.576

Table 2.8. ANOVA.

		F	Sig.	*t*	Difference
Q6. How much time do you spend looking at your reflection in a reflective surface that is not a mirror?	Equal variances assumed	11.616	0.001	1.688	
	Equal variances not assumed			1.623	

Table 2.9. Income and Environmentalism.

	N	Mean	Std. Deviation
a. 0–20K	107	1.21	0.583
b. 21K–35K	210	1.35	0.690
c. 36K–50K	120	1.50	0.767
d. 50K–100K	67	1.70	0.871
e. More than 100K	9	2.22	1.302
Total	513	1.42	0.748

Table 2.10. ANOVA.

Q5. How Much Time do You Spend per day Looking in a Real Mirror (Not a Screen, or Window, or Accidental Reflective Surface)?

	Sum of Squares	df	Mean Square	*F*	Sig.
Between groups	17.464	4	4.366	8.237	0.000
Within groups	269.265	508	0.530		
Total	286.729	512			

5.2.3 Education

Contrary to the results regarding environmental attitudes, the results of the ANOVA analysis we employed the results didn't indicate any influence of education on vanity (Tables 2.11 and 2.12).

5.3 Relationship Between Vanity, Environmentalism and Gender

In order to determine the complicated relationship between vanity, environmentalism (environmental attitudes) and gender we ran a multiple linear regression, using environmentalism as the dependent variable and vanity and its interaction with gender as independent variables. The regression method we used was partial least squares. The results of the analysis show that pro-environmental attitudes are influenced negatively by vanity. That means that people with a higher degree of vanity will develop worse attitudes on environmentalism and people with a lower degree of vanity will develop better attitudes on environmentalism. Moreover, gender was found to be a moderator of the aforementioned relationship. Specifically, it was found that for men the negative influence of vanity on environmentalism is stronger than for women (Tables 2.13 and 2.14).

Table 2.11. Education and Vanity.

	N	Mean	Std. Deviation	Std. Error
Elementary school	10	1.40	0.516	0.163
GSCE	118	1.36	0.712	0.066
A levels	181	1.43	0.739	0.055
PG degree (MA, MSc, PG diploma)	191	1.41	0.755	0.055
PhD	13	1.77	1.166	0.323
Total	513	1.42	0.748	0.033

Table 2.12. ANOVA.

Q5. How Much Time do You Spend per day Looking in a Real Mirror (Not a Screen, or Window, or Accidental Reflective Surface)?

	Sum of Squares	df	Mean Square	*F*	Sig.
Between groups	1.979	4	0.495	0.883	0.474
Within groups	284.750	508	0.561		
Total	286.729	512			

Table 2.13. Model Summary.

Model	R	R Square	Adjusted R Square	Std. Error of the Estimate
1	0.114[a]	0.013	0.009	0.78407

[a]Predictors: (Constant), ModVanity, Q5. How much time do you spend per day looking in a real mirror (not a screen, or window, or accidental reflective surface)?

5.4 Relationship Between Vanity, Environmentalism, Income and Education

Similarly, to examine the complicated relationship between vanity, environmentalism (environmental attitudes), income and education gender we employed a multiple linear moderated regression, using environmentalism as the dependent variable and vanity and its interactions with income and education as independent variables. Again, the regression method we used was partial least squares. The results indicate that there is no significant moderating effect of education and income on the relationship between vanity and environmentalism (Tables 2.15 and 2.16).

5.5 Influence of Social Values and Conservative Values on Environmentalism

Aiming to examine the simultaneous influence of vanity, social values and conservative values on environmentalism we employed a multiple linear regression, using environmentalism as the dependent variable and vanity, social values and conservative values as independent variables. The results of the regression analysis confirm the significantly negative influence of vanity on environmental attitudes and revealed a significant positive impact of positive social values (power, achievement, hedonism, self-direction, stimulation, universalism, benevolence) and conservative social values (Tradition, Conformity, Security) on environmentalism. That means that people who consider these types of values more important they will develop more pro-environmental attitudes. This is an integrated model that works really well with Environmentalism as the dependent variable and vanity, positive social values and conservative values as the independent (Tables 2.17 and 2.18).

5.6 Social Values and Demographics

5.6.1 Gender

The only important difference between the two genders were found for Tradition and Security. For both women score higher. So that means that, in our sample, women value more tradition and security than men. All other positive or conservative values were equal for two genders (Tables 2.19 and 2.20).

Table 2.14 Coefficients.[a]

Model		Unstandardized Coefficients		Standardized Coefficients		
		B	Std. Error	Beta	*t*	Sig.
1	(Constant)	3.968	0.074		53.422	0.000
	Q5. How much time do you spend per day looking in a real mirror (not a screen, or window, or accidental reflective surface)?	−0.223	0.087	−0.212	−2.576	0.010
	ModVanity	0.090	0.044	0.167	2.026	0.043

[a]Dependent Variable: Environmentalism.

Table 2.15 Tests of Between-Subjects Effects.

Dependent Variable: Environmentalism					
Source	**Type III Sum of Squares**	**Df**	**Mean Square**	***F***	**Sig.**
Corrected model	10.354[a]	19	0.545	0.874	0.616
Intercept	1,313.110	1	1,313.110	2,106.552	0.000
Q0005	0.154	3	0.051	0.082	0.970
Q0001	2.275	4	0.569	0.912	0.457
Q0005 * Q0001	6.821	12	0.568	0.912	0.535
Error	307.309	493	0.623		
Total	7,939.840	513			
Corrected total	317.664	512			

[a]R Squared = 0.033 (Adjusted R Squared = −0.005).

Table 2.16. Tests of Between-Subjects Effects.

Dependent Variable: Environmentalism					
Source	**Type III Sum of Squares**	**df**	**Mean Square**	***F***	**Sig.**
Corrected model	12.330[a]	17	0.725	1.176	0.280
Intercept	1,023.534	1	1,023.534	1,659.329	0.000
Q0005	1.313	3	0.438	0.710	0.547
Q0003	2.406	4	0.602	0.975	0.421
Q0005 * Q0003	6.295	10	0.630	1.021	0.425
Error	305.334	495	0.617		
Total	7,939.840	513			
Corrected total	317.664	512			

[a]R Squared = .039 (Adjusted R Squared = .006).

Table 2.17. Model Summary.

Model	***R***	***R* Square**	**Adjusted *R* Square**	**Std. Error of the Estimate**
1	0.390[a]	0.152	0.147	0.72728

[a]Predictors: (Constant), Conservativism, Q5. How much time do you spend per day looking in a real mirror (not a screen, or window, or accidental reflective surface)?, SocietalValues.

Table 2.18. Coefficients.[a]

Model		Unstandardized Coefficients		Standardized Coefficients		
		B	Std. Error	Beta	*t*	Sig.
1	(Constant)	2.806	0.143		19.639	0.000
	Q5. How much time do you spend per day looking in a real mirror (not a screen, or window, or accidental reflective surface)?	−0.106	0.044	−0.101	−2.442	0.015
	SocietalValues	0.060	0.029	0.100	2.056	0.040
	Conservativism	0.183	0.027	0.323	6.710	0.000

[a]Dependent Variable: Environmentalism.

Table 2.19. Group Statistics.

	Q2. What Is Your Gender?	N	Mean	Std. Deviation	Std. Error Mean
Q37.8. Tradition	Male	215	4.66	1.762	0.120
	Female	298	4.99	1.896	0.110
Q37.10. Security	Male	215	5.55	1.628	0.111
	Female	298	6.01	1.734	0.100

Table 2.20. *T*-Test.

		t	df	Sig. (2-Tailed)
Q37.8. Tradition	Equal variances assumed	−2.048	511	0.041
	Equal variances not assumed	−2.073	479.696	0.039
Q37.10. Security	Equal variances assumed	−3.049	511	0.002
	Equal variances not assumed	−3.080	477.271	0.002

5.6.2 Income

The results show that income has a significant positive impact on Power, Stimulation and marginally on Universalism. It wasn't found to have any influence on all other positive or conservative values (Tables 2.21 and 2.22).

Table 2.21. Income and Values.

		N	Mean	Std. Deviation
Q37.1. Power	a. 0–20K	107	3.80	1.974
	b. 21K–35K	210	3.75	1.948
	c. 36K–50K	120	4.06	2.100
	d. 50K–100K	67	4.24	2.168
	e. More than 100K	9	5.56	1.810
	Total	513	3.93	2.029

Table 2.21. *(Continued)*

		N	Mean	Std. Deviation
Q37.4. Stimulation	a. 0–20K	107	4.39	1.897
	b. 21K–35K	210	4.69	1.699
	c. 36K–50K	120	5.09	1.796
	d. 50K–100K	67	4.99	1.863
	e. More than 100K	9	5.33	1.732
	Total	513	4.77	1.799
Q37.6. Universalism	a. 0–20K	107	4.22	1.900
	b. 21K–35K	210	4.50	1.675
	c. 36K–50K	120	4.84	1.763
	d. 50K–100K	67	4.72	1.791
	e. More than 100K	9	5.11	1.833
	Total	513	4.56	1.770

Table 2.22. ANOVA.

		Sum of Squares	Df	Mean Square	*F*	Sig.
Q37.1. Power	Between groups	40.478	4	10.120	2.487	0.043
	Within groups	2,066.995	508	4.069		
	Total	2,107.474	512			
Q37.4. Stimulation	Between groups	35.110	4	8.777	2.749	0.028
	Within groups	1,621.748	508	3.192		
	Total	1,656.858	512			
Q37.6. Universalism	Between groups	26.706	4	6.677	2.150	0.074
	Within groups	1,577.609	508	3.106		
	Total	1,604.316	512			

5.6.3 Education

As the results indicate, educational level has a significant impact on Stimulation, Universalism, Hedonism, Self-direction, Benevolence and marginally on Conformity (Table 2.23).

Table 2.23. ANOVA.

		Sum of Squares	df	Mean Square	*F*	Sig.
Q37.1. Power	Between groups	11.272	4	2.818	0.683	0.604
	Within groups	2,096.202	508	4.126		
	Total	2,107.474	512			
Q37.4. Stimulation	Between groups	41.788	4	10.447	3.286	0.011
	Within groups	1,615.069	508	3.179		
	Total	1,656.858	512			
Q37.6. Universalism	Between groups	71.416	4	17.854	5.917	0.000
	Within groups	1,532.900	508	3.018		
	Total	1,604.316	512			
Q37.2. Achievement	Between groups	24.414	4	6.104	1.734	0.141
	Within groups	1,787.754	508	3.519		
	Total	1,812.168	512			
Q37.3. Hedonism	Between groups	33.808	4	8.452	2.790	0.026
	Within groups	1,539.175	508	3.030		
	Total	1,572.982	512			
Q37.5. Self-direction	Between groups	31.739	4	7.935	2.756	0.027
	Within groups	1,462.506	508	2.879		
	Total	1,494.246	512			
Q37.7. Benevolence	Between groups	49.475	4	12.369	3.682	0.006
	Within groups	1,706.693	508	3.360		
	Total	1,756.168	512			

Table 2.23. *(Continued)*

		Sum of Squares	df	Mean Square	*F*	Sig.
Q37.8. Tradition	Between groups	7.140	4	1.785	0.521	0.720
	Within groups	1,739.601	508	3.424		
	Total	1,746.741	512			
Q37.9. Conformity	Between groups	27.739	4	6.935	2.118	0.077
	Within groups	1,663.435	508	3.274		
	Total	1,691.173	512			
Q37.10. Security	Between groups	20.122	4	5.031	1.742	0.139
	Within groups	1,466.654	508	2.887		
	Total	1,486.776	512			

6. Discussion and Conclusion

In summary, the results show that people show vanity views regardless of their educational level and this is linked to income so the more one earns the more vanity one tends to show. What is more, the results of the analysis show that pro-environmental attitudes are influenced negatively by vanity. That means that people with a higher degree of vanity will develop worse attitudes on environmentalism and people with a lower degree of vanity will develop better attitudes on environmentalism. Moreover, gender was found to be a moderator of the aforementioned relationship. Specifically, it was found that for men the negative influence of vanity on environmentalism is stronger than for women.

The results of our regression analysis confirm the significantly negative influence of vanity on environmental attitudes and revealed a significant positive impact of positive social values (power, achievement, hedonism, self-direction, stimulation, universalism, benevolence) and conservative social values (Tradition, Conformity, Security) on environmentalism. That means that people who consider these types of values more important will develop more pro-environmental attitudes. Moreover, the only important difference between the two genders was found for Tradition and Security. For both, women score higher. So that means that, in our sample, women value more tradition and security than men. No significant differences were found for all other positive or conservative values.

Our results are well situated in the pertinent literature. For example, in a Brazilian study, Machado-Borges (2009) argued that vanity and a focus on beauty can also support women in entrepreneurial attempts with participants from the study showing that the beauty business has helped them deal with social and economic inequality, which goes against the usual perception of vanity and beauty interests being frivolous and vanity being imposed by the mass culture and imposed consumption (Brownmiller, 1985; Code, 1991; Morgan, 1991; Wolf, 1991). This paper shows a different side of the story and opens a potential for further research asking whether the beauty industry is the only culprit for environmental destruction and whether we focus too much on traditionally feminine industries, such as fashion and beauty, when discussing environmental affairs.

In addition to that, our findings have significant theoretical and practical implications. The confirmation of a significantly negative influence of vanity on environmental attitudes suggests that individuals who prioritize self-admiration and superficial appearance may be less likely to adopt pro-environmental behaviours or attitudes. This underscores the importance of addressing personal values and motivations when promoting environmental awareness and action. The significant positive impact of positive social values (such as power, achievement, hedonism, self-direction, stimulation, universalism, benevolence) and conservative social values (like Tradition, Conformity, Security) on environmentalism suggests that individuals who prioritize these values are more likely to exhibit pro-environmental attitudes. This finding highlights the potential effectiveness of framing environmental issues within the context of these values to engage a broader audience and promote sustainable behaviours.

Furthermore, the finding that women in the sample scored higher than men on the Tradition and Security scale suggests that, in this specific population, women are more likely to cherish traditional values and a sense of security. By adjusting messaging to appeal to the values that are most important to each gender, customized methods for environmental communication and advocacy can be informed by an understanding of these gender disparities. With the exception of Tradition and Security, it appears that men and women in the sample have similar values regarding environmental attitudes. This is supported by the lack of substantial gender differences in other positive or conservative values. This research emphasizes the necessity for gender-specific marketing to take a nuanced approach that takes into account the shared and diverse values of various demographic groups.

Overall, our research offers insightful information about the intricate interactions among gender, personal values, and environmental attitudes. This information can be used to inform the creation of more potent campaigns to raise environmental awareness and encourage behaviour change.

Acknowledgements of Funding

This research has been funded from internal funding by Leeds Business School, Leeds Beckett University, UK. The data has been analyzed and the chapter has been written at the University of Alabama and Liverpool John Moore University.

References

Bandyopadhyay, J. (1999, April 10). Chipko movement: Of floated myths and flouted realities. *Economic and Political Weekly*, *34*, 880–882.

Boulding, K. (1966). The economics of the coming spaceship earth. In H. Jarrett (Ed.), *Environmental quality in a growing economy* (pp. 3–14). Resources for the Future/Johns Hopkins University Press. http://www.zo.utexas.edu/courses/THOC/Boulding_SpaceshipEarth.pdf

Brownhill, L., & Turner, T. E. (2020). Ecofeminist ways, ecosocialist means: Life in the post-capitalist future. *Capitalism Nature Socialism*, *31*(1), 1–14.

Brownmiller, S. (1985). *Femininity*. Fawcett Columbine.

Calder, L. G. (1990). *Financing the American dream: A cultural history of consumer credit*. Princeton University Press.

Code, L. (1991). *What can she know? Feminist theory and the construction of knowledge*. Cornell University Press.

Davis, J. J. (1993). Strategies for environmental advertising. *Journal of Consumer Marketing*, *10*(2), 19–36.

Diani, M. (1989). Italy: The "list Verdi". In F. Muller-Rommel (Ed.), *New politics in Western Europe: The rise and success of green parties and alternative lists*. Westview Press.

Diaz, A. K. (2020). Further problematizing the #metoo movement. *Facta Universitatis. Series: Philosophy, Sociology, Psychology and History*, *19*(3), 199–209.

Đurđević, G., & Marjanić, S. (2020). Predgovor ekofem-zborniku: na rubu zenskih I zelenih studija. In S. Marjanić & G. Đurđević (Eds.), *Ekofeminizam - između ženskih i zelenih studija*. Durieux.

Durvasula, S., & Lysonski, S. (2008). A double-edged sword: Understanding vanity across cultures. *Journal of Consumer Marketing*, *25*(4), 230–244.

Ewen, S., & Ewen, E. (1992). *Channels of desire: Mass images and the shaping of American consciousness*. University of Minnesota Press.

Fakier, K., & Cock, J. (2018). Eco-feminist organizing in South Africa: Reflections on the feminist table. *Capitalism Nature Socialism*, *29*(1), 40–57.

Faludi, S. (1991). *Backlash: The undeclared war against American women*. Doubleday.

Finger, M. (1994). From knowledge to action? Exploring the relationships between environmental experiences, learning, and behavior. *Journal of Social Issues*, *50*(3), 141–160.

Fornell, C., & Larcker, D. F. (1981). Evaluating structural equation models with unobservable variables and measurement error. *Journal of Marketing Research*, *18*, 39–50.

Geiger Zeman, M., & Holy, M. (2014). »Kako to nije zaživjelo? Zašto to nije zanimljivo?«–snaga i obećanje ekofeminizma u Hrvatskoj. *Ekonomska i ekohistorija: časopis za gospodarsku povijest i povijest okoliša*, *10*(1), 94–112.

Gaard, G. (1997). Toward a queer ecofeminism. *Hypatia*, *12*(1), 137–155.

Giacomini, T. (2014). Ecofeminism and system change. Women on the frontlines of the struggle against fossil capitalism and for the solar commons. *Canadian Woman Studies*, *31*(1–2), 95–100.

Gifford, R., & Nilsson, A. (2014). Personal and social factors that influence pro-environmental concern and behaviour: A review. *International Journal of Psychology*, *49*(3), 141–157.

Glazebrook, T. (2002). Karen Warren's ecofeminism. *Ethics and the Environment*, *7*(2), 12–26.

Godfrey, P. C. (2008). Ecofeminist cosmology in practice: Genesis farm and the embodiment of sustainable solutions. *Capitalism Nature Socialism*, *19*(2), 96–114.

Goldstein, J. (2006). Ecofeminism in theory and praxis. *Capitalism Nature Socialism*, *17*(4), 96–102.

Green Belt movement. (n.d.). The Official website. http://www.greenbeltmovement.org/

Griffin, S. (2020). Održivost i duša. In S. Marjanić & G. Đurđević (Eds.), *Ekofeminizam - između ženskih i zelenih studija*. Durieux.

Henderson, K. A. (1997). Ecofeminism and experiential education. *The Journal of Experiential Education*, *20*(3), 130–222.

Hirsh, J. B., & Dolderman, D. (2007). Personality predictors of consumerism and environmentalism: A preliminary study. *Personality and Individual Differences*, *43*(6), 1583–1593.

Holy, M. (2007). *Mitski aspekti ekofeminizma*. TIM Press.

Holy, M. (2008). Žene – Glasnogovornice Životinja? *Treća*, *1*(X), 87–106.

Industry Growth Report. (2023). *Mirrors market size projected to surpass US$ 5032.4 million by 2031, by 2031, with increasing CAGR of 7.59%*. https://www.linkedin.com/pulse/mirrors-market-size-projected-surpass-us-50324-7half/

Jain, S. (1984). Women and people's ecological movement: A case study of women's role in the Chipko movement in Uttar Pradesh. *Economic and Political Weekly*, *19*(41), 1788–1794.

Jin, S. V., & Ryu, E. (2020). Instagram fashionistas, luxury visual image strategies and vanity. *Journal of Product & Brand Management*, *29*(3), 355–368.

Kim, S., & Seock, Y.-K. (2009). Impacts of health and environmental consciousness on young female consumers' attitude towards and purchase of natural beauty products. *International Journal of Consumer Studies*, *33*(6), 627–638.

Kirk, G. (1998). Ecofeminism and chicano environmental struggles: Bridges across gender and race. In D. G. Peña (Ed.), *Chicano culture, ecology, politics: Subversive kin* (pp. 177–200). University of Arizona Press.

Konstantopoulou, A., Rizomyliotis, I., Konstantoulaki, K., & Badahdah, R. (2019). Improving SMEs' competitiveness with the use of Instagram influencer advertising and eWOM. *International Journal of Organizational Analysis*, *27*(2), 308–321.

Krstić, M. (2018). Dimensions of sustainable development. *Economics of Sustainable Development*, *2*(2), 19–29.

Krstić, B., & Krstić, M. (2017). Theoretical frameworks of sustainable development. *Economics of Sustainable Development*, *1*(1), 1–9.

Leahy, T. (2003). Ecofeminism in theory and practice: Women's responses to environmental issues. *Journal of Interdisciplinary Gender Studies*, *7*(1–2), 106–125.

Ling, C. (2014). The background and theoretical origin of ecofeminism. *Cross-Cultural Communication*, *10*(4), 104–108.

Machado-Borges, T. (2009). Producing beauty in Brazil vanity, visibility and social inequality. *Vibrant*, *6*(1), 208–237.

Mallory, C. (2012). Locating ecofeminism in encounters with food and place. *Journal of Agricultural and Environmental Ethics*, *26*, 171–189.

Mann, S. A. (2011). Pioneers of U.S. ecofeminism and environmental justice. *Feminist Formations*, *23*(2), 1–25.

Marjanić, S. (2020). Ekofeminizam o 'etici' medijski zataškane priče: utjecaj mesne i mliječne industrije na globalno zatopljenje. In S. Marjanić & G. Đurđević (Eds.), *Ekofeminizam – između ženskih i zelenih studija*. Durieux.

Martinez-Alier, J. (1995, May/June). Political ecology, distributional conflicts, and economic incommensurability. *New Left Review*. https://newleftreview.org/issues/i211/articles/j-martinez-alier-political-ecology-distributional-conflicts-and-economic-incommensurability

McKinsey. (2023). The beauty market in 2023: A special state of fashion report. https://www.mckinsey.com/industries/retail/our-insights/the-beauty-market-in-2023-a-special-state-of-fashion-report

McMahon, M. (1997). From the ground up: Ecofeminism and ecological economics. *Ecological Economics*, *20*, 163–173.

Meadows, D., Meadows, D., Randers, J., & Behrens, W. W. (1972). *The limits to growth*. Universe Books.

Meadows, D., Randers, J., & Dennis Meadows, D. (2004). *Limits to growth: The 30-year update*. Chelsea Green Publishing.

Mellicker, R. (2016). The feminism of fashion. https://www.huffpost.com/entry/the-feminism-of-fashion_b_9705262

Merchant, C. (1992). Perspectives on ecofeminism. *Environmental Action*, 18–19. https://nature.berkeley.edu/departments/espm/env-hist/articles/37.pdf

Mishra, T. K., Maiti, S. K., Banerjee, S., & Banerjee, S. K. (2021). From genesis to awaited success of joint forest management in India. In P. K. Shit, H. R. Pourghasemi, P. Das, & G. S. Bhunia (Eds.), *Spatial modeling in forest resources management. Environmental science and engineering*. Springer.

Mitchell, B., & Topić, M. (2019). *Generation Z & consumer trends in environmental packaging*. The Retail Institute, Leeds Beckett University. https://eprints.leedsbeckett.ac.uk/id/eprint/6066/1/GenerationZAndConsumerTrendsInEnvironmentalPackagingPV-TOPIC.pdf

Mont, O. (2004). Institutionalisation of sustainable consumption patterns based on shared use. *Ecological Economics*, *50*(1–2), 135–153.

Moore, N. (2011). Eco/feminism and rewriting the ending of feminism: From the Chipko movement to clayoquot sound. *Feminist Theory*, *12*(1), 3–21.

Morgan, K. P. (1991). Women and the knife: Cosmetic surgery and the colonization of women's bodies. *Hypathia*, *6*(25), 53.

Nunnally, J. (1978). *Psychometric methods*. McGraw.

Parasuraman, A., Grewal, D., & Krishnan, R. (2006). *Marketing research*. Cengage Learning.

Parkins, I. (2006). Building a feminist theory of fashion. *Australian Feminist Studies*, *23*(58), 501–515.

Poole, K. T., & Harmon Zeigter, L. (1985). *Women, public opinion, and politics: The changing political attitudes of American women*. Longman.

Purnamaningsih, P., Choirisa, S. F., Rizkalla, N., & Lestari, E. D. (2024). Role of parasocial interaction and credibility in beauty influencer to improve purchase intention. *Environment-Behaviour Proceedings Journal*, *9*(SI19), 45–51.

Radford Ruether, R. (2012). Ecofeminism – The challenge to theology. *DEP*, *20*, 23–34.

Roszak, T. (1992). *The voice of the earth*. Simon and Schuster.

Ryzomiliotis, I. (2024). Consumer trust and online purchase intention for sustainable products. *American Behavioral Scientist*. https://doi.org/10.1177/00027642241236174

Stoddart, M. C. J., & Tindall, D. B. (2011). Eco-feminism, hegemonic masculinity and environmental movement participation in British Columbia, Canada, 1998-2007, "Women always Clean Up the Mess". *Sociological Spectrum*, *31*(3), 342–368.

Saed. (2017). From the october revolution to revolutionary rojava: An ecosocialist reading. *Capitalism Nature Socialism*, *28*(4), 3–20.

Salleh, A. (1984). From feminism to ecology. *Social Alternatives*, *4*(3), 8–12.

Sandberg, L. A., & Sandberg, T. (Eds.). (2010). *Climate change – Who's carrying the burden? The chilly climates of the global environmental dilemma*. Canadian Centre for Policy Alternatives.

Sandiland, C. (1999). *The good-natured feminist: Ecofeminism and the quest for democracy*. University of Minnesota Press.

Schahn, J., & Holzer, E. (1990). Studies of individual environmental concern: The role of knowledge, gender and background variables. *Environment and Behaviour*, *22*(6), 767–786.

Schultz, P. W., Gouveia, V. V., Cameron, L. D., Tankha, G., Schmuck, P., & Franěk, M. (2005). Values and their relationship to environmental concern and conservation behavior. *Journal of Cross-Cultural Psychology*, *36*(4), 457–475.

Shapiro, R. Y., & Mahajan, H. (1986). Gender differences in policy preferences: A summary of trends from the 1960s to the 1980s. *Public Opinion Quarterly*, *50*, 42–61.

Sharda, N., & Bhat, A. (2019). Role of consumer vanity and the mediating effect of brand consciousness in luxury consumption. *Journal of Product & Brand Management*, *28*(7), 800–811.

Sheth, J. N., Sethia, N. K., & Srinivas, S. (2011). Mindful consumption: A customer-centric approach to sustainability. *Journal of the Academy of Marketing Science*, *39*, 21–39.

Shiva, V., & Bandyopadhyay, J. (1986). The evolution, structure, and impact of the Chipko movement. *Mountain Research and Development*, *6*(2), 133–142.

Statista. (2023). Smart mirror market value worldwide in 2018 and 2023 (in billion U.S. dollars). https://www.statista.com/statistics/1016654/global-smart-mirror-market-value/

Steger, M. A., & Witt, S. L. (1989). Gender differences in environmental orientations: A comparison of publics and activists in Canada and the US. *Western Political Quarterly*, *4*, 627–649.

Topić, M. (2020). Ekofeministička analiza vrijednosti i filozofija globalnih eko-selâ: Jesu li žene sklonije kolektivizmu i anti-hijerarhiji nego muškaraci? [An ecofeminist analysis of values and philosophies of global eco-villages: Are women more inclined towards collectivism and anti-hierarchy than men?]. In G. Đurđević, & S. Marjanić (Eds.), *Ekofeminizam: Između zelenih i ženskih studija* [*Ecofeminism: Between green and women's studies*]. Durieux.

Topić, M. (2021). *Corporate Social responsibility and environmental affairs in the British Press: An ecofeminist critique of neoliberalism*. Routledge.

Topić, M., Diers Lawson, A., & Kelsey, S. (2021). Women and the squander cycle in food waste in the United Kingdom: An ecofeminist and feminist economic analysis. *Social Ecology* [*Socijalna Ekologija*], *30*(2), 219–253.

Topić, M., Kostopoulos, I., & Krstić, M. (2024). Sustainability, sociodemographic differences, and consumer behavior. *American Behavioral Scientist*. https://doi.org/10.1177/00027642241235822

Trentmann, F. (2016). *Empire of things: How we became a world of consumers, from the fifteenth century to the twenty-first*. Penguin UK.

Tyner, K. E., & Ogle, J. P. (2009). Feminist theory of the dressed female body: A comparative analysis and applications for textiles and clothing scholarship. *Clothing & Textiles Research Journal*, *27*(2), 98–121.

Von Werlhof, C. (2013). Destruction through "Creation" – The "Critical Theory of Patriarchy" and the collapse of modern civilization. *Capitalism Nature Socialism*, *24*(4), 68–85.

Wang, P. Z., & Waller, D. S. (2006). Measuring consumer vanity: A cross-cultural validation. *Psychology & Marketing*, *23*(8), 665–687.

Warren, K. (2000). *Ecofeminist philosophy: A western perspective on what it is and why it matters*. Rowman and Littlefield.

Warren, K. (n.d.). *Introduction to ecofeminism*. Lilith Press Magazine. http://www.lilithpress.ca/Environment-Introduction-to-Ecofeminism.html

Wolf, N. (1991). *The beauty myth: How Images of beauty are used against women*. Vintage/Penguin Books.

Wright, C., & Nyberg, D. (2015). *Climate change, capitalism and corporations: Processes of creative self-destruction*. Cambridge University Press.

Xiao, Y., Wu, B., Deng, Z., & Liu, M. (2024). Can social appearance anxiety promote the online impulse buying of beauty products among young females? A moderated mediation model of sense of control and perceived coronavirus stress. *Current Psychology*. https://doi.org/10.1007/s12144-024-05650-0

Chapter 3

Evidence-Based Functional Marketing Claims in Beauty Products Advertising: A Memorandum for Good Practice

Michal Chmiel

Royal Holloway, University of London, UK

Abstract

The goal of this chapter is to review the connections between beauty industry marketing communication and science with a particular focus on advertising. In the realization of that, I will contextualize my argument against the current post-truth communication landscape and its characteristics: the declining trust of science and traditional sources of credible information. Implications for marketing theory and the role of truth in marketing will be presented to explain how a fluid and subjective definition of beauty leads marketers to develop persuasive advertising communication that fits the mechanism of knowledge acquisition of consumers making purchase decisions. Through observing a potential for creating consumer-facing communication that has a potential to mislead, first, indirect speech acts will be discussed in the context of beauty products marketing claims. Then, four groups of typical inaccuracies observed in marketing claims that are typically used to provide substantiate product communication will be reviewed. Social psychological methodology will be used to provide guidance for creators of truthful marketing claims and specific recommendations will be included to adjust the design of studies, number of participants, type of evidence used and reporting of findings. Lastly, general considerations of marketing communicators and brand public relations professionals will be presented against the backdrop of the responsible communication challenge of the beauty industry.

Keywords: Marketing claims; truth; psychology; cosmetics; implicatures; methodology

Beauty Industry, 69–86

doi:10.1108/978-1-83608-940-720251017

1. Introduction

Despite the apparent crisis of science credibility and low trust in scientific sources (Nichols, 2018; Sunstein, 2017), the beauty industry frequently uses scientific references to persuade consumers to buy their products (Fowler et al., 2015). Although it can be argued that people pursue beauty for biological reasons (Etcoff, 2000), consumers often chase distorted beauty ideals through the use of commodities (Vacker & Key, 1993). Worryingly, the beauty industry itself contributes to diffusing fake news and pseudo-facts by selectively using and omitting information (de Regt et al., 2020).

On the one hand, several models have sought to understand the factors influencing the effectiveness of persuasive attempts on audiences (Chaiken, 1987; Fiske & Taylor, 1991; McGuire, 2000; Petty & Cacioppo, 1986). Toulmin (1958; Toulmin et al., 1979) focused on arguments and identified six aspects to explain their effectiveness: claim, grounds, warrant, backing, qualifier and exceptions. Also, Areni (2002) proposed a model that involves data supporting claims and inference rules to explain how they influence subjective beliefs of consumers to predict the acceptance of a message. On the other hand, guidance from US Federal Trading Associations, European Commission and UK's Advertising Standard Association (CAP, 2010) seems lagging behind the methodology of social sciences, which – I will argue – requires adequate and necessary knowledge for developing truthful, evidence-based marketing claims. It is further argued that the current regulations leave too much room for subjectivity and the existing guidelines need to be reviewed and corrected.

In this chapter, specific methodological guidelines will be provided to counsel advertising and marketing professionals on the development of truthful and evidence-based beauty product claims. In order to achieve this goal, generic examples of claims that are built on logical shortcuts and fallacies will be discussed. More specifically, current advertising practices found in beauty products advertising will be reviewed to aid the development of better understanding of what is supporting evidence (grounds) and what inference rules should be used to develop credible and honest advertising communication. After reviewing most common types of implicatures contained in beauty products claims, four aspects of methodology required to produce substantiated claims will be proposed: sample size (1), causality (2), subjective vs. objective evidence (3), and research design (4).

2. Beauty, Health, and Science – A Short History

Beauty and personal care goods are projected to generate an impressive profit of $646.20 bn in 2024 (Beauty and Personal Care - Worldwide, n.d.). Considering the subjective character of beauty, beauty products marketers are faced with the following challenge: How can an undefined, elusive, contested or sensitive topic be promised whilst providing relevant evidential information? In response to that problem, brands often resort to science which shows health relevance of their product; this association is not new. Stewart (2020) recalls the meaning of the

Latin word *medicamentum*, which stood for beauty products and, among other meanings, included a medical remedy or enchantment. Also, the ancient Greek synonym of *medicamentum* was *kosmeticos* "implied a sense of order and harmony, the balance of the humors in Greek medicine [. . .] (and) produced a pleasing and healthy appearance (Stewart, 2020, p. 9)." People used early cosmetics, for example make-up, for various purposes: religious, ceremonial, social – but also for personal vanity, to attract the opposite sex and also as camouflage. Throughout history, medical use has also been noted. Sources are not in agreement whether the book about beauty preparations was written by Cleopatra, but a book contains references to a cure of baldness containing ingredients like oak gum, nitre and red sulphuret of arsenic. Otzi, the iceman from 3250 BC found in Alpine glacier had marks, which could have had a therapeutic function and suggest a treatment of arthritis. "Throughout recorded history cosmetics have been used to create the beauty ideal of each passing age and for centuries a daily routine of beauty care has been an accepted 'ritual' within a social context" (Gunn, 1973, p. 19).

In the modern era, psychologists propose mechanisms explaining consumer behavior as a function of information received from influential social figures, the environment and credible scientist sources suggesting a link between the beauty industry and science. Take the example of how Helena Rubinstein advertised her cream in 1903:

> VALAZE BY DR LYKUSKY, the most celebrated European Skin Specialist, is the best nourisher of the skin. VALAZE will improve the worst of skin in one month. . . Available from Helena Rubinstein & Company, 138 Elizabeth Street. (Tungate, 2011, p. 20)

Public relations consultants sought endorsements from popular figures and looked for scientific backing of their products since the evolution of the discipline of modern PR. For example, in the 1920s Elizabeth Arden supposedly wanted the Queen of Romania to endorse her cream. In parallel, however, the beauty industry used deception to attract consumers. For example, Helena Rubinstein developed her Crème Valeze's brand narrative around a work done by Dr Lykusky in Krakow (Poland). However, contemporary investigation could not find evidence of Lykusky's operating in Krakow at that time (Tungate, 2011). The subjective and malleable nature of beauty comes with risks for consumers. Consumers are frequently turning to celebrities and SMIs (who hold no formal qualification) for health and lifestyle advice, creating many implications for their health and well-being. Unfortunately, it is not only influencers who create information that misleads or is based on pseudo-science. Perhaps unknowingly, some advertisers participate in the deception because of different approaches to the concept of truth.

3. Truth and Deception in the Beauty Industry

Although Gamble et al. (2011) demonstrated that there are discrepancies in how marketing is defined, it can be argued that the societal aspect (as well as an implicit responsibility for consumers) has been present in the definitions of the concept at least since the 1960s. Rogers saw marketing as value exchanges between different, also non-business, parties (Rogers, 1963). Kotler (1967), Eldridge (1970), Mandall and Rosenberg (1981), as well as Baker (1991), pointed to the goal of satisfying consumer needs. Finally, Shultz (2007) explained marketing as a societal function that involves delivering value to customers. One of the aspects of marketing, vigorously debated by scholars, is the concept of truth. Following Hunt's "pursuit of truth" postulate (Hunt, 1990, p. 8), a discussion started among scholars to establish if marketing science should be founded on constructivist or realist theory of truth. The main focus of this chapter, however, are functional marketing product claims, and the key question is not about the foundations of marketing, but "if marketers have an [. . .] obligation not to lie and deceive" (Anker, 2016, p. 19). In my argument, I will follow the perspective expertly laid out by Anker (2016) and the propositional theory of truth that he uses.

Anker opens his argument by referring to the ICC Code, which states that all "All marketing communications should be legal, decent, honest and truthful" (ICC, 2024) and considers truth as "a fundamental principle endorsed by all key stakeholders" (Anker, 2016, p. 1). He then follows to define the propositional theory(ies) of truth "as analyzable in terms of the content of a statement or belief, P, and P's relationship to the external world or the content of other statements or beliefs" (Anker, 2016, p. 2). In strategic brand management, consumer needs are analyzed and firms select different brand meanings to match these needs (Park et al., 1986). Needs of consumers belong to one or more categories: symbolic (representing psychological, emotional or social needs), behavioral (related to consumer's engagement with the brand or an activity performed as a function of using the brand) and functional (satisfying a specific material or immaterial need by using the brand; Anker, 2016). To provide a reason to believe that a consumer need will be satisfied with or by using a particular product, brand communicators formulate claims – assertions that something will happen as a consequence of using the product.

Anker (2016) argues that truth in marketing may not be a problem isolated to individual wrongdoing, but a larger systemic issue. The reasons behind this diagnosis could be multifold. For example, Baudrillard questions the classical notion of truth and considers its irrelevance to marketing (Baudrillard, 1998), one particular area which almost explicitly requires applying the propositional theory of truth are science-based marketing claims and functional marketing claims developed for science health beauty products. Especially in this – as explained in the introduction to this volume – subjective area of consumer decisions, audiences could be presented as players engaged in a form of subjective game of symbolic meanings. Perhaps some consumers even play this game rather skillfully, but I believe there exists a considerable subset that is not fully aware of rhetorical devices used in marketing communication or simplifications allowed by current regulations. This prevents them from making evidence-based decisions regarding their beauty. To Anker's excellent point, "Such sociological theories of the role of truth in social systems are relevant to the critique of the foundational premises of those systems...but have little practical relevance for an individual consumer" (Anker, 2016, p. 3).

Continuing the metaphor of a game with consumers, surely, there are a few rotten apples among marketers whose only motivation is to increase purchase. But my perspective in this chapter is different. Primarily, I believe marketers may not be familiar with what kind of evidence is needed to substantiate their claims. Moreover, creators of marketing claims can seek support from their legal departments but as I will argue, regulations, especially in the EU, USA and United Kingdom leave some room for interpretation (e.g., The Committee of Advertising Practice, 2010). The ultimate goal of this chapter will be to offer social sciences methodological commentary that helps establish the relationship between product statements (e.g., claims about a product making skin smoother) and external world phenomena (e.g., the concept of skin smoothness) with particular focus on functional marketing claims. While studies of consumers' perceptions suggest that substantiated and approved marketing claims lead to higher purchase intentions (van Buul & Brouns, 2015), a negative impact of persuasive claims on health has also been noticed (Chandon, 2013). Indeed, advertising claims of beauty products differ in the degree of truthfulness (Belamarich et al., 2016). In a study of advertising claims conducted by Fowler et al. (2015), only 18% of analyzed claims were acceptable and 23% were categorized simply as lies.

De Regt et al. (2020) explicitly name the beauty industry as being particularly affected by the spread of fake news, interest in pseudoscience and – "exploitation of regulatory loopholes" (de Regt et al., 2020, p. 169). One of the key elements of the architecture of spreading fake news in the beauty industry cited by these authors is scientific denialism, which simply involves rejecting science, which in its active form leads to the spreading of misinformation and rumors to manipulate public opinion. While denialism undoubtedly plays a role in distorting reality and undermining scientific discovery, in this chapter it will not be discussed. Primarily, the notion of denialism involves making specific assumptions about the motivations of those who create or disseminate untruthful information. In the present overview, I take a different stance, which is evidenced within the literature (e.g., Lewandowsky et al., 2017). It is believed that the spread (but not creation) of misinformation or fake news can be to a large extent explained by alternative systems of beliefs, which often coincide or originate in political beliefs. In other words, the spread of misinformation is not an intentional act of manufacturing doubt but simply shows a lack of knowledge on a topic or support of different viewpoints. Consequently, the selective use of information, for example to give evidence supporting a product claim, may not be a sign of ill intentions of marketers but their poor methodological training. The three examples used by de Regt et al. (2020) to develop their model of the spread of fake news in the beauty industry motivated by denialism also do not fit the most commonly experienced errors found in advertising claims. Tobacco products, indoor tanning and using detox to lose weight have been all shown to have a negative impact upon health. Today, advertising these products and services will involve denying science. This is to say, there exists evidence that smoking cigarettes kills, indoor tanning leads to cancer and (some) detox ingredients are harmful. In the majority of promotional communications designed to support cosmetics an opposite mechanism can be observed. Evidence communicated as supporting a marketing claim is either missing, incorrect or poorly (inadequately) developed. Finally, one may argue that some marketers and advertisers who create communication have adopted an eristic approach to their work and are focused on persuading audiences to choose their product and leave the notion of truth separate from their endeavors.

Advertisers include various linguistic and psychological tools to imply causality effects, effectiveness of beauty products, and credibility of testimonials. While functional claims used in advertisements of popular brands are not mostly technically incorrect, either evidence behind those claims is not satisfactory or claims often involve the use of presuppositions and implicatures to imply effectiveness of beauty products. But, as Anker suggests, claims can only be true if a consumer understands how these claims are made true (Anker, 2016, p. 2). It seems that the area of functional claims related to health requires particular scrutiny from advertisers. The first step to achieve this is a basic understanding of psychological factors influencing consumer decisions.

4. Consumers Searching for Evidence

From the perspective of social cognitive psychology, human behavior can be thought of in terms of knowledge acquisition that is limited by various internal and external factors. For example, Kruglanski based his construct of Need for Cognitive Closure on an assumption that every human activity is guided by knowledge construction (Kruglanski, 1989). In his Theory of Lay Epistemics he proposed a mechanism whereby building knowledge about the social world involves a hypothesis generation and testing mechanism. In other words, much like scientists, consumers build judgments about products based on available evidence. This holds true also about beauty cosmetics and advertisers use this mechanism by providing their audiences with evidential information that supports claims about products. Research evidence in support of the fact that the process of collecting evidence to build knowledge, form evaluations and make purchase decisions by consumers has been reviewed elsewhere (Chmiel, 2023), so the following section provides only an example of typical characteristics of this mechanism.

Imagine a consumer that is interested in improving the condition of their skin. In the first stage of this quest for new judgment, an individual may want to establish what defines a good condition of skin. This can be translated into the following: If attribute 1 or attribute 2, attribute 3 (search for premise) then my skin is in good condition (conclusion). This is the first moment beauty brands may want to aid their consumers with information (knowledge). For example, a good level of moisture may be an indicator of a desirable condition for skin. When a brand has gathered consumer research to confirm that the level of moisture is a desired characteristic, the second and more difficult part of hypothesis testing occurs: providing consumers with evidence that a product will improve it. From the perspective of a consumer, this process may take the following form of hypothesis testing: "If product X contains ingredient Y [premise], the product will lead to making my skin moist [conclusion]."

Kruglanski (1989) further assumes that people differ in an extent to which they engage themselves in hypothesis testing activity as this process may be arduous and lead to unpleasant tension resulting from not having a clear answer on a given question. For one individual only scarce information is necessary to form a judgment on an object, for other extensive research prior to giving an answer is needed. The underlying force responsible for those differences, the need for cognitive closure, is defined as intolerance for ambiguity, confusion and a preference for any answer (Webster & Kruglanski, 1994). A high need for cognitive closure manifests itself in shortening the phase of information gathering, using less information and relying on the most accessible features of objects. The need is said not only to differ between people but also intra-individually, as a function of situational characteristics. In fact, recent analyses suggest that the modern advertising environment has established a very short time frame of exposing consumers to a single brand information which is only eight seconds (cite). That would mean that most consumers, especially users of social media live with the constant need to seize information and close their minds quickly. The aforementioned characteristics of the process of information acquisition led to greater reliance on heuristics, stereotypes or knowledge elements, with which a person is already familiar with. In the context of advertising of beauty products, it could translate into ads being based on particularly evocative cues. Indeed, for each generation of consumers, certain words seem to be particularly popular in their promise to be relevant for beauty. Several of them – *new, organic, dermatologically tested or youth* – will be reviewed in the next section of the chapter.

5. Presuppositions, Implicatures and Limitations of Rational Choice

The perspective that ties knowledge acquisition with consumer behavior and considers that poor choices can be made by collecting biased or incorrect information was also present in the work of Gardner (1975). In his view, deception in advertising exists when an advertisement leaves a consumer with a different impression than what would be expected if they were equipped with reasonable knowledge. However, often presenting all information that would be necessary to produce a good decision is not possible due to limited attention span of consumers, budget constraints or specifics of marketing communication channels. Partly as a function of that, advertisers often employ persuasive devices and look for mental shortcuts to produce favorable responses based upon minimal information and within the shortest period of time.

Think quickly, *how many animals did Moses take to his ark*? This is the most famous example of a presupposition (Reder & Kusbit, 1991), something a speaker assumes to be true before producing a sentence. In this instance, the presupposed element is the fact that Moses took animals to arc. However, this (according to the Bible) is not what happened as it was Noah who was saved from the flood along with his family and all living animals. For example, Peccei defines presuppositions as "a necessary precondition for the sentence to be true" (Peccei, 2002, p. 18). From the perspective of psychology, the effectiveness of asking questions of this type can be explained in terms of increasing cognitive accessibility of the presupposed meanings (Fitzsimons & Shiv, 2001). In other words, just by asking a question, meanings associated with it are activated. In advertising, this technique is frequently employed to increase the effectiveness of persuasive appeals (Yingfang, 2007). Consider the following question from an existing print advertisement: when will you start using Brand Y shampoo? The sentence presupposes that you will start using the shampoo and it is only a matter of time when this is going to happen. The advertiser wants their consumer to focus on the *when* of behavior instead of *if* it is going to happen at. But presuppositions used by advertisers can be far more misleading and manipulate consumers.

Consider the following sentence: *Not all women dye their hair*. While literal meaning suggests simply a negation of the sentence *All women dye their hair*, meaning that the percentage of women dying their hair can be anything from 0% to 99.99%, an implied meaning of the sentence would be that there is a noticeable number (percentage) of women who perform the act of dying their hair. In pragmatics, implicatures are indirect acts of speech and are defined as "acts of meaning one thing by saying something else" (Blome-Tillmann, 2013, p. 2). For example, when asked on a date on Saturday, a person might respond by saying *On Saturday I wash my hair*. Although not communicated directly, an implied meaning suggests a refusal. Grice (1975) proposed his idea of conversational implicatures to explain conditions and expectations people implicitly agree on in conversations. He argued that when people talk, they accept certain principles that make the conversation more cooperative. These four principles were quantity, quality, relation, and manner. These implied rules suggest that we should provide a required *quantity* of information, be truthful (*quality*), relevant (*relation*), and communicate in an orderly manner that does not lead to confusion (*manner*). When consumers are faced with promotional communication, say advertising, their expectations follow the same principles. In other words, they expect to be presented with enough information about the product to make a purchase decision as much as they expect not to be lied to. But on top of somewhat obvious characterizations of what is expected from advertising, they consider information to be relevant to the purchase decision, which translates, for example, into considering product claims, information about attributes or methods of testing as meaningful (relevant).

In the process of creating a persuasive claim, apart from the obvious truthfulness criterion, relevance of product attributes should play a significant role. Indeed, marketers seek for such product characteristics that would convince consumers to buy. Several characteristics have been frequently used in many different product categories and their effectiveness is fairly stable. One such attribute – novelty – produces universally positive results and is well founded in psychological research. The word *new* captures attention of consumers and their natural curiosity as it is a response to a universal human drive of exploring the environment (e.g., Berlyne, 1954). As a result, products, especially in the cosmetics category are frequently equipped with the label of innovation or stickered with a tag "new." Although novelty of a product can be easily assessed, even when questioned the consequences of misleading consumers do not seem serious. There are other product attributes that the beauty industry uses to increase the influence of product communication, but their relevance appears limited at closer examination.

In 1967 Estee Lauder introduced the Clinique brand whose marketing communication strategy was built on links with science. Two elements of the strategy were the claim "the first dermatology-tested" brand and the endorsement from Dr Norman Orentreich, who recommended that skin needs to be exfoliated and moisturized, on top of cleaning. Tungate (2011) suggests that the pale green packaging of Clinique was deliberately invoking associations with hospital wards and the brand's positioning was a response for a need of scientific solution to skincare from consumers (Tungate, 2011).

While the strategy of connecting a beauty brand with science and health seem understandable, at closer examination, many contemporary brands seem to use the phrase "dermatologically tested" or "approved by dermatologists" purely as implicatures. Let us first look at what could be the meaning expected by a consumer who learns about a product that is dermatologically tested or approved. The implied meaning most likely would involve dermatologists testing the product to either ascertain its safety, prove efficacy, or both. However, the literal meaning only refers to a basic idea of some dermatologists (i.e., more than one person with a degree in dermatology) who performed tests on the product. As one can see, the difference between what consumers may see as a promise of a brand (the implicature) and the literal, actual meaning is considerable.

Another example of using cue words that implicate connection with scientific evidence and efficacy is hypoallergenic. However, the term "hypoallergenic" is neither scientifically defined nor legally regulated. Semantically, the term denotes something that contains less allergens or leads to fewer allergic reactions. However, despite efforts of the US Food and Drug Administration (FDA) to require adequate scientific testing of products using the label "hypoallergenic," no such tests are now required, and any brand can use it without any scientific evidence.[1] But hypoallergenicity is not the only implicature that the beauty industry uses to imply certain meaning in consumers. For example, the use of the words *organic* (Meriam-Webster definition: of, relating to, yielding, or involving the use of food produced with the use of feed or fertilizer of plant or animal origin without employment of chemically formulated fertilizers, growth stimulants, antibiotics,

[1]The Companies who opposed FDA's requirement to provide scientific evidence in this case were Almay and Clinique.

or pesticides) or *natural* is not regulated in the beauty industry. In other words, advertisers may use it freely and define what they meant without any substation or certification.

Another type of deceptive advertising claims which can be classified as a form of implicature, and more specifically, a speculative subjective speculation can take the following forms "The best Brand X make-up mascara" or "The best make-up mascara from Brand X." Although neither of these claims are technically incorrect, until presenting adequate comparative evidence, this claim is simply a speculation. But even after providing evidence, another form of deception – frequently used by advertisers – is achieved. By manipulating the structure of the sentence, both these sentences simply say that the currently marketed product by Brand X is their best so far. But the implied meanings could be different and suggest that the brand is the best on the market (when compared to competitors). Especially in the case of the second claim, various visual techniques are used to make consumers attend to the first part of the sentence only (*The best make-up mascara*) by writing the second part of the claim using smaller or lighter font.

The last quasi implicature that will provide a link with the final part of the chapter is alleged causality. Encyclopedia of Systems Biology defines it as "philosophical concept that expresses a relation or a process linking two (or more) distinct events or facts" and further clarifies that in everyday language it simply means a situation, "in which x makes y happen" (Kistler, 2013). In short, establishing a causal relationship between two events (e.g., using a product and gaining a more moisturized skin) should be important for advertisers as it can be used as evidence or persuade consumers towards a particular product choice. For consumers too, observing the effectiveness of a product they buy seems desirable. A causal link between a specific product and a desired health-related characteristic or state can be established when two conditions are met: (1) scientific measurement of the desired state/characteristic exists and (2) a correct methodology of substantiation is followed. About the first condition, in the domain of beauty products, and especially cosmetics, this task is more difficult than it would appear. Partially because the language of scientific investigations leaves an element of doubt, and partly because many complex, health-related concepts have not been developed sufficiently. Take an example of the application of cosmetics containing hyaluronic acid on the skin and consider what effect would be expected by a consumer. Then read the following excerpt from a health advice website:

> Hyaluronic acid can help increase the moisture content in your skin, which can have various skin benefits, including reducing the appearance of wrinkles and improving wound healing, among others. (Healthline.com, n.d.)

While the link between skin aging and molecules of hyaluronic acid have been established in science (Papakonstantinou et al., 2012), the direct impact of topical application of cosmetics containing hyaluronic acid is a more complex task (see, e.g., Bravo et al., 2022). This is why, in relation to this ingredient and many others, advertisers use the word help to avoid claiming direct causality. Helping is different from causing, making or producing also from a legal perspective. But, for an average consumer, help can become almost synonymous with causing an effect, thus satisfying the intended meaning and producing a persuasive effect. Establishing causality is also dependent on the choice of the correct methodology of substantiation-focused research and these guidelines will become the focus of the last part of the chapter.

These discussed types of manipulation or deception are examples of techniques that occupy a somewhat grey area of relevant regulations. While US, UK, and European regulatory bodies require advertisers not to deceive their audiences, the problem of implied meanings of consumers appears as a complex issue (e.g., Maurer, 2010) and it would be only in the hands of the most responsible brands to research all meanings implied by advertising claims to avoid misleading.

6. Methodological Guidelines on Avoiding of Deceptive Claims

It appears that the most serious violations of the relation principle (Grice, 1975) and the quality of information principle are in the domain of evidence substation and the choice of methods used to develop the evidence. Guang-Xin and Boush (2011) in their review of literature on deceptive advertising conclude that consumers "can be highly susceptible to deceptive advertising claims that lead them to acquire false information, form misperceptions, and become involved in consumptive behaviors to their detriment" (Guang-Xin & Boush, 2011, p. 293). In a related vein, searching for a remedy for problems and challenges of the scientific application of evidence-based political decisions, Sutherland et al. (2013) ponder whether science should be taught to politicians. In their view, which is a mixture of pessimism and realism, politicians never read scientific books but should be able to interrogate advisers. In response to that, 20 concepts – presented as tips – were briefly introduced with the expectation of equipping policy makers in basic research-scrutinizing skills (Sutherland et al., 2013). Several of them – *sample size, causation, significance* and *randomization* – seem particularly valuable for creators of advertising beauty claims. In the beauty industry, when regulating bodies successfully act to prevent brands from using misleading advertising, the typical response of spokespersons alludes to brands simply following the beauty industry's existing research or methodological standards. While the precise research guidelines may differ between beauty companies, a general conclusion, based on the review of the contents of advertising claims, suggests that the current standard of substantiating claims requires a considerable revision.

In the remainder of this chapter, I will use the exact wording of existing marketing claims of beauty brands. In most cases, these claims can be considered as specific instances of implicatures – they imply a certain degree of scientific evidence, which appears to be backed by relevant theories. However, even without access to original research protocols, many of these advertising claims used by beauty brands appear as poorly evidenced and can be misleading. My primary goal is to formulate actionable advice for marketers and research officers involved in the process of substantiation. In light of this, I will remove names of brands or explicit references to them. In several instances, the claims I use could be considered as containing more than one aspect that needs improvement. For clarity of communication, only one aspect that needs attention will be used at a time.

6.1 Sample Size and Type

Claim: *Super anti-aging eye serum. Brightens dark circles and visibly reduces wrinkles in 28 days.*
Evidence: *28 days* in vivo *study of 33 females with twice-daily application, in comparison to placebo group.*

The issue with recruiting too few participants in beauty marketing claims seems to be the most pervasive issue. Possibly to reduce the costs of a study, sample sizes are too small and do not allow for formulating meaningful predictions. Additionally, for a psychological effect to occur researchers need to collect enough responses to avoid producing erroneous conclusions. Also, sample size is associated with another important statistical notion – a power of a study.[2] Assuming a typical power level of 0.8, the expected sample in the present case would be 98. Also, in the claim under consideration, there is also another important information: visible reduction of wrinkles. Apart from other limitations, the study provided as evidence suggests self-assessment or assessment by a different person (e.g., a dermatologist). This could mean that the measurement was prone to a different type of phenomenon, the placebo effect, which will be explained in the last section.

Finally, it should be also noted that the claim above is not free from implicatures. After mentioning that the serum is anti-aging, a separate sentence informs about two aspects of the visible condition of the skin (brightness and wrinkles). It is worth noticing that in this case, in vivo study may mean subjective assessment of two, visible aspects of skin's appearance and should not be confused with changing the age of it.

6.2 Causation

Claim: *Amplifies the skin's hyaluronic acid levels by up to 30%.*
Evidence: *HA Content protocol: 4-week study conducted on 12 subjects ages 45–65, HA Elisa Method. Percentage reported on average result.*

Claim: *Hyaluronic acid and collagen booster for long lasting hydration. +21% of elasticity.*

[2]The concept of sample size and power and their significance is explained in great detail by Lakens (2022).

Evidence: *Evaluation of efficacy under dermatological control on 33 subjects for 28 days by clinical scoring of skin firmness, skin radiance and elasticity.*

The concept of causation (explained earlier in the chapter) should be of primary interest for advertisers. Consumers would also be interested if using a particular product (which in the above examples contain hyaluronic acid) leads to hydration of the skin. Apart from small sample sizes (12 subjects), which do not allow for establishing a link between the product and the condition of the skin, causation in the above examples is also subtly implied, rather than evidenced. In the first claim, the connection is explicated at all but rests on the existing familiarity of consumers with what hyaluronic acid levels could signify (i.e., hydration or generally positive or youthful condition). In the second claim, the apparent causation is established by placing two pieces of information in adjacent sentences. The literal meaning of the first sentence (hyaluronic acid and collagen booster) informs about an ingredient that is known to have specific properties (for hydration). The second sentence of the claim, however, does not build a direct connection between the agent, the desired effect and claim (+21% elasticity). Lastly, even if a series of assumption about the connection between hyaluronic acid, the hydration of the skin and elasticity were to be proven by additional evidence, neither the sample, size nor the design of the study would allow for ascertaining that the 21% increase in elasticity occurred based on the sample of 33 subjects.

6.3 Significance

Claim: *Deep wrinkles are visibly reduced by 50% in 4 weeks.*
Evidence: *Self-grading (Score), 4 weeks study including 41 women.*

Statistical significance is one of the most fundamental concepts in quantitative research. It refers to a situation when the obtained result is not a result of a chance (see Lykken, 1968 for a comprehensive introduction). It simply refers to a situation when an observed effect occurs with an acceptable degree of probability. In statistics, the commonly accepted level of significance is $p < 0.05$, which means that the chances of something to occur (e.g., visible wrinkles are reduced) are smaller than 5%.

Claim: *89% said skin felt soothed with moisture.*
Evidence: *Testing on 109 women for one week.*

The concept of significance is related to causality and sample size. In scientific reasoning, it is assumed that using means or averages in a meaningful way (for example, 50% of consumers agree or 73% of women in the US see the difference), a representative number of individuals from a population need to be sampled. If we want to achieve responses with an acceptable level of error (below 5%), the minimum number of participants is 384. This adds another layer of complication to using claims like the one above by advertisers.

To a large degree, social scientists agree that establishing a significant effect is possible mainly through experimentation. That means that one variable, in our case using a product, leads to certain changes in, for example, skin appearance. To design an experiment, a specific minimum number of participants needs to be recruited and they need to be assigned to at least two different groups (see randomization section below).

6.4 Randomization and Research Design

> Claim: *98% said skin looked more youthful.*
> Evidence: *Consumer testing on 160 women after two weeks.*

This claim is particularly interesting as it refers to functional (specific effect is expected) and experiential (youthfulness is measured as a function of what consumers perceive as younger) needs of consumers at the same time. The claim could be problematic from a dermatological perspective as the aging of skin is a complex process and so are the multiple symptoms that could account for that (Ganceviciene et al., 2012). To avoid this – potentially – complex and problematic measurement, the advertiser resorted to simply asking a group of consumers if their skin looked younger. However, the evidence provided in the advertisement suggests that several mistakes were made. First, the evidence suggests that the measurement occurred only once, when it should be performed at two time points. Instead of asking a group of consumers if they see a change in the appearance of their skin, they should be asked a different question (e.g., on a scale from 1 to 5, how young your skin appears to be) before and after a period of using the product. Secondly, a separate group of consumers should be given a product with no functionality and only after conducting such a study, where consumers are randomly assigned to one of the two conditions (product vs. control group), statistical analyses should be performed to ascertain that consumers are not reporting fictitious effects as consequence of a placebo effect (see Harrington, 1999, for an excellent review of the effect). Critically, random assignment to groups (Sibbald & Roland, 1998) should be performed in this case to establish causality between the agent (product) and the effect (youthful appearance), and avoid the placebo effect, for example by accidently selecting a group of consumers which had used different products aimed at improving the condition of their skin prior to the experiment.

7. Conclusions

With this chapter, I hope to aid professional marketing and public relations communicators in finding a finer line between profit and impact on the lives of consumers by giving evidence of how truthful brand communication can directly and indirectly impact different aspects of beauty experience of consumers. In my view, the formulation of marketing claims should be a cocreational process, which involves a specialized Brand PR (BPR) function (e.g., Chmiel, 2024). One of the competencies of BPR should be familiarity with the concept of truth and an applied social psychological toolkit that enables developing well-substantiated product claims. In the more advanced version of this view, communicators should also learn about implied meanings evoked by persuasive communication of beauty brands and match them to their brands' promise. While such an approach would come with additional research cost, producing meaningless or misleading communication could be avoided. The idea of placing greater responsibility for the quality and truthfulness of content is not entirely new. For example, Lamy and Beyneix (2022) advocated for extending the concept of Corporate Social Responsibility to include corporate *epistemological* responsibility, which would translate into companies fighting epistemic pollution (i.e., various forms of questionable content, fake news, rumors, etc.) by not allowing untruthful content to circulate.

References

Anker, T. B. (2016). *Truth in Marketing. A theory of claim-evidence relations.* Routledge.

Areni, C. S. (2002). The proposition–probability model of argument structure and message acceptance. *Journal of Consumer Research*, *29*(2), 168–187.

Baker, M. J. (1991). *Research for marketing.* Macmillan Education Ltd.

Baudrillard, J. (1998). *The consumer society: Myths and structures.* SAGE.

Beauty and Personal Care - Worldwide. (n.d.). https://www.statista.com/outlook/cmo/beauty-personal-care/worldwide. Accessed on June 2, 2024.

Belamarich, P. F., Bochner, R. E., & Racine, A. D. (2016). A critical review of the marketing claims of infant formula products in the United States. *Clinical Pediatrics*, *55*(5), 437–442. https://doi.org/10.1177/0009922815589913

Berlyne, D. E. (1954). An experimental study of human curiosity. *British Journal of Psychology*, *45*, 256–265.

Blome-Tillmann, M. (2013). Conversational implicatures (and how to spot them). *Philosophy Compass*, *8*(2), 170–185. https://doi.org/10.1111/phc3.12003

Bravo, B., Correia, P., Gonçalves Junior, J. E., Sant'Anna, B., & Kerob, D. (2022). Benefits of topical hyaluronic acid for skin quality and signs of skin aging: From literature review to clinical evidence. *Dermatologic Therapy*, *35*(12), e15903.

Chandon, P. (2013). How package design and packaged-based marketing claims lead to overeating. *Applied Economic Perspectives and Policy*, *35*(1), 7–31. https://doi.org/10.1093/aepp/pps028

Chaiken, S. (1987). The heuristic model of persuasion. In M. P. Zanna, J. M. Olson, & C. P. Herman (Eds.), *Social influence: The Ontario symposium* (Vol. 5, pp. 3–39). Lawrence Erlbaum Associates, Inc.

Chmiel, M. (2023). Social cognitive psychology of reputation. In U. Bihler (Ed.), *Mechanisms of action in reputation management. The importance of neuroscientific and psychological insights in reputation building* (pp. 67–82). Springer.

Chmiel, M. (2024). Societal impact of brand public relations on gender equality: Evidence for a mediation-type mechanism. *Corporate Communications: An International Journal.* https://doi.org/10.1108/CCIJ-04-2024-0059

de Regt, A., Montecchi, M., & Lord Ferguson, S. (2020). A false image of health: How fake news and pseudo-facts spread in the health and beauty industry. *Journal of Product & Brand Management, 29*(2), 168–179. https://doi.org/10.1108/JPBM-12-2018-2180

Etcoff, N. (2000). *Survival of the prettiest: The science of beauty.* Knopf Doubleday Publishing Group.

Fiske, S. T., & Taylor, S. E. (1991). *Social cognition.* McGraw Hill.

Fitzsimons, G. J., & Shiv, B. (2001). Nonconscious and contaminative effects of hypothetical questions on subsequent decision making. *Journal of Consumer Research, 28*(2), 224–238. https://doi.org/10.1086/322899

Fowler, J. G., Reisenwitz, T. H., & Carlson, L. (2015). Deception in cosmetics advertising: Examining cosmetics advertising claims in fashion magazine ads. *Journal of Global Fashion Marketing, 6*(3), 194–206. https://doi.org/10.1080/20932685.2015.1032319

Gamble, J., Gilmore, A., McCartan-Quinn, D., & Durkan, P. (2011). The marketing concept in the 21st century: A review of how marketing has been defined since the 1960s. *The Marketing Review, 11*(3), 227–248. http://doi.org/10.1362/14693 4711X589444

Ganceviciene, R., Liakou, A. I., Theodoridis, A., Makrantonaki, E., & Zouboulis, C. C. (2012). Skin anti-aging strategies. *Dermato-Endocrinology, 4*(3), 308–319. https://doi.org/10.4161/derm.22804

Gardner, D. M. (1975). Deception in advertising: A conceptual approach. *Journal of Marketing, 39*(1), 40–46.

Grice, P. H. (1975) Logic and conversation. In P. Cole & J. L. Morgan (eds.). *Syntax and semantics, Vol. 3, Speech acts*, pp. 41-58). Academic Press.

Guang-Xin, X., & Boush, D. M. (2011). How susceptible are consumers to deceptive advertising claims? A retrospective look at the experimental research literature. *The Marketing Review, 11*(3), 293–314. http://doi.org/10.1362/146934711X589480

Gunn, F. (1973). *The artificial face. A history of cosmetics.* David Charles.

Harrington, A. (Ed.) (1999), *The placebo effect: An interdisciplinary exploration* (Vol. 8). Harvard University Press.

Healthline.com (n.d.). *Hyaluronic acid: Skin benefits, products to use, and more.* https://www.healthline.com/health/beauty-skin-care/hyaluronic-acid#_noHeader PrefixedContent. Accessed on June 7, 2024.

Hunt, S. D. (1990). Truth in marketing theory and research. *Journal of Marketing, 54*(3), 1–15. https://doi.org/10.2307/1251812

ICC (International Chamber of Commerce). (2024). Advertising and marketing communication practice: Consolidated ICC Code. https://iccwbo.org/wp-content/uploads/sites/3/2024/09/ICC_2024_MarketingCode_2024.pdf

Kistler, M. (2013). Causality. In W. Dubitzky, O. Wolkenhauer, K. H. Cho, & H. Yokota (Eds.), *Encyclopedia of systems biology.* Springer. https://doi.org/10.1007/978-1-4419-9863-7_53

Kotler, P. (1967). *Marketing management: Analysis, planning and control.* Prentice Hall.

Kruglanski, A. W. (1989). *Lay epistemics and human knowledge: Cognitive and motivational bases*. Plenum Press.

Lakens, D. (2022). Sample size justification. *Collabra: Psychology*, *8*(1), 33267.

Lamy, E., & Beyneix, I. (2022, March 7). Fighting epistemic pollution (fake news, business BS) with extended corporate social responsibility. *LSE Business Review*. Blog Entry. http://eprints.lse.ac.uk/114676/1/businessreview_2022_03_07_fighting_epistemic_pollution_fake_news.pdf

Lewandowsky, S., Ecker, U. K. H., & Cook, J. (2017). Beyond misinformation: Understanding and coping with the "post-truth" era. *Journal of Applied Research in Memory and Cognition*, *6*(4), 353–369. https://doi.org/10.1016/j.jarmac.2017.07.008

Lykken, D. T. (1968). Statistical significance in psychological research. *Psychological Bulletin*, *70*(3, Pt.1), 151–159. https://doi.org/10.1037/h0026141

Mandall, M. I., & Rosenberg, L. J. (1981). *Marketing* (2nd ed.). Prentice-Hall Inc..

Maurer, S. (2010, March 12). Criteria for cosmetic product claim substantiation need to be better regulated. *BEUC, The European Consumers' Organization Position Paper*, 1–8. https://www.beuc.eu/sites/default/files/publications/2011-00007-01-e.pdf

McGuire, W. G. (2000). Standing on the shoulders of ancients: Consumer research, persuasion, and figurative language. *Journal of Consumer Research*, *27*, 109–114.

Nichols, T. (2018). *The death of expertise: The campaign against established knowledge and why it matters*. Oxford University Press.

Papakonstantinou, E., Roth, M., & Karakiulakis, G. (2012). Hyaluronic acid: A key molecule in skin aging. *Dermato-Endocrinology*, *4*(3), 253–258.

Park, C. W., Jaworski, B. J., & MacInnis, D. J. (1986). Strategic brand concept-image management. *Journal of Marketing*, *50*(4), 135–145. https://doi.org/10.1177/002224298605000401

Peccei, J. S. (2002). *Pragmatics* (1st ed.). Routledge. https://www.perlego.com/book/1626415. Accessed on June 6, 2024.

Petty, R. E., & Cacioppo, J. T. (1986). *Communication and persuasion: Central and peripheral routes to attitude change*. Springer.

Reder, L. M., & Kusbit, G. W. (1991). Locus of the Moses Illusion: Imperfect encoding, retrieval, or match? *Journal of Memory and Language*, *30*(4), 385–406. https://doi.org/10.1016/0749-596X(91)90013-A

Rogers, K. (1963). *Managers: Personality and performance*. AldineTransaction, a division of Transaction Publishers.

Shultz II, C. J. (2007). Marketing as constructive engagement. *Journal of Public Policy and Marketing*, *26*(2), 293–301.

Sibbald, B., & Roland, M. (1998). Understanding controlled trials. Why are randomised controlled trials important? *BMJ*, *316*(7126), 201. https://doi.org/10.1136/bmj.316.7126.201

Stewart, S. (2020). *Painted faces: A colourful history of cosmetics*. Amberley Publishing.

Sunstein, C. R. (2017). *#Republic: Divided democracy in the age of social media*. Princeton University Press.

Sutherland, W., Spiegelhalter, D., & Burgman, M. (2013). Policy: Twenty tips for interpreting scientific claims. *Nature*, *503*, 335–337. https://doi.org/10.1038/503335a

The Committee of Advertising Practice. (2010). Health, beauty and slimming claims substantiation advertising guidance (non-broadcast). https://www.asa.org.uk/static/uploaded/89515d0d-5635-42ef-97fd8f737fc766e7.pdf

Toulmin, S. E. (1958). *The uses of argument*. Cambridge University Press.

Toulmin, S. E., Rieke, R., & Janik, A. (1979). *An introduction to reasoning*. Macmillan.

Tungate, M. (2011). *Branded beauty: How marketing changed the way we look*. Kogan Page Publishers.

Vacker, B., & Key, W. R. (1993). Beauty and the beholder: The pursuit of beauty through commodities. *Psychology & Marketing*, *10*(6), 471–494. https://doi.org/10.1002/mar.4220100603

van Buul, V. J., & Brouns, F. J. (2015). Nutrition and health claims as marketing tools. *Critical Reviews in Food Science and Nutrition*, *55*(11), 1552–1560. https://doi.org/10.1080/10408398.2012.754738

Yingfang, W. (2007). Analysis of presupposition and its function in advertisement. *Canadian Social Science*, *3*(4), 55–60.

Chapter 4

Reflecting on Age: Societal Narratives in the World of Anti-Aging Advertising[1]

Lea Pešec

University of Graz, Austria

Abstract

Social perceptions of aging refer to the process of aging as a negative period of life during which a person loses a part of themselves and regresses both socially and culturally (Cruikshank, 2009; Gullette, 2004; Sontag, 1972). This negative perspective is closely intertwined with prevailing social beauty ideals that prioritize a youthful appearance, a narrative reinforced by media representations. This research delves into this intricate interplay, employing a dual analytical approach of semiotic and content analysis to examine the messaging within anti-aging advertisements in Croatian magazines. Examining a sample of 50 advertisements, this study identifies four main thematic categories used to promote products addressing signs of aging. These categories include (1) nature against aging; (2) magical effectiveness of anti-aging products; (3) the role of science and medicine in confirming the effectiveness of anti-aging products; (4) presentation of the aging process as a disease and illness. The findings confirmed that aging and various signs of aging are considered as undesirable and aging is presented as a negative state, rather than a process, which provides insights into what is socially desirable. Through this analysis, the findings underscore the prevailing societal narrative that views both the process of aging and signs of aging as undesirable, shedding light on the contours of social desirability. Situated at the intersection of media, societal perceptions, and aging, this research provides a broader understanding of the dynamics shaping attitudes toward aging.

[1]This chapter is based on the previously published Bachelor's Thesis titled "Analiza reklama protiv starenja u hrvatskim časopisima" (translation: "An analysis of anti-aging advertisements in Croatian magazines"). The thesis was defended in July 2020 at the University of Zadar (online), under the mentorship of doc. dr. sc. Dražen Cepić, Department of Sociology.

Beauty Industry, 87–104

Published under exclusive licence by Emerald Publishing Limited
doi:10.1108/978-1-83608-940-720251020

Beyond unraveling the semiotic intricacies of anti-aging advertisements, this study contributes to the ongoing discourse on societal ideals, beauty standards, and identity.

Keywords: Aging; anti-aging advertisements; media representations; semiotic analysis; content analysis; gender; ageism; Croatian magazines; cultural narratives

1. Introduction

Aging is not only a biological process but also a socially constructed phenomenon influenced by cultural narratives and media portrayals (Pickard, 2016). The media, as a significant social institution, play a crucial role in shaping public perceptions and attitudes toward aging (Wangler, 2013). Anti-aging advertisements, in particular, offer a unique lens through which to examine societal ideals about youth and aging, often reflecting and reinforcing cultural anxieties about the aging process (Cruikshank, 2009; Formosa, 2013). This chapter investigates the portrayal of aging in printed Croatian magazines through anti-aging advertisements, focusing on the intersection of media representations and societal attitudes toward aging. The primary objectives are to analyze how aging is depicted in these advertisements, identify the main thematic categories that emerge, and explore how these representations align with or diverge from broader cultural and social theories of aging.

In the current media landscape, aging and its representation carry significant weight in shaping societal norms and expectations. This research not only scrutinizes the direct messages conveyed through anti-aging advertisements but also delves into the subtle cues and cultural signals embedded within these media artifacts. By examining the interplay between textual and visual elements in these advertisements, insights are gained into how aging is not merely represented but also conceptualized and commodified in society. Moreover, the study of anti-aging advertisements offers a window into the pervasive impact of commercial interests on public health narratives. These advertisements often blend scientific terminology with emotional appeals, a tactic that can obscure the line between informational content and persuasive advertising. This blending raises critical ethical questions about consumer information and the responsibilities of advertisers. Additionally, the analysis of anti-aging campaigns in Croatian magazines allows for an exploration of the cultural specificities of aging narratives. While the fear of aging and the glorification of youth are global phenomena, local cultural elements can shape how these themes are expressed and perceived. Understanding these localized narratives helps in comprehending the broader cultural and social implications of aging portrayals.

This chapter also contemplates the broader implications of these representations for aging individuals. By fostering a critical discussion about the portrayal of aging, this chapter aims to contribute to a more nuanced understanding of age inclusivity in media. This research aims to challenge the stereotypes and inspire a shift toward more realistic and empowering representations of aging in media.

The fear of aging, amplified by societal ideals that idealize youth, is a central theme in many anti-aging advertisements. These ads often promote products that promise to delay or reverse the visible signs of aging, tapping into deep-seated fears and desires associated with growing older. This strategic marketing exploits societal anxieties about aging, presenting it as an undesirable condition to be fought against (Gullette, 2004). Furthermore, these narratives frequently perpetuate ageism, depicting aging as a decline that needs to be concealed or eradicated (Formosa, 2013).

Gender plays a significant role in the portrayal of aging. Sontag (1972) highlights the double standard of aging, where women face harsher societal scrutiny for aging compared to men. This gender disparity is evident in media representations, with women often depicted as needing to maintain a youthful appearance to remain socially relevant. Men, conversely, are typically shown as aging with dignity, their maturity often associated with wisdom and authority. Economic status also influences the experience of aging, as those with greater resources have better access to healthcare, wellness programs, and anti-aging products. This disparity underscores the role of socioeconomic factors in shaping individual aging experiences and societal attitudes toward aging (Twigg & Martin, 2015).

To explore these themes, this study employs a qualitative methodology that integrates content and semiotic analysis. Content analysis allows for the systematic examination of themes and patterns within the advertisements, while semiotic analysis delves into the signs and symbols used to convey messages about aging (Bignell, 2002; Chandler, 2022). Data is collected from a purposive sample of 9 Croatian magazines which feature a total of 50 anti-aging advertisements, including those targeted at both male and female audiences, ensuring a diverse representation of media content.

By analyzing these advertisements, this chapter seeks to uncover the cultural narratives and societal values embedded in media portrayals of aging. The findings aim to contribute to the broader discourse on aging, media representation, and societal ideals, offering insights into how aging is viewed and valued in contemporary Croatian culture. This research addresses critical questions about the intersection of aging, media, and culture, examining whether the portrayals of aging in Croatian magazines align with or challenge broader cultural and social theories of aging.

2. Theoretical Framework

This section explores the complex nature of aging, conceptualized as both a biological and a sociocultural phenomenon. According to Pickard (2016), aging is a dynamic process shaped by individual choices, structural conditions, and cultural influences, necessitating a multifaceted sociological perspective. Media plays a crucial role in this context, not just reflecting societal attitudes toward aging but actively shaping these narratives, as Wangler (2013) highlights. Authors such as

Sontag (1972) and Gullette (2004) highlight how anti-aging advertising exemplifies the way media narratives can influence societal perceptions of aging, often portraying it as an undesirable condition to be combated. These advertisements capitalize on societal fears and the stigma of aging, pushing a narrative that glorifies youth and portrays aging as something to be feared and medically reversed. Consequently, this perpetuates unrealistic expectations about aging, marginalizes older individuals, and fosters a youth-centric culture. The following sections will cover the pervasive fear of aging, explore the phenomenon of ageism, and discuss other related aspects. I will examine how societal pressures and media representations influence our perceptions of aging, highlighting the biases and stereotypes that often accompany the aging process. This exploration will encompass a range of topics from the fear of physical decline to the social and cultural implications of aging, providing a comprehensive understanding of how these elements interconnect within the broader societal context.

2.1 Fear of Aging, Social Ideals, and Anti-Aging Products

Cruikshank (2009) delves into the deep-seated fear of physical aging and how this fear is leveraged by the cosmetic industry, presenting it as a strategic and lucrative business model for those promoting anti-aging products. The author highlights the exploitative nature of this industry, noting, "it seems like everywhere we look, we are reminded of how old we are and what we should be looking like and doing at a certain age" (Cruikshank, 2009, p. 210). This pervasive messaging not only intensifies our collective anxiety about aging but also serves as a powerful marketing tool, capitalizing on societal insecurities to drive sales. Cruikshank (2009) further argues for a significant cultural shift, urging us to abandon the belief that aging equates to "falling from grace" (2009, p. 210). By challenging this narrative, social constructs that underpin ageism and the commercialization of age-related fears can begin to be dismantled. Additionally, Gullette (2004) explores the complexities of ageism, stating it is often seen "in the narrow sense of stimulating blind prejudice against old people" (2004, p. 7). She expands on this, noting a more insidious form of ageism, the belief that "old age is a problem" (2004, p. 7). Formosa (2013) further notes that the media perpetuates a narrative depicting old age as an undesirable condition to be resisted at all costs, suggesting that signs of aging should not only be concealed but ideally eliminated. Gullette (2004) complements these insights by addressing the discrimination against older adults, categorizing it as a form of ageism and noting that societal views often portray aging as a decline, thus positioning it negatively within the cultural discourse.

It is essential to recognize that experiences of aging are highly individualized and vary significantly across gender lines. Sontag (1972) emphasizes that men generally face fewer societal penalties as they age, due to a double standard that scrutinizes women more harshly. This disparity is rooted in societal expectations where masculinity is associated with qualities like self-esteem, autonomy, and self-control – "qualities which the disappearance of youth does not threaten" (Sontag, 1972, p. 31).

Conversely, femininity is often associated with incompetence and passivity, with aging serving to reinforce these negative stereotypes (Sontag, 1972).

Twigg and Martin introduce the concept of cultural gerontology, which examines how cultural factors crucially shape societal relations and perceptions of older people, a field constructed of both epistemological and ontological elements with the main focus on "the recognition of the way culture is constitutive of social relations and identities" (2015, p. 353). They advocate viewing aging as a lifelong process rather than merely a late-life condition. They emphasize that the human body, subject to regimes of beauty, fitness, and health, is often portrayed in a narrative promoting "successful aging," a concept frequently marketed as a moral imperative by the anti-aging industry, thereby setting and promoting unattainable physical ideals.

The fear of aging is deeply intertwined with social ideals that valorize youth and vitality, contributing to the widespread use of anti-aging products. This media-driven ideal significantly impacts women, as evidenced by studies indicating that aging anxiety and the importance of appearance are significant predictors of anti-aging product use (Muise & Desmarais, 2010). It is crucial to distinguish between legitimate scientific research on aging and the pseudoscience often found in commercial anti-aging claims, which can exploit societal fears and misconceptions about aging (de Grey et al., 2002). Historical perspectives, such as those discussed by Haber (2002), reveal that while the fear of aging is not new, it has been exacerbated by modern societal and economic conditions that frame aging as a treatable condition, thereby fueling the anti-aging industry. To conclude this section, it is important to recognize the broader implications of these findings. The pervasive fear of aging and the subsequent reliance on anti-aging products reflect deeper societal values and anxieties. The promotion of youth as an ideal not only marginalizes older individuals but also places immense pressure on younger people to maintain an unrealistic standard of beauty and vitality.

2.2 Media, Media Representations, and Aging

Lewis (2008) posits that the media are integral to everyday life, actively constructing and shaping reality. Far from being remote entities, media are deeply embedded within daily practices and significantly influence both individual and collective thought processes. Media plays a critical role in the formation and construction of contemporary culture (Lewis, 2008). This research specifically examines magazines, a dominant form of mass media. Bilić (2020, pp. 83–84) characterizes magazines as "one-way mass communication" that operates within defined social and cultural contexts, as well as temporal and spatial constraints, leaving recipients as passive participants in a structured process of symbolic transmission rather than engaged in reciprocal communication.

In exploring the theories of mediatization, a helpful distinction is made between differing analytical perspectives. Hepp (2013) and Hepp and Hasebrink (2014) categorize these as the institutional perspective, which views media primarily as influential societal institutions like journalism, and the social constructionist perspective, which sees mediatization as a broad, meta-process influenced by the totality of media in society. The institutional perspective delves into how media institutions impact other societal sectors such as politics, healthcare, and education at a meso-level, offering a focused analysis distinct from the more expansive approach of the constructionist perspective. This latter viewpoint adopts a macro-level analysis, examining the media's integration into culture and society over time, shaping all cultural and social spheres as a significant meta-process, comparable to phenomena like individualization or globalization (Krotz, 2007). Bolin (2016) introduces a third perspective – technological mediatization – "where culture and society are affected at the level of the communicative abilities of the media as technologies and the signifying codes they privilege" (2016, p. 5253). Bolin further discusses how mass media technologies foster simulations of communication, altering engagement and making full-scale symbolic exchange challenging. This analysis highlights the deep structural impacts of media technology on societal interactions and cultural perceptions.

The role of media representations in aging is pivotal as they do not merely reflect societal views but also actively generate, shape, and occasionally challenge these perceptions. Wangler (2013) explains how media portrayals of older age both mirror and influence collective and individual notions of aging, thereby framing age as a significant social construct with profound implications. Wangler (2014) and Bilić (2020) discuss the mediatization process – the pervasive infusion of media into every facet of society. This process not only disseminates information and knowledge but also establishes and reinforces collective attitudes, norms, and behavioral patterns. Media representations of aging exert considerable influence, perpetuating consistent representational patterns of older age. Wangler (2013) identifies three predominant media narratives on aging:

- Old age as human decline: This narrative highlights demographic changes associated with aging, often framed within a context of fear, thereby reinforcing the perception of aging as an undesirable process.
- Older age as superiority: In this view, old age is seen positively, recognized as a significant social factor that confers wisdom and authority in various life domains, including politics and economics.
- Old age as a new beginning: This optimistic perspective portrays aging as a phase filled with happiness, peace, and new opportunities, a time for pursuing previously unattainable goals.

Lövgren (2013) investigates how media, particularly those targeting women aged 40 and above, communicate messages about aging. She observes that the media frequently feature youthful models, reflecting and reinforcing cultural and societal preferences. This underscores the media's significant role in shaping social beliefs and opinions about aging, where the stereotypes portrayed often delineate positions of power and subordination. Furthermore, the media's role extends to promoting a consumerist culture through advertising. This research particularly focuses on advertisements for anti-aging products. Consumer culture significantly influences perceptions and practices surrounding aging and anti-aging (Twigg & Martin, 2015). The beauty and wellness industries, driven by a consumer culture that values youth and vitality, often promote products and treatments that promise to delay the signs of aging (Featherstone, 1991). This emphasis on youthfulness creates a societal pressure to maintain a youthful appearance, leading to increased consumption of anti-aging products (Twigg & Martin, 2015). Moreover, consumer culture shapes the narrative of aging as something to be fought against, rather than a natural process, reinforcing the stigma associated with aging (Gilleard & Higgs, 2014). This dynamic fosters a lucrative market for the anti-aging industry, influencing individual attitudes and behaviors toward aging. For instance, Mudrovčić (1997) remarks on how consumer culture can manifest positive or negative attitudes toward aging and old age. Östlund (2005) criticizes the generalized media depiction of older people as a homogeneous group with uniform needs and preferences, defined primarily by their age and perceived limitations. Such homogenization in media portrayals suggests that aging is a universal process characterized by typical signs of aging, promoting the notion that all individuals should use anti-aging products to mitigate or erase these signs.

The societal narratives surrounding aging, particularly through media and advertising, simultaneously stigmatize and idealize aging. Media often portray aging negatively, which can adversely affect older individuals' self-perception and exacerbate public misconceptions (Wangler & Jansky, 2023). However, anti-aging discourses in media promote a narrative of aging as a condition to be combated with technology and healthcare innovations, reflecting a persistent societal discomfort with the natural aging process. This is evident in the mixed reactions to media portrayals, where older individuals may feel disconnected from the portrayals meant to represent them, suggesting a gap between lived experiences and media representations. These conflicting narratives often fail to address the complex realities of aging, instead offering simplified, often commercialized views that may not support genuine understanding or appreciation of older age.

3. Methodology

This study addresses critical questions concerning the portrayal of aging in Croatian magazines through anti-aging advertisements, aiming to analyze how aging is represented, identify the main thematic categories emerging from the content, and explore whether the results reflect broader cultural and social theories of aging. By employing a qualitative methodology that incorporates both content and semiotic analysis, this research systematically examines media portrayals of aging.

The magazines selected for this study include the following: *Max! Germanijak* and *Men's Health*, both aimed at male audiences, and *Gloria*, *Cosmopolitan*, *Ljepota i Zdravlje* (Beauty and Health), *Sensa*, *Story*, and *Luxus*, primarily targeted toward women.[2] These selections were made based on their availability during the specific collection period from late March to early May 2020.

Advertisements within these magazines were selected based on several criteria:

- Each advertisement needed to promote an over-the-counter anti-aging product available in stores, pharmacies, or online.
- Advertisements required to explicitly exclude any treatments requiring medical interventions such as injections or surgeries.
- The advertisements must contain discourse related to aging, such as references to youth, wrinkles, or other age-related terms.

In total, nine magazines were analyzed. The total number of anti-aging advertisements across all 9 magazines is 50, 5 of which repeated across different magazines. *Luxus* had the highest number (26), followed by *Ljepota i Zdravlje* (15). Other magazines had significantly fewer, with some, like *Max! Germanijak*, having none. The total number of advertisements varied, with *Ljepota i Zdravlje* having the most (208) and *Max! Germanijak* the least (11). Despite having many advertisements, *Ljepota i Zdravlje* and *Cosmopolitan* had a lower proportion of anti-aging ads compared to *Luxus*. The high number of anti-aging ads in *Luxus* and *Ljepota i Zdravlje* goes along with the fact that these magazines target audiences concerned with beauty and wellness.

The analytical process was methodical, starting with an initial reading of the magazines to determine the appropriateness of advertisements for further analysis. This was followed by developing a system of note-taking and an analytical matrix to aid in selecting advertisements that specifically promote anti-aging products. Using open coding, the main themes within the advertisements were identified, revealing prevalent modes of representing aging. These themes were then categorized, and detailed data on the advertisement were logged.

In addition to content analysis, semiotic analysis is employed to interpret the signs and symbols related to aging portrayed in the media, following Chandler's (2022) recommendations. This method examines the connotations of visual and verbal signs used in media texts to uncover underlying messages or ideologies about aging. It focuses on how aging is symbolized and what cultural meanings are ascribed to these representations, analyzing elements such as language, dress, activities, and social interactions to decode deeper societal attitudes and values (Bignell, 2002).

Data for this analysis is collected from a purposive sample of media content that prominently features themes of aging. This comprehensive methodological framework aims to provide a nuanced understanding of media's role in shaping perceptions of aging, contributing significantly to the field of media studies and aging studies.

---

[2]The magazine's name *Ljepota i Zdravlje* translates to *Beauty and Health* in English.

4. Research Results and Discussion

The following analysis of anti-aging advertisements reveals complex interplays between consumer culture, societal expectations, and individual aspirations toward controlling the aging process. These advertisements not only promise a semblance of control over the physical manifestations of aging but also subtly influence societal norms and personal identities. Through their persuasive narratives, anti-aging products are presented as essential tools for achieving what Formosa (2013) describes as "successful aging" – a state of being that includes a healthy, active, and productive later stage of life. Additionally, these products appeal to consumers' desires to completely avoid or minimize signs of aging, a concept discussed by Calasanti and King (2007).

The profit-driven motives of the anti-aging industry are evident as these advertisements leverage social and cultural ideals to maximize impact on potential buyers. Often, these products emphasize traditional gender and age-related ideals, underscoring the differences in societal expectations for men and women as they age. The data indicates a gendered marketing strategy, with magazines for women (e.g., *Luxus*, *Ljepota i Zdravlje*, *Gloria*) featuring more anti-aging ads than those for men (e.g., *Max! Germanijak*, *Men's Health*). This analysis shows that anti-aging ads are strategically placed in magazines with a female readership, highlighting the media's role in promoting youth and beauty ideals and shaping cultural narratives around aging. Interestingly, an advertisement in *Men's Health* features a product intended for women – the *Hylauron Filler Hydrating Booster* by Eucerin. It claims to give the skin a healthy appearance and fill fine lines (2020, p. 56). According to Calasanti and King (2007), the placement of ads targeting women in men's magazines suggests an encouragement for men to purchase these products for women, thus reinforcing traditional gender roles and ideals of female beauty.

As previously discussed, Sontag (1972) highlights the double standard of aging, noting that while men are allowed to age naturally, women are often subjected to criticism for visible signs of aging. This discrepancy is further illustrated by the scant representation of aging men in these advertisements. For example, the only ad that mentions men and aging in *Luxus* promotes a perfume with the phrase, "the masculine character of wood and amber will rejuvenate your senses" (Luxus, 2020, p. 38), which focuses on sensory rejuvenation rather than physical appearance – a stark contrast to the visually oriented anti-aging ads targeted at women.[3] Smirnova's (2012) analysis of cosmeceutical advertisements provides a compelling framework for understanding the portrayal of aging in media, which closely aligns with the findings of the current study. Smirnova's research highlights three major themes: the use of scientific and medical authorities to frame cosmeceuticals as "drugs" that cure aging, the comparison between cosmeceuticals and cosmetic surgery in restoring youth, and the cultural logic that equates

---

[3]All texts quoted from advertisements have been translated from Croatian into English by the author.

youth with beauty, femininity, and power, while viewing older age as the absence of these qualities.

The findings of this research are organized into four main thematic categories:

(1) Nature against aging: this theme includes advertisements that promote natural ingredients as effective tools against aging, positioning nature as a benevolent force in the fight against the physical signs of aging.
(2) Magical effectiveness of anti-aging products: advertisements under this theme suggest that certain products can miraculously reverse or halt the aging process, presenting these solutions almost as magical elixirs.
(3) The role of science and medicine in confirming the effectiveness of anti-aging products: This category includes ads that use scientific authority and medical endorsement to validate the efficacy of anti-aging products, enhancing their appeal by associating them with professional credibility.
(4) Presentation of the aging process as a disease and illness: Finally, some advertisements frame aging as a condition or disease, suggesting that it is something to be cured, thus medicalizing the natural aging process.

Each category reflects deep-seated cultural narratives about aging and beauty, highlighting the pervasive influence of media in shaping perceptions and behaviors toward aging. This discussion not only extends the academic conversation on aging and media representation but also provides a critical lens through which to view the ethical implications of such marketing strategies.

4.1 Nature Against Aging in Anti-Aging Advertisements

The exploration of natural elements within anti-aging advertisements across nine analyzed magazines – including *Max! Germanijak*, two editions of *Gloria*, *Cosmopolitan*, *Men's Health*, *Ljepota i Zdravlje*, *Sensa*, *Story*, and *Luxus* – reveals a significant emphasis on the purported efficacy of natural ingredients in combating the signs of aging. Specifically, 17 advertisements distinctly highlight the advantages of using natural components to address aging concerns.

One notable advertisement in *Ljepota i Zdravlje* promotes a day cream by *Garnier*, which underscores the rejuvenating properties of organic lavender essential oil. The ad claims that lavender not only revitalizes the skin but also regenerates it, positioning this natural ingredient as a powerful ally against the visible signs of aging. Similarly, an advertisement in *Cosmopolitan* emphasizes the benefits of bakuchiol, a herbal equivalent to retinol but without the associated side effects. This product is acclaimed for its ability to stimulate skin cell renewal, making it particularly suitable for skin with wrinkles and pigmentation spots. The advertisement strategically places a young female model at its center, devoid of any aging signs, thereby aligning with societal beauty ideals as discussed by Gullette (2004).

Additionally, *Sensa* features an advertisement for *YSL Pure Shots*, which claims that an "urban lifestyle accelerates aging of the skin by 40 percent." The ad suggests that the product is ideal for women who are resistant to lifestyle changes and compromises, although it fails to clarify the basis for these claims or the direct benefits of the product. The advertisement mentions that the product contains potent ingredients from "Moroccan magic gardens," which are implied to rejuvenate the skin. This vague association with exotic and natural elements is designed to enhance the allure of the product.

The prevalent use of natural ingredients in these advertisements points to a strategic marketing approach that leverages the growing consumer preference for "natural" and "organic" solutions. The emphasis on natural ingredients not only caters to this preference but also suggests a form of "green" credibility or the notion that these products are healthier or more ethical than synthetic alternatives. However, the actual impact of these natural ingredients on the aging process remains ambiguously presented, often without sufficient scientific backing or detailed explanation in the advertisements. This raises critical questions about the authenticity and effectiveness of such claims, reflecting a broader trend in consumer goods where natural ingredients are invoked more for their marketing appeal than their proven benefits. This discussion underscores the need for a deeper investigation into the efficacy of natural ingredients in anti-aging products, as well as a more transparent presentation of these benefits in advertisements. The implication that natural ingredients can significantly alter the natural aging process warrants further scrutiny, both from a scientific perspective and a consumer rights angle, to ensure that such claims do not exploit consumer trust or mislead about the capabilities of the products.

4.2 The Magical Effectiveness of Anti-Aging Products

The allure of anti-aging advertisements often resides in their promise of miraculous transformations, suggesting that aging can be effortlessly reversed with "magical" ingredients. This enchanting narrative is prominently featured in various magazines, including *Ljepota i Zdravlje*, *Sensa*, and *Luxus*, where terms such as "anti-aging wizard" ("Anti-age čarobnjak," *Ljepota i* Zdravlje, 2020, p. 29), "beauty elixir" ("eliksir ljepote," *Ljepota i Zdravlje*, 2020, p. 29), and "fountain of youth" ("vrelo mladosti," Luxus, 2020, p. 19) are not just promotional phrases but are indicative of the fantastical solutions offered to the aging problem.

The advertisement for *Yasenka Skinage Collagen Prestige 10,000* in *Ljepota i Zdravlje* magazine is a striking example of how anti-aging products are marketed as essential tools for those seeking to uphold societal beauty standards. Described as a "beauty elixir," the product is said to deliver a "wonderful youthful glow," appealing directly to consumers' desires for a visible manifestation of youth. This promise goes beyond suggesting mere effectiveness; it positions the supplement as a crucial element for anyone who prioritizes maintaining a youthful appearance. The ad's messaging does more than just promote a beauty product; it reinforces a pervasive societal norm where aging is seen not just as undesirable but almost as a failure of self-care. The implication is strong and clear: to age visibly is to neglect the personal duty of maintaining one's youthful appearance. This reflects a deeper cultural narrative that equates youth with beauty and, by extension, personal worth. Furthermore, the advertisement underscores its appeal by stating it is "an excellent choice for women who take care of themselves, with a priority of not only feeling youthful but also looking it" (2020, p. 29). This statement is particularly telling, as it links self-care with the outward display of youth, suggesting that true self-care is synonymous with efforts to inhibit visible signs of aging. It subtly shifts the concept of health and wellness from a holistic approach to one narrowly focused on esthetics. Such messaging plays into and perpetuates the societal pressures on women to continually strive for youthfulness as part of their identity and value in society. It also reflects a broader societal discomfort with aging, particularly among women, where aging is not seen as a natural process but rather a battle to be fought against. This marketing strategy not only capitalizes on but also amplifies fears of aging, turning personal insecurities into commercial opportunities. By dissecting the underlying implications of this advertisement, it becomes evident how deeply entwined consumer culture is with our perceptions of aging. This critical examination reveals the ethical concerns and cultural impacts of such marketing, highlighting the need for a shift toward more inclusive and realistic portrayals of aging in media.

Luxus magazine further extends this narrative by dedicating a section to the "fountain of youth" (2020, p. 18), showcasing a range of products alongside images of young models whose flawless skin belies the natural aging process. Such imagery reinforces the myth that these products can halt or reverse aging, embedding a deep-seated fear of growing old while promoting a singular, often unattainable beauty standard.

Moreover, the use of regal metaphors like "royal treatment" and "royal youth" connects the consumption of these products with luxurious and elite lifestyles, suggesting that the battle against aging is not just about looking young but also about feeling aristocratic and prestigious. This association between anti-aging products and royal imagery taps into deeper cultural narratives that equate youth with social status and success.

The critical perspective provided by Smirnova (2012) highlights that the fantasy element in anti-aging advertising not only captivates consumers but also establishes a paradigm where aging is viewed as a defeatable adversary. The narrative of combating aging with magical potions parallels fairy tales, constructing a reality where eternal youth is not only possible but also ideal. Searing and Zeilig (2017) further explain that such symbolic language is a potent marketing tool, crafting an illusion that these products can deliver timeless beauty.

In conclusion, the thematic analysis of anti-aging advertisements under the rubric of magical effectiveness reveals a complex interplay of fantasy, societal expectations, and consumer behavior. These ads do not simply sell products; they propagate an ideology that venerates youth and vilifies aging, influencing both personal identity and societal norms. As these advertisements continue to shape perceptions about aging, it becomes crucial to critically assess their impact on societal values and individual self-esteem, questioning whether the pursuit of eternal youth should overshadow the natural and dignified process of aging.

4.3 The Role of Science and Medicine in Confirming the Effectiveness of Anti-Aging Products

In the realm of anti-aging advertisements, the invocation of scientific authority and medical endorsement plays a critical role in validating product claims and enhancing consumer confidence. These advertisements often feature endorsements from professionals such as dermatologists, specialists, and researchers, whose authority is leveraged to substantiate the effectiveness of anti-aging products.

For example, the advertisement for bakuchiol in *Cosmopolitan* not only highlights the natural composition of the product but also emphasizes its legitimacy by noting that a dermatologist from Yale University has confirmed its efficacy. This pattern of endorsement is mirrored in another advertisement for *Yasenka Skinage Collagen Prestige 10,000*, which boasts collaboration with "the best dermatologists, cosmetologists, nutritionists, and other experts." These professionals are said to have contributed to the development of a formula that combats aging signs, adding an additional layer of credibility to the product.

Additionally, *Ljepota i Zdravlje* advertises an anti-age booster from *Laboratories Novexper Paris*, supposedly approved by dermatologists, and *Luxus* magazine discusses the *L'occitane Immortelle Night Reset Booster*, which was validated through a "satisfaction test conducted on 31 women." Such claims are designed to assure consumers of the product's tested and proven benefits.

The strategic use of scientific and professional titles in the branding of these products, such as "Dr Brandt Hyaluronic Facial Cream" and "Eveline Gold Lift Expert," further enhances their perceived legitimacy. By associating these products with medical and scientific expertise, the advertisements create a strong impression of efficacy and safety, suggesting that these products are not only effective but also recommended by health professionals.

According to Smirnova (2012), the inclusion of medical endorsements makes the product appear more legitimate and desirable by establishing a parallel to the doctor-patient relationship. This framing suggests that aging is a condition requiring medical intervention, where the product serves as a prescribed remedy. However, despite these endorsements, many advertisements fail to provide detailed information about the endorsing professionals, such as their names or specific roles in product testing, which could be a potential area for more transparent communication. The strategic positioning of these endorsements within advertising narratives plays a pivotal role in constructing a medical discourse around aging. By presenting aging as a medical issue that can be treated or prevented with the right products, these advertisements not only reinforce the medicalization of natural biological processes but also promote a narrative that aging is a "disease" that needs to be cured. This narrative shift has profound implications for societal perceptions of aging, positioning older adults in a space where their natural aging process is viewed through a lens of pathology rather than a normal, healthy stage of life. Furthermore, the commodification of scientific credibility in these advertisements raises ethical concerns. It prompts critical questions about the integrity of marketing practices and the potential conflict between commercial interests and the ethical responsibilities of healthcare professionals. As such, consumers are encouraged to critically evaluate the veracity of these claims and the qualifications of the endorsers, looking beyond the surface to understand the scientific basis, if any, behind the products advertised. In summary, while endorsements from the scientific and medical community can lend a veneer of credibility to anti-aging products, they also raise ethical issues concerning the commodification of science and the medicalization of aging. It is crucial for both consumers and regulators to scrutinize these endorsements and demand greater transparency and accountability in advertising practices, ensuring that these powerful tools are used responsibly and ethically.

4.4 Presentation of the Aging Process as a Disease and Illness

In the discourse of anti-aging advertisements, aging is frequently portrayed not merely as a natural part of life but as a medical condition or disease that requires intervention. This categorization of aging as a pathological state to be combated with products marketed as cures forms a compelling narrative in the cosmetic industry. Advertisements often frame these products as essential remedies capable of restoring youth and eradicating the undesirable signs of aging.

For example, the advertisement for *Eucerin's Hyaluron Filler Hydrating Booster* in *Men's Health* claims that the product "fills fine lines for smooth, healthy-looking skin" (2020, p. 56), insinuating that fine lines and wrinkles are indicators of unhealthy skin. This implication suggests a problem that needs correction, aligning the natural aging process with a decline in health. Similarly, the advertisement for *Skinage Collagen Prestige 10,000* in *Cosmopolitan* promises that its use will give the skin a "healthier glow," implying that without such products, the skin's health is compromised (2020, p. 31).

The language used in these advertisements often incorporates medical or therapeutic terms such as "healing," "revitalizing," and "treatment," which are strategically employed to medicalize the aging process. For instance, *Ljepota i Zdravlje* refers to the *Yasenka Skinage Collagen Prestige 10000* as having magical properties that make the skin look "natural and healthy as in your best years" (2020, p. 29), while an article in *Luxus* describes the *Apivita Queen Bee Anti-Aging Night Cream* as something that "heals and revitalizes" (2020, p. 20). These descriptions not only promise rejuvenation but also suggest that aging without intervention is a departure from health.

Lövgren (2013) highlights a critical aspect of media representation: older individuals are the least represented, and when they are, it is often in a context that excessively emphasizes youthful appearances, employing young models that do not reflect the demographic realities of aging. This skewed portrayal not only shapes what is deemed socially acceptable and desirable but also reinforces a narrow view of beauty that aligns closely with youth. Such media practices contribute to the formation and support of individual aspirations that favor youth over the natural aging process, effectively turning youth into a form of commercial capital. This trend dovetails with the broader issues identified in anti-aging advertisements, where aging is often framed as a disease or a defect that needs correcting. These advertisements typically present their products as miraculous solutions capable of reversing visible signs of aging, such as wrinkles, fine lines, or sagging skin. This narrative establishes unrealistic expectations about the effectiveness of skincare products and perpetuates a stigma around aging, presenting it as something undesirable and fearful. According to Calasanti and King (2007) and Smirnova (2012), these narratives exploit societal fears of aging, manipulating individuals into seeing aging as a condition requiring a medical or pharmaceutical remedy. Moreover, Searing and Zeilig (2017) discuss how the anti-aging industry capitalizes on these fears by marketing solutions that promise to "reverse time," thereby fostering a culture where aging is viewed as something to be combated. This approach not only drives sales but also shapes cultural perceptions, reinforcing the notion that aging is a condition that diminishes personal value and should be fought against.

The portrayal of aging as a problem requiring a solution contributes to a cultural misunderstanding of aging, misrepresenting it as a condition that needs curing rather than an inevitable, natural part of life. This is further complicated by media practices that prioritize youth and associate aging with a loss of beauty and vitality. Twigg and Martin discuss the implications of such representations, noting that "the bodies of older people are disciplined and made subject to regimes of fitness and health in which responsibility for aging well becomes a moral imperative" (2015, p. 355). This perspective underscores the need for a critical evaluation of societal views on aging and challenges us to consider the ethical implications of marketing strategies that exploit these views for profit. In sum, the combination of media practices that idolize youth and advertising strategies that frame aging as a defeatable condition works synergistically to maintain a youth-centric culture. This culture not only marginalizes older individuals but also skews public perceptions about the natural process of aging, necessitating a reevaluation of how aging is depicted and discussed in public and commercial discourses.

5. Conclusion

This research, through a detailed content and semiotic analysis of anti-aging advertisements in nine Croatian magazines, analyzed the representations of aging within media discourses. A total of 50 advertisements were examined and categorized into 4 distinct themes: (1) nature against aging, (2) the magical effectiveness of anti-aging products, (3) the role of science and medicine in confirming the effectiveness of these products, and (4) the presentation of the aging process as a disease and illness.

Many advertisements emphasize the use of natural ingredients, suggesting these as powerful tools against aging. This theme reflects cultural narratives that valorize natural and organic solutions, positioning them as inherently beneficial and potent. The actual efficacy of these ingredients, however, is often ambiguously presented, raising questions about the authenticity of such claims. Furthermore, the portrayal of anti-aging products as magical solutions to aging is a prevalent theme. Advertisements frequently use terms like "beauty elixir" and "fountain of youth," creating a fantasy of effortless, miraculous transformations. This language not only captivates the imagination but also reinforces the myth of eternal youth, promising consumers the allure of a perpetually youthful appearance through regular application of these products. Additionally, a number of advertisements leverage scientific authority and medical endorsements to validate their claims. By associating products with dermatologists, specialists, and scientific studies, these advertisements enhance their credibility and appeal. However, the frequent absence of specific details about these endorsements often undermines their legitimacy, highlighting the need for more transparent communication. Lastly, a significant portion of the advertisements frame aging as a pathological condition that needs to be treated or cured. This medicalization of aging perpetuates the stigma around natural aging processes, suggesting that aging is an undesirable state requiring medical intervention. This narrative reinforces ageism and promotes the idea that aging is something to be feared and fought against.

The analysis also underscores the gendered nature of aging portrayals. Women are disproportionately targeted by anti-aging advertisements, which emphasize the need to maintain a youthful appearance to remain socially relevant. In contrast, advertisements for men often focus on enhancing vitality or sensory experiences rather than physical appearance. This disparity reflects and reinforces societal double standards regarding gender and aging.

The findings of this study contribute to the broader discourse on aging, media representation, and societal ideals. By revealing how anti-aging advertisements reflect and shape societal attitudes toward aging, this research underscores the powerful role of media in constructing cultural narratives about aging. These portrayals often promote unrealistic and unattainable ideals, reinforcing negative stereotypes and ageism.

In conclusion, this study highlights the need for a critical examination of how aging is portrayed in media. Through a comprehensive analysis of anti-aging advertisements, it is evident that these advertisements are not merely selling products; they are propagating specific cultural and social ideologies. By promoting youth and denigrating aging, these advertisements influence societal perceptions and contribute to a cultural climate that fears aging rather than embracing it as a natural part of life. Such findings underscore the need for a broader cultural shift toward a more inclusive and realistic portrayal of aging, celebrating it as a natural, dignified, and integral part of the human experience. Future research should continue to explore the impact of media representations of aging across different cultural contexts and media platforms. Additionally, there is a need for more transparent and scientifically backed communication in advertisements to ensure consumers are not misled by exaggerated claims. Understanding the broader implications of these portrayals can help develop more inclusive and realistic representations of aging.

References

Bignell, J. (2002). *Media semiotics: An introduction* (2nd ed.). Manchester University Press.

Bilić, P. (2020). *Sociologija medija: Rutine, tehnologija i moć*. Naklada Jesenski i Turk, Hrvatsko sociološko društvo.

Bolin, G. (2016). Media Times| The rhythm of ages: Analyzing mediatization through the lens of generations across cultures. *International Journal of Communication, 10*, 5252–5269.

Calasanti, T., & King, N. (2007). Beware of the estrogen assault: Ideals of old manhood in anti-aging advertisements. *Journal of Aging Studies, 21*(4), 357–368.

Chandler, D. (2022). *Semiotics: The basics* (3rd ed.). Routledge.

Cruikshank, M. (2009). *Learning to be old: Gender, culture, and aging* (3rd ed.). Rowman & Littlefield Publishers.

de Grey, A. D., Gavrilov, L., Olshansky, S. J., Coles, L. S., Cutler, R. G., Fossel, M., & Harman, S. M. (2002). Antiaging technology and pseudoscience. *Science, 296*(5568), 656. https://doi.org/10.1126/science.296.5568.656a

Featherstone, M. (1991). *Consumer culture and postmodernism*. Sage Publications.

Formosa, M. (2013). Positive aging in an age of neo-liberalism – Old wine in new bottles? In U. Kriebernegg & R. Maierhofer (Eds.), *The ages of life: Living and aging in conflict* (pp. 21–35). Lit Verlag.

Gilleard, C., & Higgs, P. (2014). *Aging, corporeality and embodiment*. Anthem Press.

Gullette, M. M. (2004). *Aged by culture*. The University of Chicago Press.

Haber, C. (2002). Anti-aging: Why now?: A historical framework for understanding the contemporary enthusiasm. *Generations: Journal of the American Society on Aging, 25*(4), 9–14. https://www.jstor.org/stable/26555096

Hepp, A. (2013). The communicative figurations of mediatized worlds: Mediatization research in times of the "mediation of everything". *European Journal of Communication, 28*(6), 615–629.

Hepp, A., & Hasebrink, U. (2014). Human interaction and communicative figurations. The transformation of mediatized cultures and societies. In K. Lundby (Ed.), *Mediatization of communication* (pp. 249–271). De Gruyter Mouton.

Krotz, F. (2007). The meta-process of "mediatization" as a conceptual frame. *Global Media & Communication, 3*(3), 256–260.

Lewis, J. (2008). *Cultural studies: The basics* (2nd ed.). Sage.

Lövgren, K. (2013). Celebrating or denying age? On cultural studies as an analytical approach in gerontology. In U. Kriebernegg & R. Maierhofer (Eds.), *The ages of life: Living and aging in conflict* (pp. 37–55). Lit Verlag.

Luxus. (2020). Luxus magazine. Müller trgovina zagreb d.o.o.

Ljepota i Zdravlje. (2020). Ljepota i Zdravlje magazine. MEDIATOP INTERNATIONAL d.o.o.

Mudrovčić, Ž (1997). Starost i starenje ljudskog roda: žensko-muški aspekti starenja. *Revija za Sociologiju, 28*(3–4), 193–205. https://hrcak.srce.hr/154472

Muise, A., & Desmarais, S. (2010). Women's perceptions and use of "Anti-Aging" products. *Sex Roles, 63*, 126–137. https://doi.org/10.1007/s11199-010-9791-5

Östlund, B. (2005). Design paradigms and misunderstood technology: The case of older users. In B. Jaeger (Ed.), *Young technologies in old hands: An international view on senior citizen's utilization of ICT* (pp. 25–39). DJOF.

Pickard, S. (2016). *Age studies: A sociological examination of how we age and are aged through the life course*. Sage.

Searing, C., & Zeilig, H. (2017). Fine lines: Cosmetic advertising and the perception of ageing female beauty. *International Journal of Ageing and Later Life*, *11*(1), 7–36. https://doi.org/10.3384/ijal.1652-8670.16-290

Smirnova, M. H. (2012). A will to youth: The woman's anti-aging elixir. *Social Science & Medicine*, *75*(7), 1236–1243. https://doi.org/10.1016/j.socscimed.2012.02.061

Sontag, S. (1972). The double standard of aging. *Saturday Review of the Society*, *55*(39), 29–38.

Twigg, J., & Martin, W. (2015). The challenge of cultural gerontology. *The Gerontologist*, *55*(3), 353–359. https://doi.org/10.1093/geront/gnu061

Wangler, J. (2013). Representation of old age in media – Fear of aging or cult of youth? In U. Kriebernegg & R. Maierhofer (Eds.), *The ages of life: Living and aging in conflict* (pp. 107–120). Lit Verlag.

Wangler, J. (2014). Internalization or social comparison? An empirical investigation of the influence of media (re)presentations of age on the subjective health perceptions and age experiences of older people. In U. Kriebernegg, R. Maierhofer, & B. Ratzenböck (Eds.), *Alive and kicking at all ages: Cultural constructions of health and life course identity* (pp. 117–130). Verlag Bielefeld.

Wangler, J., & Jansky, M. (2023). Media portrayal of old age and its effects on attitudes in older people: Findings from a series of studies. *Humanities & Social Sciences Communications*, *10*(165), 1–9. https://doi.org/10.1057/s41599-023-01671-5

Chapter 5

Beauty and Body in Fashion Photography: The Covered Body and New Bodily Practices

Petra Krpan

University of Zagreb, Croatia

Abstract

The beauty industry has maintained a longstanding relationship with photography, shaping the portrayal of what is considered 'beautiful' or 'in fashion' at any given time. The analysis examines various changes of beauty and representational practices in fashion photography and film, with a focus on women's beauty practices from the 1920s to contemporary fashion. Specifically, it will explore the concepts of the clothed body and the covered body and how these ideas have altered the appearance of the body while blurring traditional notions of feminine and masculine attributes in contemporary fashion. From the exposure of the body to its full coverage, this paper will investigate the role of beauty in the works of numerous fashion photographers, concentrating on the period from the 1960s to the 1990s. Furthermore, photography has served as a medium for presenting changeable beauty standards and the emergence of new bodily representations (Pultz, 1995). This transformation of the body was particularly significant, as there was a notable shift in beauty ideals. The liberated and revealing body of the 1960s through the 1980s, coinciding with the growing emphasis on athleticism and the physical form, redefined conventional notions of beauty through photography and cinema. As experimental photography techniques emerged in the late 1980s and early 1990s, beauty standards, along with fashion, began to change. Finally, with the rise of Japanese deconstruction, the portrayal of body and beauty began to involve concealing the body and face, enclosing them in fabric and textiles, thus obscuring flesh and reshaping gender perceptions.

Beauty Industry, 105–122

Published under exclusive licence by Emerald Publishing Limited
doi:10.1108/978-1-83608-940-720251022

Keywords: Beauty; fashion photography; gender; the covered body; bodily representation; make-up

1. Introduction

Fashion photography throughout the 20th century has played a pivotal role in shaping social perceptions of beauty, showcasing a diverse array of beauty standards. Across the decades, a myriad of fashion trends and stylistic approaches have left their mark on the notion of beauty within fashion photography. This chapter aims to research changes of beauty ideals from the 1960s onwards, while also providing an introductory exploration spanning the entirety of the 20th century within the realm of fashion photography. This historical contextualization is crucial or understanding the trajectory of beauty standards and cosmetic practices depicted in fashion photography. As British theorist and photographer Eugénie Shinkle (2008) argues, photographic images are a driving force behind the fashion system, and they play a key role in defining global fashion culture and thus have a significant impact on beauty standards. This chapter will explore and contextualize various beauty practices in fashion photography from the 1920s to the 1990s, examining their representation within the intricate fashion system.

2. Representation of Beauty and Body in Fashion Photography From the 1920s to the 1980s

From the 1920s flapper girls to the 1960s hippie movement, women's beauty and fashion practices underwent significant changes within the structured fashion system. Throughout this period, fashion played a significant role in shaping social perceptions of beauty, reflecting changing cultural norms and values. Furthermore, fashion involves various cultural and artistic practices, and it is never fully finished (Kaiser, 2012). As fashion changed, the beauty industry gradually emerged as a distinct and lucrative sector, establishing itself as an indispensable partner within the fashion system. As author and cosmetics historian Gabriela Hernandez argues 'Any woman concerned with fashion wears make-up' (2017, p. 93). Beauty products and cosmetics became integral components of the fashion industry, catering to the diverse needs and preferences of consumers. This symbiotic relationship between fashion and beauty contributed to the expansion and diversification of both industries, fuelling innovation and creativity in the pursuit of aesthetic ideals. Together, they propelled the transformation of beauty and fashion practices, leaving an enduring impact on the fashion system, and marking beauty products as luxury elements. Luxury is thus connected to wealth and social control (Calefato, 2014) applying Thorstein Veblen's concept of conspicuous consumption, where individuals display wealth and status through their consumption patterns, including fashion. This behaviour is particularly evident among the leisure class, who consume luxury goods to signify their social status (Veblen, 1899).

From the 1920s to the early 1990s, beauty standards, particularly concerning women, underwent significant transformations as social roles shifted and women increasingly broke free from traditional constraints and expectations. The concept of beauty became intricately intertwined with women's social roles and professional lives, a connection that persists to this day. The 1920s marked the onset of the quest for youth. Mature women were no longer considered genuinely fashionable. The ideal of beauty became closely linked with youthfulness, prompting women to strive for a younger appearance (Hernandez, 2017). Fashion photography emerged as a powerful tool in disseminating and popularizing these evolving beauty ideals, making them accessible to a broader audience. The history of beauty in 20th century fashion photography serves as a reflection of the cultural, social, and artistic currents of each era, illustrating the dynamic and ever-changing nature of beauty within the industry. Photography in fashion emerged as the primary medium for capturing and portraying various representations of beauty, particularly in relation to women's fashion (Hernandez, 2017). Fashion and photography collaborated closely to define and promote prevailing notions of beauty and fashionability.

While this research primarily focusses on the 1960s onwards, with special accents on the end of the 1980s and beginning of the 1990s and explores the evolution of beauty standards within fashion and photography during that period, it is imperative to contextualize this subject within the broader scope of the 20th century. Understanding how photography has shaped the representation of the body over the course of the century is crucial for comprehending the complexities of beauty portrayal and bodily practices in fashion.

Art movements such as surrealism and futurism exerted significant influence on fashion photography in the early 20th century. During that time, fashion used photography and window displays to showcase beauty standards of the time, and utilized the art of fashion advertising (English, 2013). Beauty standards often mirrored elements of fantasy and dreams, with a focus on enhancement rather than realism. Elizabeth Arden advertisements of the 1920s often presented the look of this period: the hair was cropped short in a smooth bob, the eyes were enhanced with make-up, the brows were plucked, and the mouth was painted a vivid shade (Gunn, 1973, p. 143). Renowned photographers like Edward Steichen and Horst P. Horst skillfully blended fashion and art in their images, infusing them with a sense of romanticism and ethereal fantasy (Ang, 2022, p. 110). During the early 20th century, fashion photography primarily served the utilitarian purpose of documenting fashion designs, rather than emphasizing models or beauty. Esteemed photographers such as Steichen and Baron Adolf de Meyer played crucial roles in elevating fashion photography to an art form. They experimented with lighting, composition, and body poses to create visually captivating images, exuding elegance and sophistication (Ang, 2022). A notable innovation in early 20th-century fashion photography was the use of elaborate sets and backdrops to construct fantasy worlds which complemented the display of fashion. This approach introduced a theatrical element to the photographs, laying the groundwork for the more stylized and glamorous fashion photography of subsequent decades. Furthermore, a type of face-lifting, as a means of rejuvenation, came into fashion during the 1920s and, although plastic surgery was in an elementary stage of development, the experience gleaned from operations on scarred soldiers after the war proved to be an invaluable aid to the advance of cosmetic surgery (Gunn, 1973, p. 152). Surrealism emerged as a prominent aesthetic in fashion photography during the 1920s, characterized by dream-like imagery, unexpected juxtapositions, and non-linear elements. Visionary photographers such as Man Ray and Dora Maar utilized surrealistic techniques like photomontage, double exposure, and distortion to create avant-garde and thought-provoking images that challenged traditional notions of beauty. Man Ray's work 'Glass Tears' from 1932 represented a cropped photograph of mascaraed lashes, making the woman's eye surreal (Ang, 2022, p. 147), while Maar paved the way to a more experimental approach to beauty representation. Maar's portraits frequently featured subjects with unconventional beauty, emphasizing natural imperfections and unique characteristics rather than adhering to traditional standards of perfection. This influence is evident in her use of unusual perspectives, photomontage, and manipulation of images. The influence of surrealism persisted into contemporary photography, with photomontage becoming an established practice in the 1990s, especially in fashion. Additionally, futurism left its mark on fashion photography during this time, emphasizing movement, dynamism, and technological innovation. The geometric shapes, clean lines, and bold designs of futurist fashion photography reflected the era's excitement and optimism about the future, inspiring the dynamic imagery of the 1960s and beyond. Photographers of this period explored novel perspectives, angles, and lighting techniques to convey a sense of progress and modernity in their work. From 1915 to 1939, photographers used several images to form a single photograph, thus creating photomontages, opening new dimensions of facial and bodily expression (Ang, 2022). These types of facial and bodily photograph manipulations would later appear in the 1960s pop art movement, and with Nick Knight's work in contemporary fashion photography.

Even though the 1930s witnessed significant transformations in fashion photography, profoundly influencing the portrayal of beauty and style in imagery, bizarre and distorted images of bodies were still very present in magazines. In 1935 and 1936, German artist Hans Bellmer created a series of dolls that protested against physical perfection and represented a shift towards older modes of expression. However, this era marked a transition towards a more opulent and refined aesthetic, inspired by the burgeoning film industry and the allure of Hollywood glamour. John Berger, in his seminal work 'Ways of Seeing' (1972), offers a profound critique of how women have been objectified in visual media, including photography. Berger discusses the concept of the male gaze, which refers to the way visual arts are often created from a male perspective, presenting women as objects of male pleasure and desire. In that context, Bellmer's approach to the body's deconstruction involved disassembling and reconfiguring the female human form in ways that challenged traditional notions of beauty, identity, and desire. By fragmenting the body and then reassembling it in unnatural ways, during the 1930s, Bellmer highlighted the artificiality and constructed nature of physical forms (Krpan, 2021, p. 196). His 'dolls' and the concept of the unconscious influenced beauty standards, especially in contemporary fashion practices, which we will address later on.

In the 1930s, the production of better quality cosmetics continued to be the main aim of toiletry manufacturers, and by this time the beauty business had become a thriving and lucrative industry (Gunn, 1973, p. 152). Puls of the time was marked by eyeshadows, violet and silver tints to provide women a touch of glamour, and pale complexion was very much present in photography and cinema. Beauty standards in old Hollywood during the 1930s were heavily influenced by the film industry, which played a significant role in shaping collective perceptions of attractiveness. The advent of talking pictures in the late 1920s and early 1930s brought a new era of stardom, with a focus on glamorous appearances. Commercial Hollywood portrait studios began photographing various stars, thus directly influencing beauty and fashion standards to a wider audience. Greta Garbo's cool and sophisticated look with a pale complexion and the usage of dark eye pencils influenced beauty standards, of the time and Josephine Baker, the first African American entertainer to star in a major motion picture enjoyed great popularity in Europe and the United States due to her visual presence in magazines and particular style. Foundation was lighter than one's natural colour because of the influence of cinema and early cameras. During that time film cameras could not realistically present the natural skin tone, so make-up helped to even out the tone of the skin in the image. Cinema and its stars made a significant impact in shaping beauty standards and feminine looks, actress Louise Brooks became extremely known for her short bob hairstyle and dark lip while Clara Bow, American silent movie star, became the 'IT' girl, 'IT' referred to her sex appeal (Hernandez, 2017, p. 97). These particular beauty practices were adopted and copied carefully thus creating a wider understanding of the, previously mentioned, *trickle-down* theory in by Thorstein Veblen and Georg Simmel. Both Simmel and Veblen were influential sociologists whose theories on class and social structure have significantly contributed to understanding fashion, style and beauty practices. *Trickle-up* theory created a framework of adopting various influential styles, created by the higher class. As Simmel states, 'fashion is a form of imitation and so of social equalization' (Simmel, 1957, p. 541). According to Simmel (1957), fashion serves as a means for the upper class to assert their superiority and for the lower class to aspire to higher status through imitation. According to Veblen, the upper classes engage in conspicuous consumption by adopting costly and extravagant clothing and accessories to display their economic power and differentiate themselves from lower social classes. This behaviour creates a trickle-down effect, where lower classes imitate the styles of the wealthy to enhance their own social standing, leading to a continuous cycle of fashion change and social emulation (Veblen, 1899). Paul Blumberg's trickle-up theory, also known as the *bubble-up* theory, suggests that fashion trends originate within lower-income or marginalized groups and progressively gain popularity, ultimately impacting mainstream fashion and higher social classes. In contrast to the traditional trickle-down theory, where trends emerge from the elite and spread downward, the trickle-up theory underscores the profound influence of street style, subcultures, and youth movements on widespread fashion trends (Blumberg, 1974).

This methodological framework by Simmel, Veblen and Blumberg and their classical theories of fashion's dispersal, can be easily applied to beauty practices, as both are the same structural element of the fashion system (Barthes, 1967). Through photography and film, beauty practices became more visible than ever and wider audiences would copy what was in fashion. As Hernandez cites 'Fashion trends of the decade were influenced by the movies. Women wanted the clothing of the stars, but most could only afford fashions that were more practical for everyday wear' (2017, p. 105). Beauty products were essential elements of wealth and status, and women were drawn to them through fashion and advertisements.

A notable development in 1930s fashion photography was the adoption of natural light and softer focus techniques in portraits, contributing to a romantic and ethereal ambiance that emphasized facial beauty (Ang, 2022, pp. 182–184). Esteemed photographers such as Horst P. Horst and George Hoyningen-Huene embraced this softer style, capturing models in graceful poses that exuded elegance and sophistication (Ang, 2022, p. 182). Horst's influence on capturing and creating beauty standards involved various elements such as crossing shadows, smooth gradation, making the background strong and the body sensual. His sculptural bodies, due to dramatic lighting, were very popular in fashion magazines, especially for their accent on body shaping, since Horst photographed women models in bathing suits quite often. The 1930s also witnessed the ascendance of influential fashion publications like Vogue and Harper's Bazaar, which played essential roles in promoting *haute couture* and shaping beauty trends. These magazines featured meticulously curated fashion editorials that not only showcased clothing but also conveyed narratives through imagery, establishing new benchmarks for beauty and style in photography. As author Nancy Hall-Duncan argues 'Faced with the problem of presenting fashion for the first time, the earliest fashion photographers drew on established conventions such as those used in portraiture' (1979, p. 18). These portraits provided insight into current beauty standards and what was 'in fashion'.

Moreover, this decade witnessed the emergence of fashion icons like Marlene Dietrich, who epitomized the refined and sophisticated beauty of the era. Their distinctive facial features, portraits and charismatic personas left an indelible mark on the depiction of beauty in fashion photography, setting unprecedented standards of elegance and allure. Facial beauty in the 1920s continued the trends of the previous decade, with thin, plucked eyebrows and heavily coated eyelashes remaining popular (Gunn, 1973, p. 145). This look was heavily influenced by cinema, exemplified by American film actress Jean Harlow. Hollywood costume designers, such as Edith Head and Adrian, played a crucial role in defining the aesthetics of the time as their designs complemented the beauty normative by accentuating the desired body shapes and features. Fashion photography in the 1930s embraced a spirit of escapism, luxury, and glamour, mirroring the shifting social and cultural landscape of the time. Photographers and models embraced a more stylized and polished approach to beauty, laying the groundwork for the evolution of fashion photography in subsequent decades (see more in Hall-Duncan, 1979).

Towards the end of the 1930s, and during the 1940s, photography, and beauty underwent profound changes due to the impact of World War II and the resulting changes in social norms and attitudes and during this time the body was portrayed in terms of race, class, and nationhood (Pultz, 1995, p. 89). This era was filled with patriotism and hope, even though beauty products were scarce. In that context, women's beauty companies were focussed on natural beauty. The fashion industry faced challenges during this decade, such as fabric rationing and production limitations, which influenced the aesthetics of fashion photography and beauty standards. However, as Hernandez argues 'Hollywood found a way to provide entertainment and reassurance by portraying sultry women and exotic locales in their films. The movies continued to influence cosmetic trends' (2017, p. 119). During this time, a blend of practicality and elegance was present, as fashion adapted to the constraints of wartime rationing and then transitioned to the optimism of the post-war years. During the early 1940s, the focus in fashion photography shifted towards more practical and functional clothing styles due to the war's constraints. With materials rationed, women had to be resourceful. Clothing became more practical, with an emphasis on utility and durability. Make-up was still important, serving as a morale booster, but it was used sparingly. Hair styles were simple and practical while red lipstick became a symbol of feminine strength and resilience (Gunn, 1973, pp. 160–161). Utility and simplicity became key characteristics in fashion, reflecting the need for practicality and efficiency. This change was reflected in the beauty standards of the time, with a more natural and understated look becoming prevalent. With time, fashion photography started to embrace a more romantic style, offering a sense of glamour and sophistication as a form of escapism from the harsh realities of the war. Photographers like Cecil Beaton and Erwin Blumenfeld captured this more whimsical and dreamy aesthetic, emphasizing elegance and poise in magazine images. As Ang states 'The symbiosis between magazines and advertising is most obvious in fashion. The lifeblood flowing between them is photography' (2022, p. 231). The rise of the fashion magazines thus promoting what is new in beauty was a crucial turning point during this time. Hernandez emphasizes that 'development of television spurred the creation of many niche brands as specialized products advertised in this new medium' (2017, p. 120).

After the war, and with the end of rationing products and restrictions of goods, the world of fashion and beauty started a new era. Responding to this shift, Dior's new fashion brought significant changes in the fashion system. Companies like Elizabeth Arden, Rimmel, Goya, Max Factor, Helena Rubinstein, Revlon, Coty, and Yardley introduced products that catered to the era's aesthetic demands, focussing on convenience, durability, and the iconic red lip. These brands played a crucial role in designing the beauty standards of the decade, blending practicality with glamour. Elizabeth Arden offered a wide range of matching lipstick and nail polish shades, Rimmel introduced a clever lip colour palette that included a mirror and brush and Goya, entering the cosmetics market, launched their 'Thick and Thin' lipstick (Gunn, 1973, p. 162). Fashion photography and beauty in the

1950s experienced a significant shift towards a more polished, glamorous, and idealized aesthetic of the body. This decade marked a return to prosperity and optimism after the hardships of World War II, leading to a desire for luxury, elegance, and femininity in fashion (Hall-Duncan, 1979, p. 122). In the 1950s photography embraced a more stylized and cinematic approach, again drawing inspiration from Hollywood films and celebrity culture. However, models began to advertise beauty products, and not only movie stars. Photographers like Richard Avedon, Irving Penn, and Lillian Bassman captured images that exuded sophistication, often featuring intricate lighting setups and elaborate backdrops. Beauty standards in the 1950s emphasized a flawless and refined look, with make-up trends focussing on a flawless complexion, bold red lips, and perfectly groomed eyebrows and hair (Gunn, 1973, p. 165). Hernandez detects how 'Cosmetic advertisers now used professional models in highly stylized images. As women searched for refinement in their cosmetic products, manufacturers catered to this need by focussing on chic locales, like Paris, or romantic and exciting product names that brought a sense of fantasy to the industry' (2017, p. 129). In that context, Max Factor's *Tru-Colour* lipstick offered vibrant, long-lasting colour, catering to the decade's trend of bold, red lips. Moreover, 1950s fashion photography and beauty were characterized by a sense of glamour, due to its connection to Hollywood, sophistication, and elegance, reflecting the cultural and social ideals of the time. Audrey Hepburn's doe-eyed look and short hair, brought a new type of aesthetics in fashion photography as well as the hourglass figure, epitomized by iconic figures like the actress Marilyn Monroe and Grace Kelly, became the paradigm of beauty during this era, influencing fashion and beauty normatives worldwide. The images from this era continue to influence contemporary notions of beauty and style, embodying a timeless sense of celebrity extravagance.

To understand the concept of beauty through photography in the 1960s, a decade known for socially oriented and exotic themes (Hall-Duncan, 1979, p. 158), we need to reflect how the body gained new modes of expression. The concept of beauty in the 1960s expanded to include a more diverse range of looks, celebrating individuality, freedom, and self-expression. The free-spirited era created a platform for change – in all aspects of women's beauty and body perception. Women began to change their attitude towards body awareness and became more independent than ever before. During the 1960s, a significant shift as youth culture began to exert a greater influence on cosmetic trends. The emergence of 'rock "n" roll' music from America brought a new wave of popular music that was tailored to and driven by the younger generation. Paris was still the city of high fashion, but London became the epicentre for pop culture (Hall-Duncan, 1979; Hernandez, 2017). Make-up trends became more experimental, with bold colours and graphic eyeliner defining the 'swinging sixties' aesthetic. The 1960s were a transformative era for fashion and beauty, marking a shift towards body freedom and breaking away from traditional conventions, known in beauty standards. The fashion and beauty trends of this decade continue to influence contemporary styles, embodying a spirit of freedom, creativity, and individuality. According to Gunn (1973), the 1960s, beauty manufacturers faced the ongoing challenge of capturing the attention of the ever-changing younger population. In addition to catering to the demand for make-up among teenagers, they also had to meet the needs of busy young career women. This demographic required cosmetics that were convenient and quick to use so beauty companies shifted their focus to products that were compact, easy to apply, and portable for on-the-go use. Helena Rubinstein's 'Mascaramatic', a modern alternative to traditional block mascara applied with a brush and water, quickly gained popularity and claimed how the new mascara will darken and curl lashes without a brush. Its compact size, similar to that of a fountain pen, made it particularly appealing and fashionable (Gunn, 1973, p. 168).

In the 1960s, fashion underwent a radical transformation that reflected the changing social dynamics and attitudes of the time, including a significant shift towards the liberation of the body. The 1960s marked a significant shift in beauty and fashion, driven by the youth and counterculture movements that emphasized freedom, individuality, and rebellion against mainstream societal norms. The hippie movement embraced peace, love, and communal living, while the anti-war movement protested against the Vietnam War. This movement, particularly influenced beauty standards, or to be more precise, it created new beauty practices. Hairstyle trends underwent rapid changes throughout the 1960s and many women found themselves lagging behind fashion, with their hair too short when longer styles were in Vogue magazine. They turned to false hairpieces, wigs, and half-wigs to mimic the desired length, easily discarding them if short, cropped hairstyles came back into fashion (Gunn, 1973, p. 169). False nails became a favoured choice, offering an escape from the time-consuming process of conventional manicures. Similarly, the application of false eyelashes provided a convenient alternative to curling methods. With the introduction of new home beauty preparations, women could opt out of salon visits if desired. Unlike homemade cosmetics of the past, these products were mass-produced in factories but intended for use at home. Beauty products packaged in jars reminiscent of items found in a rural pantry, cosmetic names like *Jelly Babies* by Mary Quant, and creams such as Yardley's natural 'Lipids' crafted to mimic the skin's own moisturizing process, stand out as hallmark offerings of make-up produced in the late 1960s and early 1970s (Gunn, 1973, p. 179).

Furthermore, Givenchy introduced the little black dress, a very elegant and sophisticated look which contradicted the liberation of the 1960s body but remained a type of beauty and fashion standard to this day. A significant change in the 1960s was the emergence of a young and slender model who has since dominated the fashion system and was visible in advertisements in this area. German-Australian photographer Helmut Newton marked the history of fashion with his work, representing a body liberated from all social norms and his photographic aesthetic, characterized by black-and-white photography, is very recognizable (Krpan, 2022). Thus, this paper marks this period as crucial for developing an eclectic beauty standard which later influenced many representational practices in photography. Designers like Mary Quant and André Courrèges introduced miniskirts, and innovative silhouettes that liberated the body from constrictive and traditional sartorial norms. The 1960s drew inspiration from the

1920s, particularly in the preference for a thin, boyish figure. Model Twiggy served as a prime example of this aesthetic.

Fashion photography in the 1960s also embraced this sense of liberation, with photographers such as David Bailey and Helmut Newton capturing images that challenged conventional beauty standards and celebrated their subjects' natural, unapologetic beauty (Ang, 2022). Models like Penelope Tree and Jean Shrimpton became iconic figures representing a new, more youthful, unconventional form of beauty. Helmut Newton's approach to beauty in photography was distinctive and provocative and instead of adhering to conventional standards, Newton's work often challenged artistic norms and pushed boundaries. His images frequently featured strong, confident women in glamorous yet unconventional settings, challenging traditional notions of femininity and beauty. Through his photographs, beauty was not merely about aesthetics but also about empowerment and self-expression. Helmut Newton revolutionized fashion photography by introducing multiple subjects in his photographs and moving away from traditional, static body expressions.

On the other hand, Herb Ritts made a lasting impact by capturing celebrities in black-and-white, presenting some of the earliest images of a 'covered body'. This term, as defined by Italian fashion theorist Patrizia Calefato, distinguishes itself from the 'clothed body' (2004) by emphasizing a sculptural, voluminous form always depicted with a concealed face, thus altering the body's identity and state. As Calefato states 'The clothed body, the body-as-covering, and its imagery burst into social territory' (Calefato, 2004, p. 60) and 'the clothed body expresses the way in which a subject is in and of the world through his/her aesthetic and physical appearance, his/her relation with other bodies and lived bodily experiences' (Calefato, 2004, p. 2). Departing from conventional notions of the culturally inscribed body, the 'covered body' concept delves into the shaping and designing the body with the garment directly within fashion photography, thus visually concealing the face and often the body (Krpan & Simončič, 2024). In 1963 edition of Harper's Baazar for May, Hiro's models with sunglasses are wrapped in blue chiffon scarfs (Hall-Duncan, 1979, p. 169). The body was more wrapped in dress, showing little flesh, and often had a covered face. This type of body's beauty representation became a new standard during the Japanese deconstruction in fashion, which later influenced the works of contemporary fashion designers (Krpan, 2021).

The 1970s and 1980s marked a distinct era in fashion photography, characterized by a vibrant aesthetic dominated by colour and a comeback to classic photography through the work of Guy Bourdin, Helmut Newton, Chris von Wangenheim (Hall-Duncan, 1979, pp. 198–199). This period was dominated by a new type of aesthetics. Beauty standards in 1970s photography were marked by a departure from the restrictive norms of the past, embracing authenticity, diversity, and individuality. This era introduced a new wave of creativity and acceptance in fashion and beauty photography, laying the foundation for more inclusive and empowering representations of beauty in the decades to come. The 1970s was a decade marked by a shift towards more natural and diverse representations of beauty, breaking away from the strict standards of previous decades. CoverGirl advertisements at the end of the 1970s, featured headlines 'Clean is sexy', promoting clean, glossed and tanned faces, with soft hair often with curls and pastel eye make-up (Gunn, 1973, p. 179). Photographers sought to capture a more relaxed and effortless beauty that resonated with the changing attitudes towards fashion, body image, and femininity. Models with unique features, unconventional looks, and a sense of personality were celebrated in fashion photography, challenging the traditional normatives of beauty.

The rise of the feminist movement in the 1970s also influenced beauty standards in photography. There was an increased focus on portraying women as strong, independent, and self-assured individuals, moving away from the passive and objectified representations of the past. In this context, Hernandez argues how 'the era of the strong woman fit very well with fashion models who weren't just known for their pretty faces. They spoke on current issues such as conservation and health issues, and helped with philanthropic causes' (2017, p. 154). Photographers like Helmut Newton, Guy Bourdin, Patrick Demarchelier captured women in powerful and assertive poses, redefining traditional ideas of beauty and femininity (Jobling, 1999, p. 22). Furthermore, the 1970s saw a growing emphasis on diversity and inclusivity in beauty standards. Models of different ethnicities, body sizes, and ages began to gain visibility in fashion photography, reflecting a more comprehensive approach to beauty. This push for diversity paved the way for a more inclusive and realistic portrayal of beauty in photography, celebrating each individual's unique qualities and characteristics.

Beauty standards in photography during the 1980s era underwent a significant transformation, reflecting the decade's bold, extravagant spirit. The decade was a time of excess and glamour, which was reflected in the beauty ideals portrayed in photography and film. The 1980s radically changed women's beauty standards, and took a step forward into experimenting, not only with cosmetics but also with hairstyles and dress silhouettes (Krpan, 2021). A toned, athletic body became an ideal, with aerobics classes and home workout videos contributing to the trend and fashion styles enhanced the athletic body. Spandex, leg warmers, and leotards became fashionable both in and out of the gym, emphasizing the importance of physical fitness, beauty and health. Fashion and beauty magazines were crucial in shaping beauty trends, with elaborate photo spreads and product endorsements (Krpan, 2022). During this period, both men and women's beauty standards became equally important and visible. The 1980s proposed new visions of femininity and masculinity (Riello, 2020) and beauty became more important than ever before. This is particularly visible in films such as *Working Girl* (1988) which presented strong female characters, and *American Gigolo* (1980) where beauty and wellness practices represented an essential part of the times lifestyle, especially in men's fashion. This film played an essential role in shaping the beauty, fashion, and wellness trends of the 1980s in general (Krpan, 2021, p. 98). Through its stylish portrayal of its lead character and the luxurious world he inhabits, the film influenced audiences to aspire to a polished, well-groomed appearance and a sophisticated lifestyle. Both cinema and photography in the 1980s embraced a more glamorous and polished aesthetic, emphasizing bold colours, and exaggerated poses due to the fashion's silhouette thus representing new sartorial practices

(Bruzzi, 1997). Beauty standards during this era often featured larger-than-life hairstyles, vibrant make-up looks, and high-fashion styling that exuded confidence. Supermodels like Cindy Crawford, Naomi Campbell, and Christy Turlington rose to prominence during the 1980s, embodying the era's glamorous beauty standards. These models were known for their sculpted features, athletic bodies, and confident attitudes, setting a new benchmark for beauty in fashion photography. German photographer Peter Lindbergh with his iconic black and white photographs of supermodels created a new narratives and aesthetics and played a crucial role in establishing beauty standards (see in Jobling, 1999).

The 1980s also marked the rise of fitness and wellness culture, which influenced beauty standards in photography. Healthy skin and radiant smiles became vital elements of beauty ideals, as reflected in the popularity of fitness-inspired fashion shoots and athletic wear campaigns. As Hernandez states how 'Beauty became a competitive sport, and a woman believed that the body needed to be well toned to get ahead in the world. Being beautiful required work, and women were willing to feel the pain to gain a perfect figure. Physical activity became a necessity as aerobics and jogging were the most popular forms of exercise' (2017, p. 167). American actress Jane Fonda was the pioneer of this decade due to her, very popular, exercising video tapes 'Workout with Jane Fonda', starting in 1982, and continuing today. Regarding diversity, beauty standards were still primarily centred around traditional notions of beauty, focussing on youth, symmetry, and glamour but cosmetic procedures were more accessible to women, more than ever. However, there were efforts to introduce more diverse representations of beauty, with models of different ethnicities and backgrounds beginning to gain visibility in the fashion industry which started in the 1970s. Beauty standards in 1980s photography were characterized by an extravagant aesthetic that celebrated confidence, boldness, and luxury. The era's iconic imagery continues to influence modern beauty ideals, showcasing a mix of nostalgia and timeless elegance that inspires fashion and photography today. However, a new experimental beauty approach appeared, changing the idea and concept of the body in fashion photography.

3. Experiment and New Beauty Standards of Japanese Fashion Deconstruction

The notion of 'deconstruction' in fashion emerged prominently during the 1980s, representing a notable departure from established fashion paradigms. Deconstruction, originally a French philosophical movement of the 1960s, based on Jacques Derrida's work, influenced a wide range of disciplines – art, architecture, fashion, design, music. In fashion, 'deconstruction', *deconstructed* the fashion system and the whole beauty aesthetics of the time. In the late 1970s, the Japanese deconstruction movement made its mark in Paris, initiating a fundamental shift in the established fashion system. Unlike previous models in fashion history, this fashion paradigm challenged established fashion silhouettes and the traditional organization of fashion elements on the body and beauty (Krpan, 2021).

Deconstruction emerged as a tool to disrupt the coherence between spoken, written, and visual expressions, fostering a departure from conventional textual interpretations (Derrida, 1967). Deconstruction found applications not only in philosophy and architecture but also in fashion design, and left significant impact on literary theory, cultural studies, and various other disciplines.

In the context of fashion, deconstruction defied conventional notions of symmetry, balance, and garment construction, opting instead for asymmetry, irregularity, and unconventional silhouettes. By deconstructing traditional forms, Japanese designers, such as Yohji Yamamoto and Rei Kawakubo, highlighted the arbitrary nature of fashion conventions and opened up new possibilities for expression, gender and identity (Krpan, 2021, p. 55). Japanese designers took traditional japanese clothing and style and transformed it into a new type of fashion (Krpan, 2021, p. 49). Yamamoto recontextualized what was beautiful and designed unisex fashion. Notion of what is beauty and what was considered beautiful rapidly changed. The face and body became more encapsulated with the garments, revealing little flesh thus becoming visually more covered. Designers deliberately manipulated fabrics, patterns, and proportions to craft avant-garde designs that changed the fashion paradigm. This departure from traditional fashion led to the creation of unexpected and exciting garments, pushing the boundaries of what was deemed fashionable.

The emergence of deconstruction in fashion heralded a departure from traditional aesthetics, embracing an unbridled and often deliberately messy appearance. This aesthetic, frequently labelled as post-punk or grunge, challenged conventional notions of beauty and gender. Fashion deconstruction played a pivotal role in shaping this new direction in late 1970s fashion, offering a fresh perspective on garment construction and the relationship between body and dress (Krpan, 2021, pp. 59–60). From the inception of the dress to its eventual deconstructive transformation, this movement liberated the body from the constraints of established fashion norms. Deconstruction paved the way for a shift in focus from the fashion body to the fashion object, facilitating the exploration of experimental visual silhouettes and alternative body structures. By deconstructing traditional garment forms, designers were able to create space for innovative approaches to contemporary fashion design and redefine the relationship between the body and dress (Krpan, 2021, p. 62). Another example of wrapping the body and face with fabric is Issey Miyake's voluminous designs. Miyake's approach and experiment with cut, textiles and fabric, led to redefining gender, especially with his 'Pleats Please' collection. With Japanese deconstruction, beauty began to be practical and simple, with the focus on the garment itself. A radical change, in comparison to previous decades where the face and body were almost always in the centre of attention. This is the essential difference in understanding beauty prior to this change in the fashion system.

Beauty in Japanese deconstruction is characterized by a departure from conventional aesthetics, embracing an unconventional and often asymmetrical allure just like in fashion. Rooted in the ethos of breaking down established norms, fashion deconstruction challenges traditional notions of beauty by celebrating imperfection, irregularity and 'untidiness'. Beauty is found in the unexpected juxtaposition of disparate elements, the deliberate manipulation of materials, and the exploration of unconventional silhouettes. Garments may feature raw edges, exposed seams, and unconventional draping techniques, creating a sense of dynamic movement and visual intrigue. With this radical change in fashion, photography of the time shifted to a more experimental approach, leaning on montage, collage and the body gained new visuality (Krpan, 2022, p. 20). Early works of Yamamoto and Kawakubo represented a voluminous body in motion, often photographed in black and white. While garments became more spacious, the body and face became less visible and less 'significant'. What deconstruction introduced into beauty was the connection between the skin and dress, and explored what happens in that space in between. Kawakubo's collection from 1997, thus titled 'Body meets dress, dress meets body', explores this subject in depth. Kawakubo's collection featured exaggerated silhouettes that distorted the natural shape of the body. These garments were padded in unusual places, creating lumps and bumps that altered the body's contours, creating a body which had altered movement. By altering the body's appearance through dress, Kawakubo invites viewers to reconsider the relationship between the physical self and the external world, highlighting the fluidity and constructed nature of identity (Krpan, 2021, p. 62). Dutch fashion designers Viktor&Rolf also designed collections with sculptural elements and even took a step forward by painting the model's faces black, in their collection 'Black hole' from 2001. With the experiment that deconstruction brought into the fashion system, photography became an essential tool for creating a new platform for understanding new images of fashion and beauty. By the end of the 1980s, at the beginning of contemporary fashion practice, beauty began a transition to a darker and more dramatic state. Fashion became traumatic and explored body sacrifice, violence, cruelty and pain. As British fashion theorist Caroline Evans, in her monumental work *Fashion at the Edge: Spectacle, Modernity, and Deathliness* (2003) argues, McQueen shows during the mid-1990s, were melancholic, and explored themes of death, sex and violence. Beauty was connected to sacrifice, body mutilations and photographs were often blurry and distorted, reflecting the spirit of the time. Beauty was not associated with products but more with the body's state and the experimental approach to design this new type of fashion. What was once not appealing, now became a new beauty standard.

4. Recontextualized Beauty Practices in Contemporary Fashion –McQueen's Traumatic Beauty and Galliano's Theatrical Body

The shift in beauty standards at the end of the 1980s, driven by punk aesthetics and Japanese deconstruction, redefined the fashion system and the diffusion of the fashion impulse. By challenging traditional notions of beauty, these two essential movements in fashion history promoted a more inclusive, individualistic, and conceptually driven approach to fashion, leaving a lasting impact on the beauty industry (Krpan, 2021). By the end of the 1980s Japanese aesthetics began to fade, even though it remains fashionable to this day, because of its remarkable multifunctionality and aesthetics. As the 1990s dawned, designers assumed a central role within the fashion system, shaping trends with their bold experimentation and incorporation of historical elements from the 19th and 20th centuries. A new type of deconstruction arrived, established by the Belgian circle – designers Martin Margiela, Ann Demeulemeester and Dries van Noten (Krpan, 2021). Margiela, known for his experimental work in fashion, introduced masks and face coverings in the majority of his collections, thus shifting focus once again to dress and less to natural facial beauty (Krpan, 2021, p. 89). Faces were no longer present and the focus was on the theatrical performance of the body and the garment. This trend is exemplified in the groundbreaking work of British fashion designers Alexander McQueen and John Galliano contemporary fashion practice after the 1990s and fashion photographers such as Nick Knight, Nan Goldin and Steven Meisel. Both designers drew inspiration from the past, particularly the *fin de siècle* period, characterized by the artistic movement of decadence. Despite their distinct fashion philosophies and approaches, McQueen and Galliano shared a common goal of revitalizing fashion history while pushing the boundaries of garment construction and creating new beauty practices, especially for women. Evans (2003) highlights how prevailing theoretical frameworks failed to encapsulate the essence of contemporary fashion and its beauty standards. Instead, she argues, near-contemporary and contemporary fashion are imbued with themes of death, trauma, and spectacle – a sentiment echoed in the works of McQueen and Galliano (Evans, 2003). Photographers, under this significant influence of the traumas of the 20th century, created images filled with elements of despair. Shinkle's book underscores the complexity of fashion photography as a cultural phenomenon and its capacity to shape and reflect various social values and aesthetics. It also addresses the impact of fashion photography on concepts of reality and affect, considering how contemporary fashion practices engage with and challenge traditional notions of beauty and identity (Shinkle, 2008).

Indeed, elements of morbidity, trauma, and spectacle are palpable in McQueen's and Galliano's creations and in their representation of beauty. Their designs evoke a sense of the macabre while challenging traditional notions of beauty and elegance. Through their visionary approach to fashion, these designers not only reshaped the beauty industry but also sparked a broader conversation about the intersection of art, culture, identity and gender. Furthermore, the concept 'covered body' (Krpan & Simončič, 2024), which we introduced earlier, and thus a new type of beauty is seen in later Margiela's work. He is particularly known for his fashionable masks where the face in unrecognizable and nowhere to be seen. The visible face was no longer essential as beauty standards shifted at the end of the 1980s, influenced by punk aesthetics and the emergence of Japanese deconstruction. These two fashion 'movements' recontextualized the fashion system in its entirety. Punk, led by designers like Vivienne Westwood, rejected conventional beauty norms, embracing a messy, anarchistic, and unisex approach to the body that challenged traditional gender distinctions and social expectations. This shift marked a significant departure from the natural and glamorous beauty standards that had previously dominated the fashion industry. Traditional beauty was considered unwelcome, as it no longer appealed to younger generations. Vivienne Westwood understood early on how to provoke the audience and consequently attract consumers by radically redefining what was considered beautiful. She used provocation and subversion to change the fashion and beauty system from within. Both McQueen and Galliano were and are known for their ability to use beauty as a means of provocation within the realm of fashion. Their designs transcended mere aesthetics, serving as powerful statements that challenged gender norms and perceptions. Galliano's work often drew inspiration from historical periods, reimagining and reinterpreting them through a contemporary lens. By researching fashion history, he not only paid *hommage* to the past but also subverted its conventions to create something entirely new and provocative. This approach allowed Galliano to explore themes of identity, power, and beauty, using the rich tapestry of history as a canvas for his creative expression in fashion. Galliano designed his paradigmatic theatrical body by incorporating elements of both the past and present, consistently challenging the notion of beauty. Galliano's latest *couture* spring collection 2024 for Maison Margiela, with its use of corsets, nudity, and wax-covered faces, epitomizes this subversive approach to beauty and fashion. By presenting models with a doll-like appearance, much like Bellmer's approach to beauty and body in the 1935, he invites viewers to question and critique conventional ideals of beauty, gender, masculinity and femininity. The 'doll look', as Evans states, came back as inspiration for many designers and 'at the end of the twentieth century, as much as at the beginning, te uncanny replication and standardisation of the female form, in the shop window dummy, the showgirl or the fashion model, brings together two ideas: the idea of femininity commodified in an age of mass production' (2003, pp. 171–172). As John Pultz argues 'Bellmer's photographs produce a female form that is without life, essence, or soul, but which is subject to a constant repositioning within the male narrative of fantasy, literalizing the objectification of the female body that is produced by the male gaze' (1995, pp. 76–77). Furthermore, photographer Peter Thal, while shooting the fashion collection for Viktor&Rolf from the Autumn to Winter of 1999, encountered waxy and unhuman models with lifeless gazes turning the women into objects.

5. Conclusion

Beauty practices in contemporary fashion photography remain consumed with notions of experiment, collage, photo manipulation, and double exposure. One of the most influential photographers who established this mode of visual thinking is Nick Knight with his mix-media photography and experimental fashion films. Beauty and body representation in contemporary fashion, as well as in photography and film, have undergone many changes due to various social, cultural, and political influences. Thanks to fashion photography and film, we have been able to witness these radical changes in women's beauty standards and the development of beauty products. Research of their visual narrative is essential as it serves as a visual essay (Shinkle, 2008) and reflects various changes in beauty and fashion. The fashion and beauty industries are inextricably linked, always overlapping within the evolving and complex fashion system. Without fashion, photography, and film, beauty would not have been as visible and relevant as well. These mediums, including fashion as a system (Barthes, 1967), elevated the notion of beauty to a status equal to fashion itself. Beauty became an integral part of the fashion system even though it is not a topic researched enough within fashion studies. Fashion studies, particularly fashion theory, often concentrate more on costume and dress rather than on beauty itself. However, fashion and beauty are inextricably linked, each shaping and defining the other regardless of the prevailing aesthetic codes of any given era. They coexist within the same system, working in tandem to influence cultural and social norms. The development of fashion photography has vividly captured the radical transformations within the beauty industry, from the early 1920s to experimental contemporary fashion practices. Without the integration of beauty into the fashion system, these changes would not have been as perceptible or impactful.

References

Ang, T. (2022). *The definitive visual history of photography*. Dorling Kindersley Limited.

Barthes, R. (1967). *Système de la mode*. Éditions du Seuil.

Berger, J. (1972). *Ways of seeing*. British Broadcasting Corporation & Penguin Books.

Blumberg, P. (1974). The decline and fall of the status symbol: Some thoughts on status in a post-industrial society. *Social Problems*, *21*(4), 480–498.

Bruzzi, S. (1997). *Undressing cinema: Clothing and identity in the movies*. Routledge.

Calefato, P. (2004). *The clothed body*. Bloomsbury.

Calefato, P. (2014). *Luxury: Fashion, style and excess*. Bloomsbury.

Derrida, J. (1967). *De la grammatologie*. Éditions de Minuit.

English, B. (2013). *A cultural history of fashion in the 20th and 21st centuries – From catwalk to sidewalk*. Bloomsbury.

Evans, C. (2003). *Fashion at the edge: Spectacle, modernity and deathliness*. Yale University Press.

Gunn, F. (1973). *The artificial face*. The Trinity Press Worcester.

Hall-Duncan, N. (1979). *The history of fashion photography*. Alpine Book Company.

Hernandez, G. (2017). *Classic beauty: The history of make-up*. Schiffer Publishing Ltd.

Jobling, P. (1999). *Fashion spreads*. Berg.

Kaiser, S. (2012). *Fashion and cultural studies*. Bloomsbury.

Krpan, P. (2021). *Contemporary fashion as an event – The new media and body transformation*. Unpublished doctoral dissertation. University of Zagreb.

Krpan, P. (2022). *Contemporary Croatian fashion photography from the 1990s to the 2020s*. Ulupuh & Adris Foundation.

Krpan, P., & Simončič, K. N. (2024). Digital archives of contemporary fashion photography. In P. Krpan &. K. N. Simončič (Eds.), *International scientific-professional symposium textile science & economy, book of proceedings – Digital fashion* (pp. 13–19). Faculty of Textile-Technology. https://aMakjsfI4pi.ttf.hr/documents/E9vfXsMnHQvV0Ao4mF1BOzhDYRvtzSslRqvDluueKUgFS3eZy0Wb/tzg-book-of-proceedings-2024.pdf

Pultz, J. (1995). *Photography and the body*. Weidenfeld and Nicolson.
Riello, G. (2020). *Back in fashion: Western fashion from the middle ages to the present*. Yale University Press.
Shinkle, E. (2008). *Fashion as photograph: Viewing and reviewing images of fashion*. I. B. Tauris.
Simmel, G. (1957). Fashion. *American Journal of Sociology*, *62*(6), 541–558.
Veblen, T. (1899). *The theory of the leisure class: An economic study of institutions* (Indian edition 2005). Aakar Books.

Chapter 6

'An Open Forum for Discussion': *Desmond's and the Representation of the Beauty Industry*[1]

Melissa Beattie

Al Akhawayn University, Morocco

Abstract

British comedy *Desmond's* (Channel 4 1989–1994) portrays the everyday lives of the Ambrose family. Desmond (Norman Beaton) and his wife Shirley (Carmen Munroe) are migrants from Guyana who run a barbershop. Because Desmond, Shirley and their friends Porkpie (Ram John Holder) and Matthew (Gyearbuour Asante) are also migrants, the barbershop functions as a space of negotiation for sociocultural norms. Barbershops in the Black communities of both the US and UK are key cultural spaces and can be read as being an element of the Black public sphere. The series reinforces the barbershop as a space of cultural expression and negotiations through its characters and their discussions as well as through their music which is another form of negotiation and communication with regard to identity. As this chapter will show through close reading of the televised text, the series illustrates both the breadth of representation of the beauty industry and the depth of the barbershop as a cultural anchor for Black communities through representing and entering the public sphere.

Keywords: Black cultural spaces; Afro-Caribbean barbershops; public sphere; media representation in British television; postcolonialism; Desmond's

---

[1]The title comes from a quote of the lead character Desmond in series 3, episode 13. The full quote is given below.

Beauty Industry, 123–141

doi:10.1108/978-1-83608-940-720251024

1. Introduction

> Desmond Ambrose (Norman Beaton): 'It's a West Indian tradition that a barbershop is an open forum for discussion'. (3.13; Worrell & Worrell, 1992, 3:00–3:10)[2]

British comedy *Desmond's* (Channel 4, 1989–1994) portrays the everyday lives of the Ambrose family. Desmond and his wife Shirley (Carmen Munroe) are migrants from Guyana who run a barbershop which caters to men and women (non-binary, transgender or other third gender people are not represented).[3] Regulars at their barbershop include their friends Porkpie (Ram John Holder) and Matthew (Gyearbuor Asante), who are also migrants from Guyana and the Gambia, respectively, part-time hairdresser Tony (Dominic Keating, who leaves at the end of series five) and Lee (Robbie Gee), who the Ambroses have known since he was a child in care (i.e., an orphan) and whose father is ultimately revealed to have been Desmond's bandmate 'Sweetsticks'. The Ambroses have three children: the conservative Michael (Geff Francis) who manages a bank, secondary student and later aspiring fashion writer daughter Gloria (Kim Walker) and the youngest son Sean (Justin Pickett), a secondary and later university student.

The series was shot at a Jamaican-owned barbershop in Peckham called 'Lloyd's' which functioned as a community hub until its closure in 2015 (Brown, 2019). Chairs were 'rented to professional barbers who had honed their trade in the Caribbean whilst keeping abreast of changes within the profession' (Brown, 2019, n.p.) illustrating the confluence of cultures and negotiations between them which were present within the shop. She further notes that the closure and sale of the shop has left 'the Windrush generation [of Caribbean migrants] who used to hang out there feeling displaced' (Brown, 2019). This underscores the importance of the beauty industry as a sociocultural institution, particularly for those of Afro-Caribbean descent in the UK. Barbershops in the Black communities of both the US and UK are key cultural spaces (Alexander, 2003) and Mills (2013) argues for them to be an element of the public sphere in the US more generally. Though the UK and US are significantly different culturally, in both places these barbershops serve as what Boehme et al. (2022) term 'community anchors', particularly at times of sociocultural stress. These anchors can serve, amongst other things, to help in crime reduction as well as in the (re)distribution of sociocultural and other resources across a wide geographic area as Wood and Brunson (2011) note, making it clear that 'community' is cultural rather than geographic in this context. Majors (2003, p. 290) notes that African-American

---

[2]For this chapter I am using the convention 'series.episode'; thus '1.4' would be 'series one, episode four'.

[3]I am using the term 'migrant' throughout this chapter as it is relatively neutral. 'Diasporant' refers to any member of a diaspora, here meaning Afro-Caribbean people, migrant Africans, African-Americans and any other members of the African diaspora.

barbershops function '...as an educational setting through which knowledge is cocreated, recreated, and shared between members' something which is accomplished through talk. Along similar lines, Mbilishaka (2018), Mbilishaka et al. (2021) and Smith et al. (2023) have all shown that the barbershop is a key area for socialisation, discussion and for psychological support against the pressures of racism for Black communities. Thus, the barbershop functions as a space of negotiation through discussion for cultural as much as personal identity.

As befits a fictionalised representation of a Black barbershop, the series shows Desmond's barbershop as a nexus of the community its cultural expressions and sociocultural and individual support as described above, particularly through characterisation, dialogue and music. The series is heteroglossic (Bailey, 2012) meaning that the characters all have different, valid perspectives in which no single character is always in the right or always in the wrong. This a key part of the discussions that all of the studies above have noted are key to the barbershop's importance within communities. Here, however, it not only mimics the public sphere in a fictional context but also functions to bring the fictional context into the wider public sphere.

To begin, it is necessary to discuss the concept of the public sphere in the context of the barbershop, music and television. Habermas et al. (1974) defines the public sphere as

> ...a realm of our social life in which something approaching public opinion can be formed. Access is guaranteed to all citizens. A portion of the public sphere comes into being in every conversation in which private individuals assemble to form a public body. [...] Citizens behave as a public body when they confer in an unrestricted fashion–that is, with the guarantee of freedom of assembly and association and the freedom to express and publish their opinions-about matters of general interest. In a large public body this kind of communication requires specific means for transmitting information and influencing those who receive it. Today newspapers and magazines, radio and television are the media of the public sphere. (Habermas, tr Lennox & Lennox, 1964, p. 49)

Thus Desmond's statement quoted above illustrates that the barbershop, in his view and his tradition, functions as part of the public sphere as well as the cultural sphere. Writing of the history of the Black barbershop in the US, Mills states:

> The modern black barber shop joined black churches, beauty shops, and the black press to anchor the black public sphere in the twentieth century. [...] Especially during the era of Jim Crow, black men had few spaces where they could congregate and deliberate freely and with a sense of privacy. [...] African Americans continue to frequent black barber shops, churches, and beauty shops because black culture guides the dynamics of

> these spaces. [. . .] barber shops [are] within what I call the black commercial public sphere. This sphere encompasses the private and public, individual and collective interests that organize these spaces. Barber shops are locations of economic exchange, but they are also spaces that facilitate public discourse. As businesses, barber shops operate as private spaces where grooming services are rendered. Yet, interactions between barbers and customers allow for public conversations between acquaintances and strangers. (Mills, 2013, n.p.)

Desmond's firmly positions the barbershop as simultaneously a business and as what Shirley half-jokingly refers to in the pilot as a social club where such public conversations can be had and used to negotiate and represent cultural identity (Majors, 2003) as well as being Boehme et al.'s (2022) community anchors. The barbershop is often a space of negotiation between economics and culture, as I explore in more depth below, but because of the setting and the production team, Black, especially Afro-Caribbean British culture(s) guide the dynamics of the production and representation. I would further argue that barbershops are represented in *Desmond's* as a key part of the British migrant and Black public sphere. In addition, because the series was on mainstream television – Osbourne and Bourne (2016) note that *Desmond's* presents the British public of the time a 'changing face' – it can also align with McGuigan (2005) who

> . . .updates the notion of a literary public sphere into an expanded concept of the cultural public sphere, including the whole range of media and popular culture. This concept refers to the articulation of politics, public and personal, as a contested terrain through affective (aesthetic and emotional) modes of communication. (McGuigan, 2005, p. 427)

I would therefore argue that, because it both represents the Black/Afro-Caribbean public sphere and, as a television series, exists as part of the wider cultural public sphere, both Desmond's the barbershop and *Desmond's* the series function as a key part of the British public sphere of that time. This aligns with Habermas' definition above and also accords with studies on how television constructs, represents, reinforces and modifies national and subnational/cultural identities for its audience (e.g., Beattie, 2017).

Though Habermas references radio in his definition he does not discuss music specifically; it would fit into McGuigan's (2005) expansion of the cultural public sphere, however and, as such, part of the barbershop's position as a community anchor and space of cultural knowledge. Indeed there has been very little work done on music and the public sphere (Fairchild, 2012 notwithstanding), despite its use as a medium of political speech and protest, especially in the Caribbean where calypso and its descendent reggae were a means of protesting British colonialism and Western capitalism in Jamaica and elsewhere (Beattie, 2022; Nidel, 2005). Guyana in particular has a history of political control and protest regarding music

(Cambridge, 2015) which is why the fact that Desmond and Porkpie are musicians who own and frequent the barbershop is relevant. They specialise in calypso – though Desmond apparently began with jazz – and a wide range of music is performed and heard within the series. Barbershops themselves are also associated with music through the barbershop quartet, which has a social function for men but which is also associated with the Victorian era of the UK (Mook, 2007) though Abbott (1992) and Hobson (2013) both argue that the barbershop quarter is instead an African-American form. Thus connecting Desmond's barbershop with music not only engages with the cultural public sphere and its ability to communicate and negotiate identity but can also be read as appropriating or glocalising a colonial-era tradition into something which serves the interests of the formerly colonised and/or as reclaiming a cultural form which had been appropriated by the coloniser.

As such, this combination not only brings Afro-Caribbean migrants into the viewers' perception but also gives a window into a representation of the Afro-Caribbean public sphere. As this chapter will show through close reading of specific episodes of the televised text, the series illustrates both the breadth of representation of the beauty industry and the depth in which the beauty industry can be represented as a microcosm of the contemporaneous time period. Through fictionalised versions of the discussions, debates and identity negotiations which pervade Black barbershops, the series shows how inextricably bound the beauty industry is and can be within a given (sub)culture and everyday life.

2. Problems Faced by the Black Community as a Whole

Though many of the characters are migrants, *Desmond's* represents the Black community (and the Peckham community) as a whole. While some issues the series discusses relate to community inaction, such as the dearth of Black bone marrow donors referenced in 6.13 (Williams & McLean, 1994), the majority of issues the series explores with regard to the Black community as a whole relate to crime. In early series two is a two-part episode in which the barbershop is the site of a hostage situation. Jackson and Benson (2014, p. 1200) note that '…Peckham is an ethnically and socially mixed area. It is renowned for gang-related gun and knife crime, as well as associated with a traditional south London working class…' which broadly fits the plotline of the episode. 2.2 (Worrell & Hanson, 1990) begins with what Desmond calls the 'Peckham Symphony', i.e., police sirens, which frames the episode. The entire first scene (0:00–5:35) discusses the relative poverty of the area contrasted with elsewhere, with Porkpie noting that the displays of wealth are like 'dangling a carrot in front of the noses of the more impoverished'. Thus the connection between wealth inequality – implied through several comments to be at least exacerbated by the UK government and those working in high finance – and crime is established. In essence, the characters are discursively connecting the two, socioeconomic inequality and crime, to illustrate that this is a systemic problem rather than the idea that criminality is due to individual factors, Desmond's assertion that 'crime is crime' regardless of motivation notwithstanding. Though

Desmond and his conservative son Michael regard the robbers as 'bad' people, the two young men who ultimately take the barbershop hostage when recognised by Beverly (Jo Ann Maynard), another Guyanese migrant who had been in the post office at the time, are characterised as impoverished and struggling which is why they had tried and failed to rob the nearby post office. Robert (Steve Sweeney) explicitly states that, because of his family situation (alcoholic father and abused, valium-addicted mother), he does not feel he has many prospects and says that his family was so poor that he and his siblings had to take up thieving to feed themselves. Though two 23-minute episodes cannot give guest characters the same depth of diegetic history as given to the regulars, both hostage-takers are treated sympathetically.

The two young men, the white Robert and the Black Lloyd (Terry Sue-Patt), are both former classmates of Gloria and Louise. Shirley tells Lloyd

> . . .a lot of people are working damned hard to improve their lot. And there are a lot of people striving to improve the image of Black people in the eyes of the general public so they don't think we're all muggers and thieves. For every hundred good things we achieve it only take [*sic*] one incident like this to cancel it all out. (16:02–16:25)

While the appeal to sociocultural matters does not get through to Lloyd, it is a clear statement to the audience of sociocultural problems within the UK with regard to representation and just as clearly evokes the discussions of racism and racial/cultural identity which pervade the discussions in the barbershop (Harris-Lacewell, 2010; Mbilishaka, 2018; Mbilishaka et al., 2021; Smith et al., 2023). Robert also notes that, after he tells his story (19:05–20:50), that 'everyone wants a [charitable] cause', because it allows them to give money once a year and then forget about others the rest of the time; there is also the implication that the money does not go to those who need it most (i.e., Robert and other impoverished people in Peckham, regardless of race). At the end of the first part of the episode armed police – a rarity in the UK – surround the shop having been alerted surreptitiously by Michael. This leads to a continuing hostage situation into the next episode.

After a brief recap, part two begins with the robbers releasing Sean and a background artist who had been using the phone when the hostage situation began. To occupy themselves, Desmond, Porkpie, Matthew and Lloyd play dominoes, Tony and Gloria work on Louise's hair and Shirley and Beverly read a magazine while, outside, Lee works with the inspector in charge of the scene. While much of this is standard generic fare for a hostage episode of a sitcom, that Lee, who is something of a con artist, not only works with the police but uses his knowledge of the community to solve the matter peacefully reinforces the overall message of the episode and a recurrent theme of the series, that the community is unfairly tarnished by outsiders and that marginalisation and socioeconomic depression are at the root of the area's problems, not anything specifically related to ethnicity, migration or the area's multiculturalism. Further, if one views Lee and the barbershop both as community anchors, then the series also reinforces what both Wood and Brunson (2011) and Boehme et al. (2022) have found, that barbershops and their spaces for negotiation and discussion are key to preventing or at least ameliorating crime.

An example of talk (i.e., conversation, Majors, 2003) being used for this purpose occurs when Shirley tells Robert a story about a coconut picker who could not resist temptation to take a coconut on a dangerous branch, the moral of which being to about temptation by the unobtainable by climbing trees that one cannot climb (14:05–15:26). While Shirley's story refutes Beverly's assertion that young people were afraid of or unwilling to engage in 'hard work', (13:46) this story also can also be read as somewhat defeatist, i.e., accepting one's 'lot' in life. I would argue, however, coupled with her earlier statement quoted above, the preferred reading would be to accept and work towards incremental change rather than a dangerous or desperate course of action; this is supported by a later assertion in 3.13 (Worrell & Worrell, 1992, 12:00–14:10) in which she and Desmond point out to Michael that 'If you deny your origins, then you lose part of your richness as a person. [...] Some people say that Black kids today, in spite of your origins, you can do anything'. Desmond follows by saying 'But we say, *because* of your origins, you can do everything' (cf Majors, 2003 on talk and construction of cultural knowledge in barbershops).

The hostage situation concludes when a television journalist runs an interview with Lloyd's mother, a migrant from St Kitts; a previous interview with Robert's mother having only enraged him. She encourages him to give up, saying that she did her best, that she feels shame over his actions but that 'deep down [he] is a good boy' and that she still loves him (19:08–20:14). This appeal leads to the hostages being released, though Shirley and Desmond remain. Lloyd says that his reasons for robbery were so that his mother need never be short of money again. Though the episode ends with the police entering because Desmond inadvertently fires the gun, the implication is that both young men surrender and go to gaol. Worrell notes in an interview that writing *Desmond's* was a response to news coverage of violence in Black communities and that this two-part episode had a very high audience share (Davies, 2019). The sympathetic treatment of the robbers, the debates over crime and its reasons plus the discussion and debate amongst the characters all serve the purpose of interrogating and critiquing crime within the Black community as well as critiquing and representing its reasons in a way which would be intelligible to a wide audience. Through this two-part episode all of that discussion which is so typical of the barbershop is brought into the wider public sphere by representing it in a fictionalised public sphere.

Racial profiling is also a brief feature in 3.12 (Worrell & Wakefield, 1992) in which two white police officers see Michael manoeuvring his drunken father into his car. Because it is an expensive car and Michael is Black, the officers ask if the car is his and implying that they believe he has stolen it. While the scene is played for comedy the fact that both Michael and Desmond are arrested does allow the series to comment on institutionalised racism but do so in such a way as to allow the audience to recognise the critique without worrying that the characters would be harmed. Along similar lines, episode 6.3 (Anoff & Askey, 1994) begins with

Sean returning after having suffered racist abuse and assault on a night out and being arrested while fleeing from the perpetrators because the police officers falsely believed he and his friend Spider (Robert McKewley) were fleeing a scene of crime. Shirley tells Sean not to separate 'them' and 'us', which Sean refuses, knowing what has happened to him and why. Gloria's boyfriend Alex (Chris Tummings) says something similar has happened to him in the past and Spider, who arrives later, says that after such events have occurred 'a couple of times' one 'chill[s] out' about it. As Majors (2003), Harris-Lacewell (2010), Mbilishaka (2018), Mbilishaka et al. (2021) and Smith et al. (2023) have all argued, the barbershop provides a safe space for discussions of racism and for psychological support when it has been experienced. That said, at the end of the episode two white police officers come to take a statement from Sean and Spider about the assault. The sergeant (Ian Dunn), a Northerner, apologises to Sean and Spider for the fact that they were not believed the previous night. That the sergeant is Northern connotes a working-class background which aligns with Peckham, his whiteness notwithstanding. This is reinforced by the sergeant disabusing Michael, who arrives later in scene, of the assumption that Sean and Spider had engaged in criminal activity; the sergeant explicitly tells Michael that he is there to apologise for other police officers making the same mistake.

The whole event upsets Shirley and Desmond, and this leads to Desmond wondering if they had made the right decision by leaving Guyana. He notes that the children 'are British', whereas he and Shirley think of Guyana as home. This precipitates him daydreaming throughout the episode about what would have happened if they had stayed in Guyana, featuring all the characters transposed from the barbershop to Desmond's 'bar' in Georgetown, all of whom in one daydream are exaggeratedly successful and in another are exaggeratedly unsuccessful. While this part of the episode is played as broad comedy it, along with Michael's incorrect assumptions which align with the white police officers who arrested Sean in the first place, underscores the concerns about the perceived consequences of migration. It is to this I now turn.

3. Problems Faced by the Migrant Community Specifically

In a 2016 interview with the BFI (archived on YouTube), series creator Trix Worrell, himself British/St Lucian, calls *Desmond's* 'a migrant story'. The theme song to the series and the opening credits over which it plays unambiguously illustrates the series as such as well as showing the blending of cultures through music, a key aspect of the cultural public sphere. While it is nominally calypso, the theme song features the record-scratching associated with hip-hop and also contains the line 'don't scratch my soca'. Soca is an outgrowth of calypso evoking African-American soul music as well as the Caribbean calypso; soca is also a blend with East Indian music (Nidel, 2005). This can be read as expressing the fusion or negotiation of identity seen in the various characters which itself can be read through a postcolonial and/or migratory lens and evokes the wider discussions of race and identity seen in Black barbershops. Bhabba (1994) refers to those impacted by colonialism as being liminal, or 'in-between' due to displacement and hybridity. We see this particularly in the Guyanese characters who consider Guyana their home but who have been changed by their migration and who express concerns over their children being 'corrupted' or at least divorced from their parents' identities. While national identity is discursive (Anderson, 2010) the perceived loss of 'roots' or heritage to Western/colonial/capitalist culture(s) is a common feature of Caribbean music (e.g., roots reggae, Daynes, 2010; King et al., 2002). As such, it is unsurprising that such concerns are a feature of *Desmond's*, albeit a feature which the heteroglossia of the characters allows to be negotiated and critiqued, with both the older Guyanese characters' concerns and the younger British characters' interests being treated sympathetically for the audience.

Ashcroft et al. (1995, p. 183) state that 'Most post-colonial writing has concerned itself with the hybridized nature of post-colonial culture as a strength rather than a weakness. Such writing focuses on the fact that the transaction of the post-colonial world is not a one-way process'. For this chapter, the two-way process can be read not simply as the representation of Guyanese and Afro-Caribbean cultures interacting with wider British culture but also the series itself functioning to give the migrant culture(s) a voice – in Spivak's (1988) terms, the series allows the subaltern to speak directly to the wider British public about their challenges through a fictionalised version of the talk which occurs within Black barbershops and, as such, both represent and enter the public sphere.

This hybridity is evident in the pilot and is present in the opening credits of each episode, thus framing the series as a whole and each individual episode. The theme song, as noted above, is soca with hip-hop record scratching. The theme is sung by Norman Beaton, illustrating that the song is from Desmond's point of view and tells of his journey from the warmth and sun of Guyana to the damp and cold of London. It also features the line 'I miss my rum/I want my coconut tree' illustrating that Desmond misses his home and that he is keenly aware of his displacement. That said, the images over which the song is played are predominantly that of London, though the lines quoted above are over archive footage of the *Empire Windrush*, a large vessel which sailed from Jamaica to the UK carrying migrants (the 'Windrush generation'). Though the images change slightly over the six series, they all feature Black British people in different jobs and at different sociocultural levels (e.g., barristers, students, etc.) and them interacting with white British people. In particular, the first few series show and white hand and a Black hand engaging in a handshake; later series feature a fist bump. After series three there are also images of the London Carnival, an iteration of the Caribbean tradition. Thus the series makes it very clear that, while Desmond misses Guyana, *Desmond's* focuses upon negotiation and integration. This is to some extent contra Harris-Lacewell (2010), who notes that, while there are rare instances of virulently anti-white sentiment, most debate in Black barbershops about racism focuses upon what Black people can do rather than on white people. *Desmond's* is fully supportive of white people entering the Black cultural space of the barbershop so long as they are supportive – recurring white characters are shown to appreciate Black culture and music while not appropriating it or being condescending. Yet the debates over what to do about racism and about the negotiations required of migrant identities and the identities of their children is rooted within and focused upon Black culture as Harris-Lacewell's (2010) respondents were.

This integrationist perspective is supported by the fact that the Ambroses are introduced in the pilot episode (Worrell & Fletcher, 1989) in the context of music styles. The very first scene (0:01–0:40) features Shirley waking Sean up for school. She sees a handwritten, hip-hop-inspired sign on his door and then raps an admonition for him to wake up which he then continues when he opens his door, finishing by identifying himself as being from Peckham. This framing of the series and characters is particularly important as it illustrates both that Shirley is able to assimilate through her use of hip-hop and that her son (and, as we later see, all of the children) identify as British rather than Guyanese. Immediately after this (0: 41–0:50), Louise (Lisa Geoghan) a white friend of Gloria's appears, having spent the night, which reinforces the ideal of racial harmony and equality expressed within the opening credits sequence.

The scene then shifts to Desmond himself (1:18–3:45), opening up the barbershop for the day, humming in no particular style as he does so. Matthew and Porkpie enter without knocking, establishing that they too are considered friends and illustrating that Africans, in this case the Gambian Matthew, also frequent the shop and it is therefore a wider Black cultural space rather than exclusively Guyanese. Porkpie turns on the radio to hear a song by Oscar Brown Jr, an American jazz and soul singer, who they compare to Desmond who was 'the best trumpeter in all of Guyana!' according to Porkpie. Desmond wore 'Miles Davis sunglasses' in an early jazz band, according to Shirley later in the episode. This again connects African-American music with Afro-Caribbean, though different generations of characters connect with different genres, something reinforced by Desmond being unable to verbally engage in one of Sean's raps later in the episode.

Over the course of the episode, Shirley half-seriously refers to the barbershop as a social club, referencing its position as a space of discussion and debate which, though a business, does not always only attract paying customers (Harris-Lacewell, 2010). Meanwhile, Desmond bans *The Sun*, a British tabloid from the shop because of 'page three' (featuring topless or nude women) and 'how many times they blame Black people for so many things' (2:42–2:44) and encourages the family friend Lee to save his money so he could go '. . .to the real Jamaica and check out your roots where you was born'. Lee counters by saying 'I've seen where I was born; I drive past it every day! King's College Hospital, Camberwell, London' (6:27–7:44). This interaction shows the crux of the series' negotiations couched within the public conversations of the barbershop; Desmond considering Guyana/the Caribbean to be his home and lineage whereas the younger characters identify as British. That said, Desmond's assertion that he 'wouldn't trust a Black man with a name like Jean-Pierre' (15:25–15:28) can be read as expressing British prejudices against the French.

Near the end of the episode, after Shirley confronts him about wanting to learn and exercise her mind with French lessons (16:30–22:46), Desmond expresses a wish to 'build a house on a plot of land back home and retire'. Desmond thus views Guyana as home and considers his time in Britain to be temporary, with migration as a means to an economic end. Shirley, however, replies 'Stop dreaming, Desmond! This is England, 1989. And we [*sic*] no nearer building a house back in Guyana now than we were in 1969'. Desmond tells her that he will build a house, if not for them then '. . .for the children. So they could know their country of origin. Their culture. Its roots'. Desmond and Shirley then teasingly call each other 'Linford Christie' and 'Daley Thompson', after a Jamaican British and Black British Olympian of Nigerian descent, respectively. This shows the depth and breadth of potential identifications within the wider Black community as well as the Afro-Caribbean community. Though Desmond and Shirley identify as Guyanese, they see no contradiction in also analogising themselves with others from the wider African diaspora. This aligns with how both are characterised through music earlier in the episode illustrating a number of different ways in which postcolonial hybridity can be represented and negotiated in the context of the barbershop and its public sphere.

Guyanese migrants are not the only ones seen within the series. Matthew is a student from the Gambia, though it is unclear what exactly his field of study is or what level of education he is pursuing. Through the occasional visit and frequently via letter, Matthew's family often demand either consumer goods or for him to return to the Gambia permanently. To accommodate the former and forestall the latter, Matthew often requires help from the other characters. He often spars with Porkpie and/or Desmond and dispenses 'old African sayings' to illustrate points of what he considers to be common sense advice. Though benign, Matthew represents and expresses both a counterpoint and a subversion to the difference between African and Afro-Caribbean cultures. In the pilot (Worrell & Fletcher, 1989, 12:27–13:25), Matthew says 'You West Indians forget that you're our direct descendants. Without us you would not exist!' 'Me know', Desmond replies, somewhat irritatedly. 'And me very grateful. But I'd be even more grateful if you was to play [dominoes]'. This type of interaction between Matthew and Desmond or, more commonly, Porkpie, is a standard part of the series' discussions. Yet the support he receives from his Guyanese friends is unconditional, implying that they view the sparring either as friendly rather than condescending and/or that they view Matthew's condescension as a feature of the wider African diasporant community resident in London. Because the relationship is played for comedy, with both characters evenly matched and clearly being friends, and because the series is heteroglossic and encourages the audience to consider the positions the characters express, the series positions such intracommunity prejudice as wrong but in such a way as to avoid making Matthew unlikeable or making the audience so uncomfortable that they stop watching. This can be read in terms of Conway's (2013) concept of the paradox of saleable diversity in which characters are limited by the (perceived) need for them to be palatable enough to not impact potential sales to domestic and/or transnational audiences (Caldwell, 1995; Turnbull & McCutcheon, 2021). Conway notes that emotional expression is particularly limited by this paradox. Yet because the series is heteroglossic this does allow for a greater range of expression as the heteroglossia encourages the audience to, as Matthew often ends his 'old African sayings' with, 'think about it'. This brings the audience themselves, regardless of their background, into the public conversations had within the barbershop and, as such, viewers, characters and the people they represent all function within the public sphere.

Matthew's prejudices against the Afro-Caribbean community also function to subvert and critique some aspects of the perception of Africa in general by both the Afro-Caribbean and African-American communities as well as the wider community. This should not be surprising as Hall (1995, n.p.) argues that different countries are differently postcolonial, something which is a key factor in the nuances of the differences within the Black community. But the sparring between Matthew and the Guyanese characters also argues against the idealisation of Africa, particularly one in which the continent full of different countries and cultures is elided. Writing of Fanon, van Robbroeck (2011, n.p.) notes that after an attempted assimilation 'the colonised intellectual retrieves an "authentic" African identity based on a romantic reconstruction of an idyllic pre-colonial African culture' which Tabensky (2008) argues is a feature of pan-Africanism. Matthew is an intellectual from a postcolonial country who does critique capitalism and the 'Western' way of life, much as Desmond and his friends do. Yet his condescension towards West Indians more generally also subverts some aspects of pan-Africanism, particularly those pan-Africanists who argued for a return to continental Africa. These specific groups tend to be associated with Rastafari, a syncretic religion which is primarily associated with independence/anti-colonial movements of Jamaica. There are no explicitly Rastafari characters within the series – Alex's dreadlocks notwithstanding (cf. Edmonds, 2003 on dreadlocks and Mbilishaka, 2018; Mbilishaka et al., 2021; Smith et al., 2023 on hair and identity for Black men) – but because of its anti-colonial stance and its ritual use of marijuana a fallacious association between crime and the religion developed in British culture (Edmonds, 2003). Rastafari is also strongly associated with dreadlocks and with reggae, particularly roots reggae (Daynes, 2010; King et al., 2002). Thus music is a key means of expressing the same sorts of debates that are present in the Black barbershop and why it serves to reinforce these debates within the series.

The Georgetown Dreamers, Desmond and Porkpie's band, are primarily calypso whose importance is 'its history as a medium of resistance, for expressing the voice of the common people in the local vernacular…and its history as the foundation for multiple later music genres…' (Beattie, 2022, p. 238). Cambridge (2015) notes that calypso is also a common genre of Guyanese music. Thus in addition to being culturally appropriate, the use of calypso eliminates the (fallacious) connection to crime as well as the association with marijuana (Edmonds, 2003) while still using calypso's connotations of resistance to oppression and its use of the vernacular. Thus the music and its negotiations serve to reinforce the spoken discussions of the characters about race and identity which are themselves fictionalised versions of those which Harris-Lacewell (2010), Mbilishaka (2018), Mbilishaka et al. (2021) and Smith et al. (2023) all note are key elements of the public sphere as expressed in the barbershop (Mills, 2013).

Guyanese calypso is also shown in direct contrast to a later offshoot of reggae called ragga. Moskowitz (2006, p. xiv) notes that in its lyrics 'Discussions of slack elements, such as womanising and gun culture, are found alongside discussions of cultural uplift and Rastafarian doctrine'. Ragga, specifically ragga hip-hop, a fusion between the Jamaican and African-American styles, is a style of music which Sean's friend Spider becomes successful with in 5.9 (Anoff et al., 1993). Rather than cultural uplift or Rastafarianism, however, the key issue is Spider's offencive lyrics, what Moskowitz (2006) above calls 'slack elements'. Spider is an ambiguous character throughout the series; in 3.13 (Worrell & Worrell, 1992) he tries to use the history of racial and colonial oppression to guilt Louise into intimacy, something which Sean tells him is unacceptable in no uncertain terms. Spider also antagonises the majority of other characters on a regular basis. Thus it is unsurprising that the rest of the family seem to view him as a bad influence. Gloria points out Spider's lyrics are 'sexist, homophobic, misogynistic' and rejects Sean's statement that 'they're only songs' (3:50–4:12) He maintains that he, as someone planning a university dance, must give people what they want, but Shirley argues that it must depend on what it is they want. This is then underscored by multiple students telling Sean to cancel Spider's concert; they include his openly gay friend Bernie (Rhashan Stone) who calls Spider a 'slack DJ', referring to the offencive content Moskowitz (2006) defines ragga as having. The students tell Sean they will protest and prevent anyone from attending the dance via a picket line (6:40–7:44). Bernie visits Sean at home – just above the barbershop – pointing out that it was Sean who had convinced him about the possibility of rap lyrics politicising Black people, and Bernie continues by pointing out that lyrics do have meaning, particularly the homophobic lyrics in Spider's songs. Bernie tells Sean that it is impossible to go to a dance without hearing slackness, but in the case of Sean's dance they do have a choice and they should 'stand up for what [they] believe in' (7:44–9:50). Sean agrees and cancels Spider's performance, illustrating the benefits the type of sociocultural discussions common to the barbershop can have.

Meanwhile, Desmond and Michael arrange to bring Spider for a 'personal appearance' for economic purposes, reminding the audience again that this is a Black economic space as much as a cultural one (Mills, 2013), but Sean protests sanctioning Spider's discrimination. Sean then joins many of his classmates in a protest demonstration and boycott of the barbershop, pointing out to Desmond that 'if you're not part of the solution, you're part of the problem' (10:00–11:30). The student demonstrators prevent the press from covering Spider's personal appearance at the shop; this leads to a confrontation between Spider and Shirley, who asks him why he sings about things he knows will offend people. He claims he is merely making a living, something Michael and Desmond support, contrasting student idealism with 'the real world'. Matthew then joins the protest while Desmond is ultimately sent outside to speak with the protesters (off-camera). In the next scene (17:36–23:39) we learn that Sean, Bernie and Matthew, along with the rest of the peaceful protestors, have been arrested. Matthew calls the treatment by the police disgraceful while Shirley tells Sean that, though she respects what he did, the protest should have been only done with police permission. The episode ends with Spider dressed as a Rastafari and expressing devotion to roots reggae and conscientiousness but still expressing sexism. While many Rastafari traditions are sexist and/or homophobic (Edmonds, 2003) what is clear is that Spider's slackness will overwhelm the social progressiveness that reggae, ragga and other forms of Caribbean music espouse. The debates within this episode illustrate the value of the barbershop and, in particular, of the series' representation with regard to the public sphere is made quite literally apparent.

Generational negotiation with regard to gender has been present since the pilot, generally contrasting Desmond's paternalism with Shirley and/or the younger characters' social progressivism. Save 3.6 (Williams & Hanson, 1991), in which Gloria and Louise try to open a men's beauty business and are denied a loan for their 'schoolgirl fantasies' by Michael, women's empowerment tends to be an underlying theme related to Shirley's strength as a character rather than a main focus. In this we can perhaps see an example of what Harris-Lacewell (2010) notes was a common theme with regard to male discussion in barbershops, the idea that explicit feminism undercuts the support the Black men in their study believe they need in order to acquire racial equality. Shirley is shown to be unfailingly supportive of her family but will take Desmond to task over his occasional paternalism, showing that it is possible to address gender and racial equality without one diminishing the other. Racialised beauty norms, however, are not generally discussed within the series (contra Randle, 2015, who discusses Black women's hair in this context) and, as such, are not explicitly entered into the public sphere. That said, as Osborne and Bourne (2016) note that *Desmond's* changes the 'face' of British television, it can be argued to have implicitly shown the breadth of Black appearances, including different beauty norms, to the wider British audience.

Homosexuality is addressed briefly through one of Sean's friends; the fallacious idea that homosexuality is new or the similar fallacy that homosexuals do not exist in Africa (Hoad, 2007; Simuziya, 2022) is lampooned in 5.9 (Anoff et al., 1993) in the barbershop in such a way as to make it very clear that the series is LGBTQIA-friendly, though, again, it is not a major part of the series. One can read the gender aspects being underlying rather than specifically focused upon in Conway's (2013) terms but I would argue it is more in the sense of normalisation of such generational and gendered negotiations within the wider British community rather than something specific to migrants or the Black community. That said, cultural fusion as represented in the Ambrose children is a constant. Sean, positioned as an amateur hip-hop musician throughout the series, joins Desmond's band on the steel pan in 2.8 (Worrell & Hanson, 1990). Though Gloria ultimately chooses not to go to university and occasionally works with her parents in the barbershop, she ultimately falls in love with Alex, an artist of Afro-Caribbean descent. Though Michael is positioned as thoroughly English and his lack of connection to his roots is a major concern throughout the series (e.g., 3.13, Worrell & Worrell, 1992); that he is a partner in the barbershop business does still connect him to this aspect of his cultural sphere and his differentiation from it, while still being a sympathetic character, allows the audience to observe these negotiations in action through his interactions and discussions with the other characters.

This series of negotiations is particularly evident in the final episode of the series (6.13, Williams & McLean, 1994) which features Shirley deciding to have a traditional Guyanese Christmas. The other characters disagree with the idea though they eventually throw a pre-Christmas party in the barbershop to accommodate Shirley's wishes as a fusion of British and Guyanese traditions (26: 32–30:20). This features Porkpie playing guitar and singing vaguely calypso-esque Christmas songs. The rest of the characters do the conga, a Cuban dance of West African roots and whose name is arguably related to the 'Kongo' ethnic group (Pérez, 1988); conga drums, though not present in the episode, are a feature of calypso. Michael, however, and his white fiancee Mandy (Mathilda Thorpe) do the cha-cha, another Afro-Cuban dance which has some elements in common with dances from the Afro-Caribbean syncretic religion Santeria (Sublette, 2004) and which is also part of international ballroom dance. Thus Michael here illustrates another successful negotiation between his Afro-Caribbean heritage and his British identity, communicated to them and to the audience through the barbershop. It is in a different manner to that of his family but it acknowledges both aspects of his identity. Similarly, the end of the episode features a reference to the Guyanese Christmas figure 'Boom Boom Sally' played by young men in drag (here Lee; 46:34–49:14) and who leads a procession of dancing and singing. This episode shows the fusion of Afro-Caribbean, West African, African-American and Black British influences that pervade the series as well as how the series shows that cultural heritage, particularly of the children of migrants, can exist harmoniously with that national/British identity, all through discussions shown, sung and spoken within the fictionalised barbershop.

4. Conclusion

In a 2019 interview with *The Guardian*, Worrell states that

> I didn't write Desmond's for black people...I wrote it for white people so they could see how black people really are. At that time, the negative press about muggings and shootings was all we seemed to get. I was fed up with it. (Worrell, quoted in Davies, 2019, n.p.)

Worrell's ambition to demonstrate the nuances of the Black community through the cultural and musical anchor of the barbershop seems to have been realised and remains pervasive today (Davies, 2019). In this chapter I have argued that Desmond's the barbershop and *Desmond's* the series illustrate how key the beauty industry can be for Afro-Caribbean and other African diaspora cultures. I have supported Mills' (2013) contentions that the barbershop can and should be viewed as part of the public sphere, particularly in the context of media representation of the industry doing so both diegetically and extradiegetically (Alexander, 2003;

Osborne & Bourne, 2016). Indeed, this paper shows that this representation of the barbershop as public sphere is what helps to include Guyanese and/or Afro-Caribbean migrants into the public sphere by showing the wider British – and, latterly, the transnational – audience the challenges they face. *Desmond's* does this through a number of modes, including characterisation, heteroglossia which allows for debate as well as through music which is another pervasive communicative expression of culture and fusion within the series.

Given the prominence of the *Empire Windrush* in the opening credits of the series, it seems both fitting and disheartening to view the series after the Windrush scandal in the UK, during which many long-term residents of the UK who had been born British colonial subjects were deported, detained or otherwise ill-treated by the British government. Desmond, Shirley and Porkpie were all of the Windrush generation and, looking back at their ambition and fierce support for their community, both migrant and not, they clearly still have much to teach us about understanding and embracing the diverse identities that we all discursively construct.

References

Abbott, L. (1992). 'Play that barber shop chord': A case for the African-American origin of barbershop harmony. *American Music*, *10*(3), 289–325.

Alexander, B. K. (2003). Fading, twisting, and weaving: An interpretive ethnography of the Black barbershop as cultural space. *Qualitative Inquiry*, *9*, 105–128.

Anderson, B. (2010). *Imagined communities* (3rd ed.). Verso.

Anoff, P. (Writer), & Askey, D. (Director) (1994, October 10). Georgetown dreaming (Series 6, Episode 3)[Television series episode]. In H. Barclay & A. Mitchell (Executive producers), *Desmond's*. Humphrey Barclay Productions. Channel 4.

Anoff, P., Worrell, T. (Writers), & Askey, D. (Director) (1993, November 22). Kiss of the spiderman (Series 5, Episode 9) [Television series episode]. In H. Barclay & A. Mitchell (Executive producers), *Desmond's*. Humphrey Barclay Productions. Channel 4.

Ashcroft, B., Griffiths, G., & Tiffin, H. (1995). *The post-colonial studies reader*. Routledge.

Bailey, B. (2012). Heteroglossia. In M. Martin-Jones, A. Blackledge, & A. Creese (Eds.), *The Routledge handbook of multilingualism*. Routledge.

Barclay, H., & Mitchell, A. (Executive Producers) (1989–1994). *Desmond's* [TV series]. Humphrey Barclay Productions. Channel 4.

Beattie, M. (2017). 'My' hero or epic fail? *Torchwood* as transnational telefantasy. *Palabra Clave*, *20*(3), 722–762.

Beattie, M. (2022). 'You can get it if you really want:' The use of Caribbean music genres in *Death in Paradise*. *Journal of Popular Television*, *10*(3), 231–246.

BFI. (2016). *Desmond's creator Trix Worrell: 'Desmond's is a migrant story'*. BFI. https://www.youtube.com/watch?v=yKX7u3srcxk&ab_channel=BFI. Accessed on 25 April 2024.

Bhabba, H. K. (1994). *The location of culture*. Routledge.

Boehme, H. M., Williams, T. V., Brown, N., Kidd, L., Hernandez, B., & Nolan, M. S. (2022). 'It's all about just creating the safe space' Barbershops and beauty salons as community anchors in Black neighborhoods: Crime prevention, cohesion, and support during the COVID-19 pandemic. *Crime & Delinquency*. https://doi.org/10.1177/00111287221130956

Brown, C. (2019). *'Lloydie's', the real life Desmond's – A tale of urban regeneration, gentrification and displacement in Peckham* (p. 5) Community Bridges.

Caldwell, J. T. (1995). *Televisuality: Style, crisis and authority in American television*. Rutgers University Press.

Cambridge, V. C. (2015). *Musical life in Guyana: History and politics of controlling creativity*. University of Mississippi.

Conway, K. (2013). Little Mosque on the Prairie *and the paradoxes of cultural translation*. University of Toronto.

Davies, R. (2019, 4 January). *Desmond's* at 30: 'I wrote it for white people'. *The Guardian*. https://www.theguardian.com/tv-and-radio/2019/jan/04/desmonds-at-30-i-wrote-it-for-white-people. Accessed on 25 April 2024.

Daynes, S. (2010). *Time and memory in reggae music: The politics of hope*. Manchester University Press.

Edmonds, E. B. (2003). *Rastafari: From outcasts to culture bearers*. Oxford University Press.

Fairchild, C. (2012). *Music, radio and the public sphere*. Palgrave Macmillan.

Habermas, J., Lennox, S., & Lennox, F. (1974). The public sphere: An encyclopedia article (1964). *New German Critique*, *3*, 49–55.

Hall, S. (1995). When was the post-colonial? *Reading the periphery*. http://readingtheperiphery.org/hall/. Accessed on November 20, 2023.

Harris-Lacewell, M. V. (2010). *Barbershops, bibles, and BET*. Princeton University Press.

Hoad, N. (2007). *African intimacies: Race, homosexuality, and globalization*. University of Minnesota Press.

Hobson, V. (2013). Plantation song: Delius, barbershop, and the blues. *American Music*, *31*(3), 314–339.

Jackson, E., & Benson, M. (2014). Neither 'Deepest, Darkest Peckham' nor 'Run-of-the-Mill' East Dulwich: The middle classes and their 'Others' in an Inner-London neighbourhood. *International Journal of Urban and Regional Research*, *38*(4), 1195–1210.

King, S. A., Bays III, T. B., & Foster, P. R. (2002). *Reggae, Rastafari and the rhetoric of social control*. University Press of Mississippi.

Majors, Y. (2003). Shoptalk: Teaching and learning in an African American hair salon. *Mind, Culture, and Activity*, *10*(4), 289–310.

Mbilishaka, A. M. (2018). Black lives (and stories) matter: Race narrative therapy in Black hair care spaces. *Community Psychology in Global Perspective*, *4*(2), 22–33.

Mbilishaka, A. M., Mbande, A., Gulley, C., & Mbande, T. (2021). Faded fresh tapers and line-ups: Centering barbershop hair stories in understanding gendered racial socialization for Black men. *Psychology of Men & Masculinities*, *22*(1), 166–176.

McGuigan, J. (2005). The cultural public sphere. *European Journal of Cultural Studies*, *8*(4), 427–443.

Mills, Q. T. (2013). *Cutting along the color line: Black barbers and barber shops in America*. University of Pennsylvania Press.

Mook, R. (2007). White masculinity in barbershop quartet singing. *Journal of the Society for American Music*, *1*, 453–483.

Moskowitz, D. V. (2006). *Caribbean popular music: An encyclopedia of reggae, mento, ska, rock steady and dancehall.* Greenwood.

Nidel, R. (2005). *World music: The basics.* Routledge.

Osborne, D., with Bourne, S. (2016). Black British comedy: *Desmond's* and the changing face of television. In J. Kamm & B. Neumann (Eds.), *British TV comedies: Cultural concepts, contexts and controversies* (pp. 167–184). Palgrave MacMillan.

Pérez, N. (1988). *El carnaval santiaguero, Tomo I.* Editorial Oriente.

Randle, B. A. (2015). I am not my hair: African American women and their struggles with embracing natural hair. *Race, Gender and Class*, *22*(1–2), 114–121.

Simuziya, N. J. (2022). A critical evaluation of the African perspectives on gay and lesbian relationships & gender. *African Renaissance*, *19*(1), 329–351.

Smith, A. M., Humphries, M. L., Mbilishaka, A. M., & Auguste, E. E. (2023). Hair messages: A context for exploring racial socialization among African American males. *Journal of Black Psychology*, *49*(5), 684–715. https://doi.org/10.1177/00957984231191847

Spivak, G. C. (1988). Can the subaltern speak? In C. Nelson & L. Grossberg (Eds.), *Marxism and the interpretation of culture* (pp. 271–313). University of Illinois Press.

Sublette, N. (2004). *Cuba and its music: From the first drums to the mambo*. Chicago Review Press.

Tabensky, P. A. (2008). The postcolonial heart of African philosophy. *South African Journal of Philosophy*, *27*(4), 285–295.

Turnbull, S., & McCutcheon, M. (2021). Outback noir and megashifts in the global TV crime landscape. In S. Shimpach (Ed.), *The Routledge companion to global television* (pp. 189–201). Routledge.

van Robbroeck, L. (2011). Beyond the tradition/modernity dialectic: African nationalist subjectivities in South African print and visual culture of the early twentieth century. In K. G. Tomaselli & H. K. Wright (Eds.), *Africa, cultural studies and difference*. Routledge.

Williams, C. (Writer), & Hanson, C. (Director) (1991, December 2). Vanity merchants (Series 3, Episode 6) [Television series episode]. In H. Barclay & A. Mitchell (Executive producers), *Desmond's*. Humphrey Barclay Productions. Channel 4.

Williams, C. (Writer) & McLean, I. (Director). (1994, December 19). O little town of Peckham (Series 6, Episode 13) [Television series episode]. In H. Barclay & A. Mitchell (Executive producers), *Desmond's*. Humphrey Barclay Productions. Channel 4.

Wood, P. B., & Brunson, R. K. (2011). Geographies of resilient social networks: The role of African American barbershops. *Urban Geography*, *32*(2), 228–243.

Worrell, T. (Writer), & Fetcher, M. (Director) (1989, January 5). French lessons (Series 1, Episode 1) [Television series episode] In H. Barclay & A. Mitchell (Executive producers), *Desmond's*. Humphrey Barclay Productions. Channel 4.

Worrell, T. (Writer), & Hanson, C. (Director) (1990, February 5). Old de front page again (Series 2, Episode 3) [Television series episode]. In H. Barclay & A. Mitchell (Executive producers), *Desmond's*. Humphrey Barclay Productions. Channel 4.

Worrell, T. (Writer), & Hanson, C. (Director) (1990, January 29). Old de front page (Series 2, Episode 2) [Television series episode]. In H. Barclay & A. Mitchell (Executive producers), *Desmond's*. Humphrey Barclay Productions. Channel 4.

Worrell, T. (Writer) & Hanson, C. (Director). (1990, March 12). For love or money (Series 2, Episode 8) [Television series episode]. In H. Barclay & A. Mitchell (Executive producers). *Desmond's*. Humphrey Barclay Productions. Channel 4.
Worrell, T. (Writer) & Wakefield, L. (Director). (1992, January 27). Too young (Series 3, Episode 12) [Television series episode]. In H. Barclay & A. Mitchell (Executive producers), *Desmond's*. Humphrey Barclay Productions. Channel 4.
Worrell, T. (Writer), & Worrell, T. (Director) (1992, February 3). Roots tradition (Series 3, Episode 13) [Television series episode]. In H. Barclay & A. Mitchell (Executive producers), *Desmond's*. Humphrey Barclay Productions. Channel 4.

Chapter 7

Ultimate Beautification: Reception of 'RuPaul's Drag Race' Show in Poland

Jacek Barlik and Dominika Sobiesiak

University of Warsaw, Poland

Abstract

This chapter has two main purposes. Firstly, it investigates the perceptions of "RuPaul's Drag Race" (RPDR), the wildly popular TV show featuring drag characters, in Poland, and its contribution to advancing tolerance for diversity and the LGBTQ+ community there. Secondly, it looks to understand how the meaning of beauty and acceptance of beautification techniques used in this TV show has changed among its fans in Poland. The study is based on an online survey conducted in May 2024 among members of Polish Facebook groups devoted to "RuPaul's Drag Race" and on a critical content analysis of their opinions about the meaning of beauty and beautification methods featured by the host and participants in the show. Even though the vast majority of Polish fans of "RuPaul's Drag Race" treat the show as just entertainment and a nice pastime, they also understand its role in transgressing and challenging the traditional meaning of beauty, not necessarily according to the established gender patterns but rather based on freedom of expression, self-acceptance, openness, diversity, and tolerance. This chapter provides insight into the role of "RuPaul's Drag Race" in normalizing and mainstreaming drag culture with its extreme beautification practices in Poland. Methodologically, the study is novel in terms of measuring the opinions and attitudes of a closely knit community of drag queen show fans in Poland.

Keywords: Beauty standards; drag queens; LGBTQ+ celebrities; queer; reality show; RuPaul's Drag Race

Beauty Industry, 143–162

doi:10.1108/978-1-83608-940-720251026

1. Introduction

The idea of cross-dressing by males pretending to be females has been present in European culture since its inception, from Achilles hidden among daughters of Lycomedes to avoid the Trojan War to all-male ancient Greek and Renaissance theater casts to Shakespearean characters swapping gender roles (with Falstaff's attempt to impersonate an old aunt and Rosalynd, Portia or Viola dressed up as males to achieve their goals) to many operatic figures (like Cherubino in Mozart's "Le nozze di Figaro" or Octavian in "Rosenkavalier" by Strauss) (Biemmi, 2023).

The first manifestations of phenomena similar to modern drag queens were described in England of the early 1700s, with gay men gathering in "molly houses" that were occasionally raided by authorities, which resulted later prosecuted in court proceedings. Cross-dressing with young men in glamorous frocks and makeup has been popular in Anglo-American culture and universities since the 1890s (Ekins, 2013). It evolved into drag shows and masquerade balls in the 1920s (and later) featuring performers swapping gender identities on stage, with drag queens who performed being women in front of an audience that knew they were men, as more common (Moncrieff & Lienard, 2017). The documentary "Paris Is Burning" about the New York drag ball scene in the 1980s, directed by Jennie Livingston and released in 1990, was not only well-known and often discussed by scholars in gender theory and queer studies but also introduced the subjects of gender subversion and racial performance to wider audiences (Bronson, 2020).

In countries like Poland, the drag queen phenomenon is relatively new, beginning in the early 1990s, when it was perceived as a Western import and a sign of progress of the post-communist society, aspiring to become an affluent European nation. Moreover, media coverage of the fledgling Polish drag scene in the 1990s proved that it had been influenced by the local gay subculture (described by the derogatory term "aunties," which is an equivalent of the American word "swishes," referring to feminine acting homosexual males) and that it still lacked the glamour and affluence of its Western equivalent (Janion, 2020).

Later, in the 2000s, the public and mainstream media interest in drag queens decreased due to a major shift in the social mood in Poland, which was no longer that enthusiastic toward all things Western. Yet, drag queens presented in media and performing at live events at clubs, cabarets, and theaters taught younger Poles about tolerance toward the LGBTQ+ community, acceptance of social transgressions, and appreciation for this form of stage expression.

2. Literature Review

Drag shows, for decades a feature of nightclub entertainment in major cities globally, stormed mass culture in 2009 and 2016 when "RuPaul's Drag Race" (RPDR), a reality TV competition among drag queens, premiered on TV channels in the US (and later in other countries). Drag superstar RuPaul is the host, mentor, and judge for the series, which looks for "America's Next Drag Superstar." Winners are expected to show the traits of "charisma," "uniqueness," "nerve," and "talent."

The show was conceived in May 2008 and premiered on February 2, 2009. It aired in Australia, Brazil, Canada, Germany, Hungary, Ireland, Italy, Latin America, Spain, Sweden, the Philippines, and the UK. The streaming service Netflix has seasons 11, 12, and 13 available online in many countries (Drag Race Wiki, n.d.). The American program has been produced by World of Wonder for Logo TV (2009–2016), later for VH1 (2017–2022), and currently for MTV (since 2023).

RuPaul Andre Charles (born in San Diego, California, on November 17, 1960), better known as RuPaul, is an American drag performer, actor, television host, and recording artist. Finding global success in the 1990s and in recent years, RuPaul has become a beacon in LGBTQ+ communities. RuPaul is well known for appearing in several films and hosting his namesake show, for which he has received 14 Primetime Emmy Awards as of 2024. RuPaul is considered the most commercially successful drag queen in the United States. In 2017, he was included in the annual Time 100 list of the most influential people in the world (Drag Race Wiki, n.d.).

It mainly was the success of the RPDR show that catapulted drag culture from the fringes to the mainstream and made its host, RuPaul, a top celebrity, with many contestants of his program following suit in the US and other countries (Feldman & Hakim, 2020). Since its launch, "RuPaul's Drag Race" as a global phenomenon focusing on people who identify as lesbian, gay, bisexual, transgender, and queer (LGBTQ+), began to challenge, question, and even dismantle established societal norms about gender, sexuality, and identity, and – at the same time – brought drag queens, their art and performance to the publics that might not have seen these types of entertainment before (Chan, 2023). RuPaul, as a legitimated, well-known artist, was instrumental in the current transition of the drag performance genre from modest, small-scale, scene-based to industry-based, huge events shown in major media (TV, streaming platforms, internet), and – as an intermediary – he also influenced the way other artists perform during drag shows (Vaughn, 2019).

Then, drag shows (mostly RPDR) moved from a niche (limited to the LGBTQ+ community and its allies) to the major media and became a popular entertainment and pastime for – predominantly – younger generations and a subject to study by scholars from various fields, spanning from cultural studies, rhetoric, sociology, marketing, communication and media, feminist, queer, and critical studies, and books on the subject (cf. Brennan & Gudelunas, 2017).

One of the examples was a plethora of celebrity studies, self-branding, and personal public relations literature about RPDR that outlined the central role that social media played in the process of celebrification of drag culture in the US and later globally (Feldman & Hakim, 2020). Especially those participants of RPDR who managed to get recognition beyond the show were skillful in – following RuPaul's suit – presenting themselves as larger-than-life, exaggerated, and simplified personas, with quotable, distinctive phrases, traits and mannerisms that could be condensed in memes, short video clips, and GIFs. As Mercer and Sarson (2020) put it, memeability – that is, the potential to lend a persona's look, quips, or announcements to becoming a meme on the net – is the modern, online celebrity's proof of charisma and success in the social media age.

However, despite the growing presence of drag culture and queerness in popular culture in the US and globally, there are still numerous examples of discrimination, oppression, and violence against the queer and LGBTQ+ communities, mostly in the form of rhetoric aimed at perpetuating established hierarchies that maintain hegemonic power (Hines, 2004). Ward (2020) pointed out a particular irony: the wildly popular TV show increased queer access to the public sphere and legitimized specific queer identities represented by drag queens, borrowing heavily from the New York ballroom culture, while simultaneously the "RuPaul's Drag Race" show mostly omitted more radical queer subcultures calling for a reconfiguration of reality and subversion of heteronormativity.

Another scholar reflected that the dominant drag culture is normative and binary, dominated by impersonating females (drag queens) who earn the most cultural capital, perform more often at bigger venues, and are better paid, in comparison to drag kings who are less popular and – to an extent – marginalized when it comes to the ability to get gigs at local bars and events (Litwiller, 2020). Zaslow (2024) went even further, stating that "RuPaul's Drag Race" – due to its massive exposure in media, the internet, and public debate – has become a drag "public," in effect – establishment, while smaller, local drag shows turned from insular subcultures to counterpublics that is – using Michael Warner's term – publics aware of their inferior and subordinate status. Thus, "RPDR" would be perceived as a part of the existing order and hierarchy of power, as opposed to smaller, guerilla-type events and shows performed by less recognized artists at smaller scenes.

Other contradictions concerning "RuPaul's Drag Race" that academics identified included cultural identity and authenticity in reality TV (Canavan, 2021), rooted in still-existing racial and other tensions. Even though show participants were eager to discuss gender, its flexibility, and performative character, issues of race and ethnicity remained more sensitive and prone to stereotyping and rewarding White/Asian characters over Black/Brown ones (Strings & Bui, 2013). Similar observations were made in connection to the musical careers of RuPaul's program participants: many white and light-skinned cast members fared much better in their recording journey after appearing on the show than their peers of color, thus equaling professionalization in pop music with contributing to entrenched liberalism and post-racial politics of the musical and recording conglomerates (Vesey, 2017).

Moreover, critical theorists analyzing "RuPaul's Drag Race" identified three stages (or levels) of how gender is represented to the public concerning show participants. The first stage is mocking drag queens and petrifying negative stereotypes about genderqueer or non-binary persons; the second – formally accepting personalities, depictions, and "otherness" of drag queens featured in "RPDR" and "normalizing" them while still sticking to heteronormative stereotypes, and the third stage – with finally portraying drag queens as holistic people, equal to their heterosexual peers, and totally free to identify and express themselves on stage and in everyday life, by behaving, styling, choosing clothes, and applying makeup according to their choices (González & Cavazos, 2016).

3. Methodology and Research Questions

As "RuPaul's Drag Race" has become a global phenomenon (predominantly among younger audiences) and emerged as a focal point for dispersed and "othered" minorities in different countries (including Poland), the show began to gather online fora, fandoms, and discussion circles of avid viewers and devoted fans. These groups evolved into sizable communities that have been debating the show, its participants, drag culture, its social, entertainment, pedagogical, cultural, and political contexts, styling, fashion, makeup, shifts in public perceptions and attitudes toward drag queens, and tolerance for "others," that is members of any disadvantaged, oppressed, and minority groupings (e.g., LGBTQ+). They are mainly based on Facebook, as private groups that can be accessed by approved members only.

The biggest Polish private Facebook group devoted to "RuPaul's Drag Race" is "Drag Race Poland," which was established on September 30, 2015, and currently has 13,700 members (Drag Race Poland, n.d.). The second biggest similar Polish Facebook group, "Drag Queen Poland Race," is a public one with 2,700 members and is less active (Drag Queen Poland Race, n.d.). "Drag Race Poland" group is administered by four people and has one moderator.

As one of the authors of this chapter belongs to the private group "Drag Race Poland," we have seized this opportunity to get in touch with people who are aware of "RuPaul's Drag Race" and – likely – willing to share their opinions and comments on subjects related to the show, its educational role in supporting tolerance, especially for queer and LGBTQ+ community.

Therefore, we thought it worthwhile to pose several questions concerning drag culture, the RPDR show, and its goals (including beautification) to the show's audience and devoted fans (mostly young people) in Poland:

RQ1. What is the main purpose of the RDPR show: entertaining audiences by featuring unusual characters or building tolerance and normalizing non-standard societal behaviors?

RQ2. What is the meaning of beauty represented by the host and participants of "RuPaul's Drag Race" show according to its devoted fans and occasional viewers?

RQ3. What methods and means of beautification are used by RDPR contestants according to the show's audience and fans?

In order to answer these research questions, we have designed an online survey among members of the "Drag Race Poland" group and among other fans of the show who were directly informed about the survey by one of the researchers. It was conducted from May 11 to May 28, 2024, following a message with the explanation posted to the group by one of the authors of this chapter and approved by its administrators.

The data for this survey were collected using the Google Forms platform for quantitative research. The questionnaire contained 27 questions, with about half directly concerning "RuPaul's Drag Race," its relationships with the beauty and fashion industries, and the LGBTQ+ community, and described below (the remaining ones were needed for a master's thesis of one of the authors).

The survey was conducted according to ethical standards and transparency rules as described by the University of Warsaw's Rector's Committee for the Ethics of Research Involving Human Participants https://en.uw.edu.pl/rectors-committee-for-the-ethics-of-research-involving-human-participants/.

Most questions were Likert-type based on a five-point scale (1–5), with 1 – strongly disagree, 2 – rather disagree, 3 – neither agree nor disagree, 4 – rather agree, and 5 – strongly agree. There were also open-ended questions on the meaning of beauty and beautification methods and questions about respondents' characteristics, genders, interests, sexual orientations, and demographics.

Of 612 respondents in the survey, 402 were females, 152 were males, and 58 declared their gender as "other" (non-binary, queer, etc.).

The majority of respondents (53.9%) were young adults aged 20–24, followed by persons aged 25–39 (37.6%), 6.9% of teenagers (15–19 years), and just 1.5% of middle-aged (40–55) fans of "RuPaul's Drag Race." Not surprisingly, the show's audience in Poland consisted of young adults and teenagers, with middle-aged and older people hardly represented at all.

More than 60% of respondents declared earning a college degree, 38.9% – a high school diploma, and the remaining 1% – a middle high or elementary school (which is understandable, as teenagers participated in the survey). Almost 75% of participants lived in big (plus 500,000 inhabitants) and mid-sized (100–500,000) cities (57.7% and 16.7% – respectively), followed by 9.5% countryside and 2.5% small town (up to 10,000 people) dwellers, 5.9% people living in smaller cities (50–100,000), and 7.8% – from towns with 10–50,000 people.

When it comes to the sexual orientation of respondents, the results showed that homosexuals amounted to 31.5% of replies, heterosexuals – 29.6%, and other orientations – 37.9% (with almost 25% of bisexuals and around 6% of pansexuals, supplemented by 7.5% of different orientations). Obviously, sexual orientations of drag queen show fans differed significantly from the general population in Poland (and in other countries), since mere 30% – the lowest share – of the sample were heterosexuals.

Polish fans of "RuPaul's Drag Race" were encouraged to participate by one of the researchers who – as an active member of the private Facebook group for some time – was credible to her peers. Respondents were directed to a website (https://docs.google.com/forms) where they completed the questionnaire, responding anonymously to – mostly – closed-ended questions (with some open-ended ones focused on different aspects of beauty and beautification techniques with reference to drag queens). Their responses to the question: "To what extent do you agree with the following statement," on a Likert-type scale ranging from 1 (strongly disagree) to 5 (strongly agree) are presented in Table 7.1 (containing also standard deviation for each statement).

The open-ended question on understanding beauty as represented by the cast of "RuPaul's Drag Race" and its host gathered 179 replies, while the one on beautification methods and techniques – had 135 replies (comments and opinions of varying length). Replies to closed-ended and open-ended questions were later exported to MS Excel (as .xlsx files) and then reviewed by the research team.

Table 7.1. Key Descriptive Statistics of the Questionnaire Items Used in the Study.

Evaluated Statements	**Mean**	**Std. Deviation**
"RuPaul's Drag Race" is mostly entertainment, fun, and relax.	4.58	0.840
Thanks to "RuPaul's Drag Race," I am expanding my knowledge about drag queen art (hairdos, makeup, styling, lip sync, dance, comedy acting, etc.).	4.56	0.802
"RuPaul's Drag Race" is my source of news about new trends in fashion, makeup, and styling.	3.28	1.328
I watch "RuPaul's Drag Race" show since it supports LGBTQ+ community, promotes tolerance, and openness.	4.25	1.052
"RuPaul's Drag Race" strengthens the standard canon of female beauty (hairdos, makeup, styling).	2.24	1.086
"RuPaul's Drag Race" challenges the standard canon of female beauty (hairdos, makeup, styling), and expands its for new dimensions.	4.15	1.028
Thanks to "RuPaul's Drag Race," I more often wear original outfits, apply a visible makeup and sport an extravagant hairdo.	2.74	1.386
Having watched "RuPaul's Drag Race," I am willing to participate in a live drag queen show at a club, cabaret, or a theater.	4.50	0.956
Styling, hairdos, and makeup from "RuPaul's Drag Race" inspire fashion shows, clothes designers, stylists, and theatrical and movie costume designs.	4.00	0.997
Drag queen art and "RuPaul's Drag Race" show influence trends in the beauty and fashion industries.	3.92	1.004

Source: Author's own creation.

Note: Responses to the question: "To what extent do you agree with the following statement?," on a Likert-type scale ranging from 1 (strongly disagree) to 5 (strongly agree) (N = 612).

Respondents' opinions and statements in replying to open-ended questions were also compiled, critically analyzed, and commented on in following parts of the chapter.

4. Findings

As mentioned, the study among Polish fans of "RuPaul's Drag Race" covered the following areas: personal motivations for watching the show, its role in supporting the LGBTQ+ community, educating about tolerance, diversity, and openness, defining beauty represented by drag queens, evaluating their beautification methods and techniques, the influence of the show on trends in clothing design, makeup, beauty industry, theatrical and movie costumes, and – additionally for the master's thesis of one author, which is not described in this chapter – reception of "Drag Me Out," a Polish TV show on drag queens, among the same respondents.

4.1 Expertise About Drag and Beauty Industry

More than 90% of respondents expressed their positive opinion on the show as improving their knowledge about drag queen art, performance, styling, makeups, hairdos, wigs, lip sync, dancing, comedy acting, etc. Appreciation for "RuPaul's Drag Race" educational and instructional role in drag queen art and performance for its fans was overwhelming: the mean score of replies to this question was 4.56 (on a 1–5 scale), the second highest in the survey.

This result was likely caused by the vivid interest of respondents in the subject and – often – by their ventures into drag (as proven by systematically observing the timeline of the Facebook private group).

"RuPaul's Drag Race" was not assessed that high by respondents, though, when they were asked about the show as a source of news on fashion, makeup, and styling. Less than 50% (45.49%) agreed with this statement, while 30% expressed the opposite view, and 24% were indifferent (neither agree nor disagree) (mean score: 3.28 on a 1–5 scale). General knowledge of fashion, makeup, styling, and the beauty industry was acquired elsewhere by Polish fans of RuPaul than on the namesake show.

4.2 Drag and Standards of Female Beauty

Almost 80% (79.58%) of inquired RPDR fans maintained that the show challenged the standard canon of female beauty and expanded it with new dimensions explored by drag queens participating in the program (with mean score: 4.15 on a 1–5 scale).

On the other hand, just 14% (13.89%) agreed with the statement that the show preserved the standard canon of women's beauty. In comparison, two-thirds of respondents (65.69%) negatively replied to this opinion (with a paltry mean score of 2.24 in a 1–5 scale). Such results clearly show that drag is perceived by its fans as a unique and different phenomenon, different than a simple mimicking of glamorous females by their male impersonators.

4.3 Drag Art as an Inspiration and Trendsetter in the Beauty Industry

According to most asked RPDR viewers, their favorite programs inspired fashion shows, cloth designers, stylists, and theatrical and movie costumes (more than 70% agreed with that) and influenced trends in the beauty and fashion industries (confirmed by almost 70% of respondents). "RuPaul's Drag Race" was simultaneously called an early pioneer and thought leader (mean score: 4.0 on a 1–5 scale) and a trailblazer and authoritative voice in the field (mean score: 3.92 on a 1–5 scale). Even though only a small number of answers was negative (both – less than 10%), the neutral replies (neither agree nor disagree) were more common (more than 20% in both cases), showing that the program was not seen as something of great importance by this group.

4.4 Drag and Personal Experience

Every third respondent in the survey (31.7%) declared a change in their dressing code, makeup, and hairstyle thanks to watching "RuPaul's Drag Race," while the remaining 68% tended to stay their ways regarding everyday habits. Flashy outfits, heavy makeup, and extravagant hairdos did not appeal as a look of choice to the majority of RPDR fans (mean score: 2.74 on a 1–5 scale), who – instead – gladly watched drag queen shows at clubs, restaurants, cabarets, or theaters.

Having watched "RuPaul's Drag Race," they were even more willing to take part in a live event featuring drag queens at their local venues: almost 90% of respondents (88.89%) concurred with this statement, while a mere 6.37% disagreed (with less than 5% indifferent answers) (mean score: 4.5 in 1–5 scale). As most RPDR fans (almost 75%) hail from major cities (with at least 100,000 inhabitants), it is relatively easy for them to locate an occasional drag performance in their area at LGBTQ+-friendly clubs, restaurants, or theaters.

4.5 More Than Just Fun

On the one hand, "RuPaul's Drag Race" was treated lightly by its fans: 91.5% respondents agreed with the statement that the show was mostly entertainment, fun, and relaxing (with more than 72% strongly agreeing). On the other hand, 81.7% of fans declared watching "RuPaul's Drag Race" due to its support for LGBTQ+ communities and promoting tolerance, diversity, and openness, thus putting the program in a broader perspective as a force to introduce social changes and raise awareness about rights of minorities (including drag queens and their milieu).

Seeing "RuPaul's Drag Race" as a predominantly entertaining, fun, and relaxing show earned the highest score in the entire survey (mean score: 4.58 on a 1–5 scale), while the show's commitment to LGBTQ+ community was also appreciated (mean score: 4.25 in 1–5 scale). It is hardly a surprise, taking into account not only the sexual orientations of respondents (roughly – one-third of homosexuals, one-third of heterosexuals, and one-third – of other orientations) but also an overwhelming support for LGBTQ+ movements declared by 92.2% of participants in the survey.

4.6 Qualitative Research – Respondents on Beauty

All answers to two open-ended questions about the meaning of beauty in the context of "RuPaul's Drag Race" and beautification techniques used by its cast and host (about 300 in total) were proofread and edited to remove repetitions, mistakes, and unclear passages. Their length was comparable to this chapter (about 7,000 words).

The collected answers were then identified (with themes from Research Questions 2 and 3), and the coding themes were analyzed to discover interesting traits, later used for critical content analyses. Transcripts were read at least three times by two researchers to find out unique opinions, thoughts, and insights, which were organized as annotations and summaries to form a consistent narrative of this study.

Summaries of the replies to two open-ended questions with conclusions about the relationship between beauty, the drag queen community, and "RuPaul's Drag Race" show are presented in the following parts.

4.7 Meaning of Beauty

The first open-ended question asked in this research concerned the meaning of beauty expressed and represented by RuPaul and the drag show participants as perceived by Polish fans and occasional program viewers. The question gathered 179 replies, which is a 29.2% response rate (out of 612 persons who took part in the survey), which is high, considering the length of the questionnaire and its detailed nature.

After reviewing and analyzing the replies to this question, the following main themes describing the essence of beauty shown in "RuPaul's Drag Race" were identified:

- daring to express yourself in your way/be yourself/be courageous,
- self-love/self-acceptance/self-expression/self-confidence/inner beauty/authenticity/originality/individualism,
- the subjectivity of beauty/freedom/non-conformism/self-presentation/individual style of clothing, makeup, and style of being,
- diversity/experimenting with your image through makeup, hairstyle, and fashion styling,
- inner beauty externalized through self-presentation/body positivity/self-confidence,
- creativity/art/extravagance/charisma (charismatic personality),

- sense of esthetics/professionalism and perfectionism in drag art/attention to detail,
- depends on the field of drag art with which a particular drag queen identifies (e.g., camp, comedy drag queen or fashion drag queen, etc.)/hyperbole of the standard canon of female beauty (exaggerated female beauty) or the individual style of a given drag queen.

According to respondents, beauty is being yourself even in someone else's disguise (a standard way of drag queens), and unconventionality and authenticity are at the core of such understood beauty. Daring to be themselves was perhaps the most crucial feature of drag queens meaning of beauty according to "RuPaul's Drag Race" viewers:

> Drag queens participating in this program understand beauty as bold self-expression - their style. Beauty is striving to be oneself and not conforming to the opinions of others. Beauty is courage, freedom, and non-conformity. It follows that beauty is diversity - not uniform because everyone expresses themselves in their own characteristic way. (Sobiesiak, 2024, pp. 109–110)

Freedom to behave as the contestants in "RPDR" felt appropriate came at a cost, though, especially for their mental health, but it is worth showing their internal females:

> I haven't watched many seasons, but I notice a trend that the contestants talk a lot about mental health issues, liking themselves, and if asked directly, I think they would talk about this beauty internally. Also, my understanding of drag (mostly based on RPDR) is that it's not about creating the 'most beautiful woman,' it's about bringing out the femininity in yourself, no matter how beautiful or imperfect it is. (Sobiesiak, 2024, p. 110)

Drag queens – as one of the fans put it – try to "fully express themselves and establish an aesthetics that fits not only their physical features but also their personality." At the same time, they promote the beauty of character shown through an original appearance that expresses their individuality:

> Beauty is subjective, as each drag queen has an original style and way of being that sets them apart from others. Beauty for them is the ability to express themselves by creating a persona that allows them to gain self-confidence, as well as the opportunity to show their creativity through costumes, wigs, makeup, and their performances. (Sobiesiak, 2024, p. 110)

According to fans, looking for beauty is an essential factor in the show, but more critical is finding "the truest version of yourself":

> Combining a creative and aesthetically pleasing look with the individual characteristics of a drag queen, i.e., her skills (dancing/comedy/design, etc.) and personality fuels the show. The meaning of beauty depends on the particular person because beauty is not the essence of this program, so it's hard to talk about it in general in its context. It is more about finding the truest version of oneself, a sense of belonging and acceptance, and besides that, it's a play on the social constructivism that is gender, which lacks drag artists who aren't drag queens and more women, but maybe they'll change that someday. (Sobiesiak, 2024, p. 110)

Beauty is, by definition, diverse and cannot be imposed on everyone in the same form, standard, or pattern, although costumes and general look matter, too: "It is more a reflection of inner beauty – hence its diversity, which is why it does not fit into a strict framework."

> Each of them interprets beauty in their way: some drag queens think that beauty is impeccable makeup and 'female illusion,' and others think that beauty is freedom and the ability to express themselves in any way.
>
> Most generally, beauty is considered something that everyone has within themselves. As for the costumes, though, the most beautiful ones are characterized by great attention to detail and professional workmanship. (Sobiesiak, 2024, p. 110)

Some respondents questioned whether the same beauty standards should be universally applied to females and drag queens.

> The beauty canon of drag queens and the beauty of women are two separate things. I don't think they have any influence on each other. Drag racers define beauty as the symbiosis of their inner selves and how they present themselves. It's about being themselves. Even if putting on drag somehow creates a separate persona, it comes from our experiences. Drag racers spend much time mutually criticizing someone else's appearance. Personally, it doesn't bother me; I know it's just for entertainment, and that's why I watch the show - because it's entertaining - but it certainly dilutes the message regarding beauty itself. (Sobiesiak, 2024, p. 110)

Feminine beauty standards are not generally supported by fans of "RPDR": "Opinions are divided. Some participants adhere to the standard canons of beauty (the so-called pageant queen beauty), while some are much more open to the diversity of beauty." They also comment: "I believe that every drag queen understands beauty differently. For one, it will be a complete illusion of being a beautiful, shapely woman, and for another, it will be crazy makeup and outfits" (Sobiesiak, 2024, pp. 109–110).

> For each participant, beauty is expressed differently, but most often, it comes down to hyperbole of femininity (large symmetrical breasts, hourglass figure, full shiny hair, impeccable posture, etc.). One can see favoritism toward people who choose 'standard' beauty (typically 'feminine').
>
> When it comes to the American version of the show, beauty is quite stereotypical. There were no drag kings but more and more typical glamour queens; perhaps the biggest departure from the canon gates was Gottmik with their black and white makeup. It's a bit better in the British edition, where there has been much more diversity since the first season. (Sobiesiak, 2024, p. 111)

Drag queens don't need to be fashionable and trendy, even though some choose to follow these ways.

> Some performers are totally commercial, thus fitting in with current trends and being nothing different than what is 'popular.' Others cultivate classic and timeless styles. On the one hand, it is ultra-feminine, and on the other, it is an exaggerated, larger-than-life look. There's also all the kitsch in between. (Sobiesiak, 2024, p. 110)

The show itself also evolved when it comes to understanding beauty, from parroting divas to a more open and diverse approach:

> The first seasons were characterized by a 'more rigid' understanding of beauty in terms of imitating femininity in its traditional sense. Now, the idea of beauty is expressed in a wider range of drag and is more diverse, while 'femininity' is not so strictly understood and has become more inclusive.
>
> I have the impression that a few seasons back, most participants understood beauty according to standard canons. Some of them tried to exaggerate features perceived as typically feminine. Fortunately, many contestants rely on originality and promote a different kind of beauty by often impersonating imaginary, fantastic characters. Many of them are also experimenting with makeup. (Sobiesiak, 2024, p. 111)

Originality and diversity count, as these characteristics make a good show and amplify, exceed, and challenge the traditional standards of beauty.

> I feel that each drag queen understands beauty in her unique way. We have campy weird queens, typical beauty queens; we have queens inspired by other stars (e.g., Derrick Barry, Chad Michaels) and those who create their own completely innovative drag style.

> It seems to me that the vast majority of RPDR cast in part conventionally perceives beauty (long hair, makeup, dresses, bright colors expressive), but processes it through the filter of being a drag queen that is five times amplified than just being a girly girl or a woman goddess. However, more and more chicks go beyond the pattern, e.g., Sasha Velour or Cheddar Gorgeous, where being a drag queen goes beyond the girly look, draws literally from everything, and often conceptualizes these in a new way. (Sobiesiak, 2024, p. 111)

Perhaps the most comprehensive yet succinct description of beauty as implemented by "RuPaul's Drag Race" cast and perceived by their Polish viewers and fans straddles two worlds: the one of freedom, self-expression, and diversity, and the other of more conventional, feminine beauty:

> They understand beauty as the courageous expression of themselves - their style of being. Beauty is striving to be oneself rather than conforming to the opinions of others. Beauty is courage, freedom, and non-conformity. Beauty is diversity - it is not uniform, as everyone expresses themselves in their own characteristic way. Most of the show's drag queens express themselves through colorful, feminine styles in the form of long or short colorful dresses and wigs that mimic lush, long hair. Sometimes, they also put on ornate colorful bodysuits to emphasize the feminine shapes that drag queens have given themselves by using special techniques (fabric fillers, special pads, etc.). (Sobiesiak, 2024, pp. 109–110)

4.8 Beautification Techniques

The second open-ended question on beautification techniques and methods used by the cast of "RuPaul's Drag Race" was more specific, required a more profound knowledge of fashion, cosmetics, and beauty industries, and therefore was not as often replied to as the first one. Consequently, it was answered by 135 people, which is a 22.1% response rate (out of 612 persons who took part in the survey), still quite a high percentage taking into account the length and detailed nature of the filled form.

After reviewing and analyzing the replies to this question, the following main themes describing the beautification methods and techniques applied in "RuPaul's Drag Race" were identified:

- dressing up in fancy, extravagant costumes, often designed and even tailored by drag queens themselves,
- using body shaping techniques to change the silhouette to become more female-looking/applying inserts (fake or artificial add-ons) to accentuate some parts of the body and tucking supplies (gaffs or medical tape) to hide the male sex organs,

- heavy, expressive makeup/contouring the face with cosmetics/facelifting with duct tape to alter the facial features/baking makeup/lip contouring/eyebrow blocking,
- showy and flamboyant hairdos, coiffures, and wigs imitating lush hair, often loose wavy hair, usually much bigger than in reality,
- esthetic medicine/prosthetics/plastic surgery.

Respondents seemed to possess an expert knowledge of beautification techniques used by drag queens, which are based on three pillars: makeup, wigs, and costumes.

> Makeup of drag queens varies: there are known queens who wear delicate makeup, closer to the stereotypical canon of femininity, but there is also a group known for heavy or smoky makeup. The wigs that drag queens wear span from more natural to ridiculous, using innovative hairdressing methods to build large structures often. Costumes also express the originality of drag queens; many were designed and sewn by themselves, putting their creativity into fabric. Their ability to draw attention to details, even such as gluing individual crystals to fabric, allows them to create fantastic, unique creations that set them apart from the crowd and give them confidence. (Sobiesiak, 2024, p. 112)

In addition to clothing, makeup, and hairdressing techniques, numerous body-shaping and changing methods are popular among drag performers.

> Modeling their figure using typical drag queen techniques (using fillers and other specialized materials to achieve the desired effect, i.e., giving feminine shapes); applying expressive artistic makeup on their own, which is visible even from a distance: artificial eyelashes, colored eye shadow, lipstick, face contouring – foundation, concealer, highlighter, and bronzer; an eye-catching wig, which is usually characterized by high volume, to achieve the effect of lush long loose hair - often curls; an important element of the styling is usually an original long or short dress, often made independently by the drag queens themselves, to which accessories in the form of jewelry - for example, large earrings, a head ornament - for example, a hat of unusual shape, and shoes with heels - all these usually in intense colors. Some of the show's drag queens go beyond the standard canon of feminine beauty and wear long gowns less often, and create styles reminiscent of punk and rock or goth subculture: dark makeup, studs, etc. (e.g., Gottmik or Aiden Zhane). Such drag queens are the minority in the RPDR program, with most positioning themselves as elegant ladies, alluding to celebrity styling from the so-called 'red carpet.' (Sobiesiak, 2024, pp. 112–113)

> Padding - using soft padding to accentuate hips and buttocks. Tucking - a technique for hiding the male sex organs. Makeup techniques, some of course, include non-drag style makeup: baking - using a very thick layer of powder to fix clear facial makeup, contour, and create 'cut-offs'; covering the eyebrows, which men tend to have quite low, to create the illusion of a new, much larger eyelid. (Sobiesiak, 2024, p. 113)

Beautification techniques in "RuPaul's Drag Race" range from costumes (inspired by high fashion or popular culture but also completely original designs) to makeup and fine wigs and corrections of body and limp shapes (including all kinds of filling, tights, padding, or patching prosthetics, or other non-standard materials).

> Patching, filling in curves, leg-slimming tights, push-ups, fancy hairstyles that require much work and skill. Beautiful outfits that sometimes look much better than from the best designers.
>
> Contouring, which can completely change the shape of the face. Lip contouring, which gives the effect of larger lips. Proper eye makeup, which optically enlarges the eye. Padding, which can change or give a new body shape. (Sobiesiak, 2024, p. 113)

According to their fans, drag queens spend a lot of time on facelifts, makeup, and body-shaping techniques.

> The most distinctive makeup element is eyebrow blocking, which allows the eye to be exaggerated and enlarged. Queens also use modeling underwear and padding to create the desired silhouette. These techniques have been used in European women's fashion for centuries, but since the 1960s, they have ceased to be part of standard women's clothing. (Sobiesiak, 2024, p. 113)

Other beautification methods used by drag queens include:

> Facelift using duct tape, tucking, pushing out the hips with a sponge, shaving/hiding the eyebrows, sharp contouring of the face.
>
> Sticking eyebrows with glue to draw a new shape, several pairs of false eyelashes, inserts imitating breasts or hips.
>
> Richly stylized wigs, original costumes, expressive and original makeup, figure beautification - artificial breasts, hips, corsets, etc.
>
> Extensive use of tape, blocking or even shaving eyebrows, eccentrically made-up and unusual styling of wigs. (Sobiesiak, 2024, p. 113)

However, there was also a dissenting voice that questioned the idea of beatification as an excessive and lavish styling that uses all available (preferably expensive-looking) outfits, materials, cosmetics, and accessories.

> Beautification is not necessarily a good term for drag, even in the context of RuPaul's program. Attention to detail is mentioned, but the criterion of beauty is not crucial. In many cases, beautification was understood as the lack of excess material in outfits - a better/effective fit under one's proportions. (Sobiesiak, 2024, p. 113)

5. Conclusions

The RPDR show – especially its original, American version – required contestants to perform, look, and dress according to conventional Western standards of beauty and – in a way – to promote the idea of the diva, embodied by Hollywood stars, opera singers, supermodels, socialites, and celebrities (Campana et al., 2022). The essence of the RDPR is – besides the competition – the beautification process of all participants supervised by RuPaul, the host, master of ceremony, mentor, role model, and judge simultaneously. At the same time, drag queens (DQ) are associated with transgressions of societal norms and standard behaviors, especially concerning gender and sexual orientation, masculinity and femininity, performative acts, and breaking social habits and taboos (Logan & Ciszek, 2021).

However, as the online survey and critical content analysis of opinions expressed by Polish fans of the program proved, the show is perceived chiefly as entertainment; viewers know that its host strongly supports the LGBTQ+ community and promotes tolerance, diversity, and openness. Therefore, in answering RQ1 about the program's main purpose, both options (juxtaposing elements of fun and relaxation vs. education about tolerance) have to be ticked, with more emphasis on the former.

When the research question on the meaning of beauty (RQ2) is answered, most of the respondents refer to the self-acceptance of drag queens, freedom of their flamboyant self-expression through the art of drag, with their style of makeup, hairstyles, and clothing, and personality of the drag queen. Therefore, the very concept of beauty is being deconstructed and questioned, and it is no longer uniform and universal, at least in the context of "RuPaul's Drag Race" cast. Beauty has become diverse, as the contestants in the show, because each presents themselves in an individual way and in accordance with their drag style.

Some interviewees pointed out that in earlier seasons of this show, most drag queens showed the standard canon of female beauty. In comparison, in newer seasons, especially in the British edition, there are more diverse drag queens who represented a different sense of esthetics and types of drag art (for example, camp drag queen, fashion drag queen, comedy drag queen, classic drag queen, drag queens inspired by the appearance and behavior of celebrities or stars, drag queens with innovative style, etc.). The respondents noted that drag queens participating in "RuPaul's Drag Race" beautify their stage personas with expressive, heavy makeup, wigs that mimic a large volume of hair, original styling, and using professional material fillers to give them a proper (feminine) shape. However, most respondents thought that drag queens featured in "RPDR" rather challenged the existing standard of female beauty than petrified it, even though comments in open-ended questions suggested otherwise.

Respondents and interviewees are knowledgeable about the original beautification methods of these drag queens (which is the subject of the last research question, RQ3). Numerous techniques and methods of beautification of drag queens were listed: starting from smoky and baking makeup, facelifting, and contouring, eyebrow blocking, application of false eyelashes, to extravagant and oversized coiffures and wigs, to modeling one's figure to give it a standard feminine shape (emphasized waist, bust, hips, buttocks, etc.) by padding (based on inserts that accentuate the hips or buttocks and other parts of the body) and tucking (hiding the male sex organs), and even undergoing plastic surgery.

As the survey showed, the meaning of beauty with reference to "RuPaul's Drag Race" show, its host, and its cast changed and extended to include other factors that are not strictly from the area of esthetics but instead focus on openness, self-acceptance, self-confidence, and freedom of choice. Self-expression of drag queens in their artistic, personal, and identity journeys has also brought a liberating effect on the viewers of the show, who admitted that they are more likely to support a drag community and participate in local drag shows, thus further spreading tolerance and openness toward the LGBTQ+ community.

References

Biemmi, L. (2023). *Opera as Sexualwissenschaft: sexology, the 'third sex', and the intermediary voice in Strauss and Hofmannsthal's Der Rosenkavalier (1911) and Ariadne auf Naxos (1916)*. Doctoral Thesis. The University of Western Australia.

Brennan, N., & Gudelunas, D. (Eds.). (2017). *RuPaul's Drag Race and the shifting visibility of drag culture*. Palgrave Macmillan. https://doi.org/10.1007/978-3-319-50618-0_15

Bronson, M. L. (2020). *Drag queen discourse: Social circulation, restorative literacies, and rhetorical space (Publication No. 27955803)*. Master's thesis. California State University, Fresno. ProQuest LLC.

Campana, M., Duffy, K., & Micheli, K. M. (2022). 'We're all Born Naked and the Rest is Drag': Spectacularization of core stigma in RuPaul's Drag Race. *Journal of Management Studies*, *59*(8), 1950–1986. https://doi.org/10.1111/joms.12848

Canavan, B. (2021). Post-postmodern consumer authenticity, shantay you stay or sashay away? A netnography of RuPaul's Drag Race fans. *Marketing Theory*, *21*(2), 251–276. https://doi.org/10.1177/1470593120985144

Chan, A. S. W. (2023). RuPaul's Drag Race: A cultural phenomenon that challenges gender norms and sparks conversations across borders. *Journal of Homosexuality*, *71*(8), 1863–1866. https://doi.org/10.1080/00918369.2023.2216336

Drag Queen Poland Race. (n.d.). About this page [Facebook page]. *Facebook*. https://www.facebook.com/groups/238858803314227/about. Accessed on June 8, 2024.

Drag Race Poland. (n.d.). About this page [Facebook page]. *Facebook*. https://www.facebook.com/groups/427487394107983/. Accessed on June 8, 2024.

Drag Race Wiki. (n.d.). *RuPaul's Drag Race*. https://rupaulsdragrace.fandom.com/wiki/RuPaul%27s_Drag_Race. Accessed on June 8, 2024.

Ekins, R. (2013). On male femaling: A grounded theory approach to cross-dressing and sex-changing. In D. Denny (Ed.), *Current concepts in transgender identity* (pp. 181–205). Routledge.

Feldman, Z., & Hakim, J. (2020). From *Paris is burning* to #dragrace: Social media and the celebrification of drag culture. *Celebrity Studies*, *11*(4), 386–401. https://doi.org/10.1080/19392397.2020.1765080

González, J. C., & Cavazos, K. C. (2016). Serving fishy realness: Representations of gender equity on *RuPaul's Drag Race*. *Continuum*, *30*(6), 659–669. https://doi.org/10.1080/10304312.2016.1231781

Hines, S. (2004). *Transgender identities, intimate relationships and practices of care*. PhD thesis. University of Leeds.

Janion, L. (2020). The rise and fall of the progressive drag queen: Westernization of cross-dressing in 1990s Poland. *Sexualities*, *23*(7), 1179–1198. https://doi.org/10.1177/1363460719888438

Litwiller, F. (2020). Normative drag culture and the making of precarity. *Leisure Studies*, *39*(4), 600–612. https://doi.org/10.1080/02614367.2020.1800798

Logan, N., & Ciszek, E. (2021). At the intersection of race, gender and sexuality: A queer of color critique of public relations habitus. *Journal of Public Relations Research*, *33*(6), 487–503. https://doi.org/10.1080/1062726X.2022.2051174

Mercer, J., & Sarson, C. (2020). Fifteen seconds of fame: RuPaul's Drag Race, camp and 'memeability'. *Celebrity Studies*, *11*(4), 479–492. https://doi.org/10.1080/19392397.2020.1765102

Moncrieff, M., & Lienard, P. (2017). A natural history of the drag queen phenomenon. *Evolutionary Psychology*, *15*(2), 1–14. https://doi.org/10.1177/1474704917707591

Sobiesiak, D. (2024). *Komunikowanie o marce osobistej (personal PR) celebryty ze społeczności LGBTQ+ na przykładzie reality show RuPaul's Drag Race* [*Communication about personal brand of a celebrity from LGBTQ+ community: Case study of the reality show RuPaul's Drag Race*]. Unpublished master's thesis. University of Warsaw.

Strings, S., & Bui, L. T. (2013). "She Is Not Acting, She Is": The conflict between gender and racial realness on *RuPaul's Drag Race*. *Feminist Media Studies*, *14*(5), 822–836. https://doi.org/10.1080/14680777.2013.829861

Vaughn, M. P. (2019). Supermodel of the world: The influence of legitimacy on genre and creativity in drag music videos. *Social Psychology Quarterly*, *82*(4), 431–452. https://doi.org/10.1177/0190272519869314

Vesey, A. (2017). "A Way to Sell Your Records": Pop stardom and the politics of drag professionalization on RuPaul's Drag Race. *Television & New Media*, *18*(7), 589–604. https://doi.org/10.1177/1527476416680889

Ward, J. (2020). Serving 'Reality' television 'Realness': Reading RuPaul's Drag Race and its construction of reality. *Comparative American Studies. An International Journal*, *17*(1), 23–40. https://doi.org/10.1080/14775700.2020.1720407

Zaslow, S. (2024). Mainstream novelty: Examining the shifting visibility of drag performance. *Sexualities*, *27*(1–2), 330–355. https://doi.org/10.1177/13634607221091447

Chapter 8

Red Lipstick as a Communication Tool of (Self)-presentation: Gender and Power Perspectives

Nikolina Borčić

Faculty of Political Sciences, University of Zagreb, Croatia

Abstract

This chapter explores the interplay between the symbolic metaphorical representation of red lipstick as a tool for communication within public discourse, specifically examining how it contributes to shaping a public figure's image. Societies develop unique modes of communication, habits, and semantic relationships, depending on the zeitgeist. The use of symbolic messages, such as wearing red lipstick as a message not only reflects but also could shape perspectives. In line with this, this chapter approaches the analysis of use of red lipstick as a communication tool for (self-)presentation of public figures from gender and power perspectives within media communication. The term (self)-presentation includes the protagonist's self-presentation regarding the use of red lipstick as a beautification tool and a message. Presentation furthermore refers to the depiction of this usage within the media text and narrative, which are products of the media content creator. This approach investigates the tactics of labeling and description as part of the discourse strategies of self-representation. Key findings indicate that red lipstick functions not merely as a cosmetic item but as a powerful communication tool that can communicate authority, rebellion, sensuality, and professionalism. In analyzed article, red lipstick is often employed by women to communicate confidence and authority, thereby serving as a potent symbol of empowerment. In addition to the above, in the texts make-up and appearance are packaged as an image element that serves for the presentation and promotion of femininity, sexuality and daring.

Beauty Industry, 163–181

Published under exclusive licence by Emerald Publishing Limited
doi:10.1108/978-1-83608-940-720251028

Keywords: Beauty discourse; self-presentation strategies; red lipstick as a tool and message; gender perspective; power dynamic; media qualitative text analysis; media communication and meaning-making

1. Introduction

Media communication theories, including McQuail's (2010) mass communication theory and Hall's (1980) encoding/decoding model, further deepen our understanding of how media shapes and is shaped by public perceptions. These theories, for example, highlight the creation, dissemination, and interpretation of media messages which in turn generate the discursive practices associated with a particular topic, occasion or individual. In light of this, this paper explores the content regarding the red lipstick as a communication tool of (self)-presentation for image production purposes in media texts from a gender and power perspective. In celebrity discourse, beauty discourse, and discourse related to various social or political issues in media content, the mention of red lipstick can ascribe additional associations to the protagonist or topic. The communicative role of red lipstick from the perspective of power has the potential to create meaning in terms of the construction or deconstruction of common behavior in a certain period, society, and culture. Borčić (2023) states that language and communication play a key role in the creation of social reality, and thus in creating the meaning of the elements of that reality. In this context, it is important to mention how the German linguist Leo Weisberger uses the term "wording" (German: *das Worten*) to describe the process of naming and describing everything that surrounds us, from behavior and space to actions and interpersonal interactions (Borčić, 2023; Glovacki-Bernardi, 2008). When applied to the media context, the way media texts discuss a topic and the context in which authors place a term such as red lipstick potentially affects the visibility, awareness, and understanding of certain societal elements. In this context, the meaning and associations that red lipstick implicitly or explicitly carries in media content contribute to the creation of the discourse of a certain time. Moreover, contemporary media, internet content, and advertising campaigns have both challenged and reinforced these notions.

The historical journey of red lipstick is emblematic of its multifaceted role within societal and individual contexts. As a communication tool, red lipstick has continuously adapted, reflecting and influencing changes in social attitudes toward gender, power, and identity. Its use intersects with gender and power dynamics, historically symbolizing "disobedience" (Wu et al., 2024) while also being tied to the ongoing effort to maintain an attractive and respectable appearance (Hurd Clarke & Bundon, 2009). Beauty plays a central role in women's lives due to societal emphasis on physical appearance and the pressure to conform to ever-changing ideals (Bartky, 1990). As Peiss (2001) suggests, the bold color is not merely a fashion statement but a form of non-verbal communication, indicating rebellion against patriarchal norms and serving as a metaphor for strength and self-esteem. Accordingly, the use of lipstick as an embodied practice marks the body and serves multiple functions: enhancing appearance, attracting attention, disguising, amplifying, and seducing (Benoit, 2013, p. 112). Its meaning is (de)constructed depending on the focus of individual feminist or social periods (Humm, 1992; cf. Scott, 2005). Consequently, the relevance of red lipstick in today's media landscape is multifaceted. Red lipstick can be seen both as an artifact of gendered expression and as a dynamic instrument wielded in the power plays of public life. Accordingly, the theoretical part of this work delves into the topics of (self)-presentation as an image communication tool from gender and power perspectives, with a particular focus on red lipstick as a communicative element for the purpose of (self)-presentation. The research provides an analysis of recent media discourse, using examples of mentions of red lipstick in texts aimed at a wide audience.

2. (Self)-presentation in Media as an Image Communication Tool From Gender and Power Perspectives

Media play a key role in shaping social norms, needs, and consumption habits of audiences by using compelling narratives and characters to promote certain values and behaviors. Geiger Zeman and Zeman (2015) point out that media representations, such as those in the series "Sex and the City" and movies like "Legally Blonde" and "Confessions of a Shopaholic," contribute to the idealization of a certain lifestyle and consumer habits, especially among young women. In this way, media not only reflect existing social norms but also actively shape them, creating new needs and expectations for the audience. Characters from popular culture thus become role models that dictate fashion trends and lifestyles, potentially affecting the consumerist habits of the audience and creating behavioral patterns. If this is put in the context of using red lipstick as a means of self-presentation, it can be assumed that this topic encourages the preference for topics or elements of the public image that can be interesting and meet public expectations. (Self)-presentation in media, therefore, is a tactic that creates an image of oneself, with the associations attributed to it, consequently shaping the image of the subject, the protagonist, or the topic as well. Martin Rüdiger and Astrid Schütz (2016) identify three common communicative strategies, assertive, defensive, and offensive, that are employed in the context of media (self)-representation. Assertive strategies highlight strengths and competencies of the individual or entity, serving purposes of self-presentation and creating a political image in line with public expectations. Defensive strategies offer reinterpretations of perspectives or apologies for certain outcomes. Offensive strategies point to scapegoats or blame, redirecting audience focus through causal arguments based on the fault of "others" or circumstances (Rüdiger & Schütz, 2016).

In the context of mentioning red lipstick and placing it within the symbolic transmission of meaning through the appearance and public performance of the person using it, the media can influence the reinforcement of the symbolism of red lipstick among the audience. Depending on whether it is used for affirmation or criticism, it can be assumed that these associations may also be transferred to the audience. McQuail (2010) suggests that media are powerful tools in the socialization process, shaping individuals' perceptions of reality through the framing of symbols and events. This theoretical framework explores how media messages are crafted, disseminated, and received, considering the active role of the audience in interpreting, and reshaping these messages. This approach is vital for understanding how the representations of red lipstick in media are communicated in relation to the concept of media framing, as discussed by Entman (1993). Communication in the media takes place within the media frames. Framing involves the selective presentation of events, symbols, or issues, which can significantly influence how they are perceived by audiences. In the case of red lipstick, media might frame it as a symbol of empowerment, sexuality, professionalism, or rebellion, depending on the narrative being constructed. Each framing carries different implications for how gender and identity are perceived and understood by the public. For instance, if red lipstick is consistently depicted as a staple of successful and assertive women in media, audiences may come to associate wearing red lipstick with professional and personal success. This model can be applied to the consumption of media surrounding red lipstick, where different audiences may decode the same media messages in varied ways, potentially reinforcing or challenging their pre-existing beliefs about gender norms.

Lipstick is one of the most used cosmetics, closely associated with female attractiveness and influencing people's perceptions and behaviors. Although wearing red lipstick is mostly associated with women (Carter, 2021), in history, but also in recent times, wearing red lipstick is also associated with men who wear red lipstick. In this context, from a gender perspective, it is important to consider the role of Judith Butler's theory of performativity. Rather than seeing gender as a fixed and natural category, Butler understands it as a dynamic process, an act that is continuously repeated and constructed within social and discursive frameworks (Butler, 1990). Butler distinguishes performativity from performance. Performance implies the existence of a subject who performs an act, while performativity denies the existence of a subject before the act itself (Salih, 2002, p. 45). One way to understand the performativity of gender is through the practice of drag. Drag performances parody gender norms and expose them as imitations without originals. Butler (1990) argues that such performances can destabilize heteronormative assumptions, pointing out that all gender identities are, in essence, imitative and constructed. Gender is not something a person "has" or "performs" but is the result of repeated acts that constitute what we recognize as gender identity. In this context, this paper discusses whether the use of red lipstick in today's media texts is a tool for the self-presentation of femininity, cis women and trans women or if it is used by men as a tool within celebrity discourse or popular culture to (de)construct the gender concept. Considering this, the use of red lipstick could be considered a (self)-presentation tool to construct or deconstruct gender identity through continuously repeated use, thereby constructing meaning within social and discursive frames in media texts. Utilizing Butler's framework, the paper explores how wearing red lipstick can be a deliberate act of identity construction, where individuals may use the boldness of the color to assert confidence, professionalism, or femininity.

Kandiyoti (1988) argues that women strategize within a set of concrete constraints that reveal and define the blueprint of what she calls the patriarchal bargain of any given society (p. 275). Wearing red lipstick could be considered one of such strategies, whereby "a woman conforms to gender-based rules in order to gain benefit or power from the system" (Gurrieri & Drenten, 2019, p. 226). In this context, engaging in beauty rituals could be seen as a strategic move or a form of tacit consent, allowing women to assert control over their lives and consciously enjoy the benefits (Davis, 1995; Dellinger & Williams, 1997, as cited in Gurrieri & Drenten, 2019, p. 226). It is in this context the nuanced ways in which red lipstick is utilized to convey and reinforce specific narratives are in focus. Lazar (2006) delved into the portrayal of female empowerment in advertisements, particularly examining representations within the realm of post-feminism, on example of the research centered on "beauty ads" that promote products aimed at enhancing female attractiveness. While these advertisements could be interpreted as objectifying, they endeavor to portray women as embracing their own beauty and exerting influence through their attractiveness, which can be considered a strategy of (self)-presentation.

3. The Communicative Potential of Red Lipstick

Red lipstick has marked gender identity, status, and political affiliation, reflecting changing ideas about social mores, citizenship, femininity, female liberation, and sexuality. Its controversy stems from whom wears it and why, as well as the distinctions and symbolic value it bestows upon its wearer. Despite this, its basic composition has changed very little, with technical adjustments mainly for safety and comfort. Historically, wearing lipstick has served as a barometer for measuring the social climate (Benoit, 2013, pp. 112–113). The history of red lipstick began with the Sumerian Queen Schub-ad around 3,500 BC, a practice adopted by the Sumerian people who continued this tradition (Cohen Ragas & Kozlowski, 1998). Following them, the Assyrians, both women and men, also began using red lipstick. Subsequently, the Egyptians utilized red lipstick primarily to denote social status rather than gender (Corson, 2005). The contextual surrounding red lipstick can be attributed to its bold visual impact, which has often been perceived as challenging social norms and boundaries (Gurrieri & Drenten, 2019). The portrayal of wearing lipstick, especially bold red lipstick, as an assertion of agency finds its roots in the suffragette movement. Initially depicted as unfeminine and radical, suffragettes faced criticism for deviating from traditional gender norms (Chapman & Nuttall, 2011, as cited in Gurrieri & Drenten, 2019, p. 227). In response, suffragettes aimed to counter these perceptions by adopting a more conventionally feminine appearance (Chapman, 2015, as cited in Gurrieri & Drenten, 2019, p. 227). However, as an act of defiance, they also embraced red lipstick, deliberately challenging societal norms that historically stigmatized its use (Schaffer, 2007, as cited in Gurrieri & Drenten, 2019, p. 226). Recognizing the symbolic power of red lipstick, retailers leveraged it as a tool of women's resistance. For example, Selfridges was the first British department store to prominently feature lipstick for sale, specifically targeting suffragettes involved in demonstrations (Blackman, 2018, as cited in Gurrieri & Drenten, 2019, p. 227).

During the Second World War, cosmetics emerged as a tool to challenge traditional notions of masculine authority in wartime settings (Delano, 2000, as cited in Gurrieri & Drenten, 2019, p. 227). In this context, when more women were actively involved in the war effort, lipstick was portrayed in advertisements as a symbol of traditional femininity. However, it also came to represent feminine defiance, resilience, independence, and bravery (Benoit, 2013, p. 118). Lipstick shades were given names like "Fighting Red!," "Patriot Red!," and "Grenadier Red!," reflecting their association with the wartime spirit. Moreover, lipstick served as a morale booster, as seen in the example of munitions factories cited by Gurrieri and Drenten (2019), where "the bathrooms of munitions factories in which women worked were stocked with red lipsticks such as Elizabeth Arden's 'Victory Red' to foster worker efficiency" (Gurrieri & Drenten, 2019, p. 227). After the Second World War, society saw a return to more traditional gender roles. The use of sexuality in advertising became more acceptable, prominent, and eventually conventional. According to Gurrieri and Drenten (2019, p. 226) a notable example is the 1952 Revlon "Fire and Ice" lipstick campaign, which featured model Dorian Leigh in posters and print ads. The ad copy asked, "Are you made for 'Fire and Ice'?" followed by 15 questions designed to gauge whether the potential wearer was suited to the lipstick. Questions included "Have you ever danced with your shoes off?" and "Do you close your eyes when you're kissed?" Answering "yes" to at least eight out of 15 questions indicated that the wearer was indeed "made" for Fire and Ice lipstick. As Karen Ragas and Meg Kozlowski note, Fire and Ice was a "red [lipstick] with real meaning that captured the feminine spirit, the good and bad nature of women." This campaign carefully balanced feminine respectability with a hint of sexual allure, as explained by Benoit (2013).

Second wave feminism, which began in the 1960s focused on a wide range of issues including workplace equality, reproductive rights, and the deconstruction of traditional gender roles. For Betty Friedan, author of The Feminine Mystique in 1963, feminism appeared to have lost its momentum. Her work, which identified the pervasive discontent among women confined to domestic roles, analyzed the "problem that has no name," which served as a catalyst for a new wave of feminist thought. The relationship between this nascent movement and the earlier "old feminism" of equal rights was intricate, as it extended the fight for equality into broader social, cultural, and personal realms, highlighting the complexities of women's liberation beyond mere legal equality (Friedan, 1963; Thornham, 2006). Second-wave feminists therefore have had a complex relationship also with beauty and red lipstick as symbols of femininity. Their efforts primarily focused on challenging the traditional roles and expectations imposed on women, which included a critical stance on beauty standards perpetuated by patriarchal society. Beauty practices, including the use of red lipstick, were often seen as tools of oppression that reinforced women's roles as objects for the male gaze. Therefore, second-wave feminists aimed to liberate women from these restrictive beauty norms, advocating for a broader definition of femininity that did not rely on external appearance and traditional markers of female attractiveness, so they adopted a "natural," un-made-up look as a form of resistance against gendered beauty norms and consumer culture (Harris, 2004). Post-feminism, since 1990, has been characterized by inclusiveness, empowerment and freedom of choice, within which is the so-called "girlie culture" which considered the reclaiming of feminine symbols like lipstick to be playful and deliberately chosen (Baumgardner & Richards, 2004). From the perspective of the struggle for social changes and a better quality of life for certain social groups, it is important to mention MAC Cosmetics' VIVA GLAM lipstick as an example for exemplifying this dual role, functioning as a beauty product and a tool for social advocacy (Benoit, 2014). Lipstick therefore has significantly influenced social and cultural norms, especially regarding gender and sexuality equality. RuPaul and k.d. lang challenged traditional norms about lipstick use, confronting its regulation as a female-only activity and mocking historical conflicts about gender disguise. MAC's advertising promoted a message of glamour, creativity, and hope about AIDS, encapsulated in VIVA GLAM lipstick. By 1998, the MAC AIDS Fund had raised $16 million (Bittar, 1998, p. 125). Furthermore, an example is one more campaign of MAC's VIVA GLAM lipstick in 2010, featuring notable figures such as Cyndi Lauper and Lady Gaga, who significantly contributed to its impact (Benoit, 2013). In 2010, Lauper and Gaga promoted safe sex practices among young heterosexual women, leveraging their influence to challenge traditional gender norms and encourage responsible behaviors. This demonstrates how consumer technologies like lipstick can impact and reflect broader cultural and social changes. VIVA GLAM effectively used celebrity influence to further its mission, showing the powerful intersection of consumer products, cultural advocacy, and social change (Benoit, 2013). One hundred percent of the profits from VIVA GLAM are donated to the MAC AIDS Fund, supporting organizations worldwide that assist those affected by HIV/AIDS (Benoit, 2013, p. 112). The involvement of influential figures such as Cyndi Lauper and Lady Gaga has highlighted the role of lipstick beyond aesthetics, using it to challenge traditional gender norms and promote responsible behaviors.

In the context of encouraging changes in the discursive practices of non-rushes in a certain period of time, it is important to talk about the communicative potential of the red lipstick as a means of (self)-presentation from the perspective of stage performance. From the perspective of red lipstick performance, celebrities often use this shade as a self-presentation tool and as part of their public image (Benoit, 2013; Turner, 2020). Red lipstick is not only a cosmetic product, but symbolizes boldness, power and self-confidence. This practice is visible through historical and contemporary examples, where public figures used red lipstick to highlight their presence and influence. One of the most prominent examples is Madonna, who used MAC's Russian Red lipstick during her Blond Ambition World Tour in 1990. According to Turner (2020), one of the key moments in the development of the MAC brand took place in 1990 when the pop icon Madonna started using their products. During this period, Madonna was preparing for the Blond Ambition World Tour, which was known for its energetic choreography, extravagant costumes designed by Jean Paul Gaultier, and bold red lipstick. To ensure lipstick that would last throughout the entire performance, Madonna contacted the founders of MAC, Frank Toskan and Frank Angelo. In response to her request, Toskan and Angelo developed an "intense matte red shade" of roses, later known as Russian Red. When Madonna began her tour in the spring of 1990, she wore Russian Red lipstick during all 57 sold-out shows in Asia, North America and Europe. This tour was not only a great success, with a total income of 62.7 million US dollars, but also contributed to the popularity of Russian Red lipstick, which soon became one of MAC's signature products. Madonna's performance with red lipstick significantly contributed to the recognition of the brand, and the shade Russian Red became a symbol of longevity and vividness, which further strengthened MAC's position on the cosmetics market (Turner, 2020). According to Benoit (2013), the use of red lipstick by celebrities not only serves an esthetic purpose, but is also a means of communication, expressing individuality and creating a strong visual identity. These examples clearly show how cosmetic products, such as red lipstick, can play a key role in the performance and public perception of celebrities. RuPaul, a famous drag performer, became the first representative of MAC's VIVA GLAM campaign in 1995. In this role, RuPaul used lipstick as a performance tool, defying traditional gender norms and highlighting the fluidity of gender. His appearance in the campaign, accentuated red lipstick, blonde wig, red bustier and high boots – was provocative and provoked discussion about sexuality and gender identities. Many famous rock stars used make up products, for example, during the 1970s David Bowie used lipstick as part of his glam rock alter-ego Ziggy Stardust. Bowie explored and promoted gender ambiguity through his performance and appearance, using lipstick and other cosmetic products to create unique stage personas that defied societal norms of masculinity at the time. The Cure's lead singer, Robert Smith, is known for his iconic look that includes smudged red lipstick. This look is part of his performative identity on stage, contributing to the band's dark, gothic image and expressing his personal esthetic vision (Benoit, 2013). Lipstick performance is a powerful concept that shows how lipstick can be used as a means of expressing identity, defying social norms and communicating important social messages. Examples from contemporary popular culture show that cosmetics can be more than just a means of beautification; it can be a performance tool that carries deep meanings and provokes reflection on gender and sexual issues.

4. Research Methodology

The primary objective of the research is to analyze the communication potential of the symbolic roles of red lipstick within the media texts on the recent Croatian web portal extension of the most-read news portal. The focus is on the news portal because of the broader audience with different interests and life perspectives. The presumption is that the media texts for that kind of audience could reflect more common beauty preferences of the recent era, specifically using the example of widely popular persons and global celebrities. By focusing on this element, the research aims to uncover deeper insights into the strategies of (self-)presentation, the interplay between gender and power, and the broader implications of esthetic choices in public discourse. The specific objectives are structured to explore both the implications and the perceptions of red lipstick as used by public figures across varied media formats. Therefore, the analysis of media texts seeks to understand the strategic use of red lipstick in crafting public and non-public personas, examining how such choices align with or challenge traditional gender roles and expectations. Focusing on the intersections of gender and power, the research questions explore how red lipstick serves as a medium for expressing or contesting power dynamics within media discourse. In accordance with that, the following research questions were asked:

To achieve these aims, the study will address the following key research questions:

- What specific characteristics are associated with red lipstick?
- What thematic elements are commonly highlighted in beauty discourse discussions around red lipstick?
- How do different contexts provide unique insights into the significance of red lipstick in media and public discourse?
- How does the symbolism of red lipstick challenge or reinforce traditional beauty standards?

The data collection for this study involves a curated selection of media texts that prominently feature red lipstick within their narrative or imagery. The selection criteria are twofold: firstly, the media texts must be publicly accessible and influential in shaping public discourse, such as feature articles in major magazines, broadcasts from significant television events, or posts from influential social media accounts. Secondly, these texts must explicitly mention or visually emphasize red lipstick in a context that is relevant to public presentation and identity. According to the results of measurements of portal attendance, available on the Gemius Audience Report website (2024) are portals vecernji.hr and jutarnji.hr. The research covers a period of six months, from May to October 2023, therefore, it is a period in which the readership of articles about celebrities grows due to vacations and summer dress habits. The selection of texts was made using the web application Retriever TakeLab (https://retriever.takelab.fer.hr) and by manual search according to keywords on articles published in the Jutarnji list (jutarnji.hr, including the portal gloria.hr and sportski.jutarnji.hr, which are connected to the portal jutarnji.hr and vecernji.hr). The unit of analysis is one text on the portal, together with the title, subtitle and photo.

Within the research, a qualitative content analysis methodology is used to explore how red lipstick is depicted and discussed in media texts. This approach allows for a detailed examination of the themes, meanings, and narratives associated with red lipstick within analyzed media texts. The process begins with the systematic coding of texts where red lipstick is mentioned or prominently featured. Coding helps identify patterns and recurrent themes that provide insights into the symbolic meanings of red lipstick in different contexts. Once the coding is completed, thematic analysis is conducted to delve deeper into the identified themes. This involves interpreting the significance of red lipstick in various narratives and understanding how it contributes to the construction of identities and social roles. By contextualizing the use of red lipstick, the analysis can uncover how it is used strategically to convey complex messages about identity and status. The qualitative content analysis approach provides a nuanced understanding of the multifaceted representations of red lipstick in media. It reveals the enduring symbolic power of red lipstick and its capacity to influence perceptions and communicate non-verbally. Each context offers unique insights into how red lipstick is leveraged to shape narratives and reinforce or challenge societal norms. Therefore, qualitative content analysis allows for a comprehensive examination of the themes and narratives that surround red lipstick, providing valuable insights into its role in contemporary media discourse.

The first level of analysis is extracting titles and subtitles. Then a linguistic analysis of the text and a manual analysis of the obtained data is carried out. Therefore, the linguistic and topic analysis is three-dimensional, which includes identifying the use of lexemes, thematic context, and discursive interpretation. Data analysis in this study follows a structured process of coding and thematic identification based on the principles of qualitative text analysis. Initially, texts are coded for instances where red lipstick is mentioned or prominently featured. These instances are categorized according to the nature of the mention – whether it is visual, textual, or both – and the associated themes, such as power, gender, rebellion, or professionalism. Following the initial coding, a thematic analysis is conducted to identify recurring patterns or narratives within the data. This involves examining the contexts in which red lipstick appears, the attributes associated with it, and how these elements contribute to the construction of gender identities and power relations in the media. Special attention is given to how visuals and language are used around these themes, examining metaphors, descriptors, and narrative structures. The final step involves an interpretation of these themes, linking them back to the theoretical framework established in the literature review. This analysis not only reveals the dominant discourses surrounding red lipstick but also highlights potential areas of resistance or counter-discourse where traditional norms are challenged or subverted.

This content analysis aims to provide nuanced insights into the symbolic significance of red lipstick in contemporary media beauty discourse. To offer insights into recent discursive practices regarding the topic, the results of the qualitative content analysis are used to interpret the research results in relation to critical discourse analysis according to Jäger (Jäger & Zimmermann, 2019). The aim of discourse analysis according to Jäger is ultimately to "analyze entire strands of discourse (and/or interconnections of several strands of discourse) historically and in relation to the present" (Jäger, 1999, p. 171). In this context, qualitative content analysis provides data on the discourse about the use of red lipstick in synergy with celebrities and influential persons, as well as other topics in texts from 2023, giving insights into part of the current beauty discourse. The results are therefore symptomatic and valid only for the analyzed media texts. Accordingly, the emphasis here is solely on the thematic analysis, which is potentially part of the analysis of social discourse as a whole and the dispositive analysis. During this initial content analysis, it should become clear which topics and subtopics recur (cf. Jäger, 1999, p. 192).

5. Findings

Media text analysis in this work was three-dimensional. The first level of research relates to the identification of individual segments of the topic within the discourse on beauty and appearance. Discourse on appearance and beauty is realized at the text level in relation to the connection between the theme and subtopic, discourse strategy and language tactics. In the context of language strategies, information, criticism, positive and/or negative evaluation of part of the topic, informing, criticizing, highlighting and/or evaluating the perspective of the use of red lipstick within the discourse on beauty and appearance are identified. In the context of discourse strategies, the context of presentation and/or self-presentation is identified in relation to the use of red lipstick and highlighting the inner or external values of a person with a special focus on appearance and social role.

The analysis included a total of 25 articles from the portal vecernji.hr and 19 articles from the portal jutarnji.hr. The articles were published during 2023, and the criterion for their selection was that the phrase red lipstick was mentioned in the text of the article as a tool of non-verbal communication for the purpose of (self-) presentation, implicit or explicit. It is important to point out here that the analysis and interpretation refers only to the analyzed articles and as such is symptomatic and cannot be considered as general conclusions for the general beauty discourse. From the protagonist's perspective, the articles can be divided into articles dealing with a communication situation with a famous persons from Croatia (11 different persons and/or teams), then articles in which the topic is non-verbal communication of globally famous persons (a total of nine different persons) and texts that highlight the commodification of the body, either through an exhibition or through a speech about sexuality (five texts in total). As far as the thematic representation is concerned, the texts deal with the protagonist's public performance at music, sports, fashion, social and film events, the protagonist's activities in his free time, and finally with topics related to the body, its presentation, and the potential of the body to achieve attractiveness, sexuality and pleasure.

The cultural and psychological implications of red lipstick, characterized by its long-standing associations with power, femininity, and sensuality, present a compelling subject for scholarly analysis within media studies. This part will examine these characteristics from a media perspective, drawing on an analysis of articles from various online portals to elucidate how red lipstick is portrayed and perceived in contemporary society. As the communication potential is the focus of the analysis, the interpretation does not separate Croatian celebrities from global celebrities but rather analyzes the context of use from the perspective of thematic and communication aspects. In the analyzed texts with famous people, red lipstick is associated with elegance and expressiveness and standing out, in this context red lipstick is noted for making her stand out and adding to her bold appearance (vecernji.hr, 2023a, b). Red lipstick is associated with elegance and expressiveness. Ana Gruica, for example, wears red lipstick, which emphasizes her glamorous and sophisticated appearance, and is cited in the text as a key addition to her image (G.L., 2023a). In all analyzed texts in which the protagonists are women, and the theme is a festive event such as an award ceremony and others, red lipstick is emphasized as a key accessory that emphasizes elegance and sophisticated appearance (B.L., 2023b; G.L., 2023a; jutarnji.hr, 2023a; S.A., 2023; Zavišić, 2023a, b).

In one text, red lipstick is emphasized as a key image of a politician, along with black eyeliner, red lipstick and a Depeche Mode tattoo. The article discusses Isabel Díaz Ayuso, the president of the Community of Madrid, known for her provocative political stance and actions. Ayuso, described as a controversial figure, has aggressively opposed leftist policies and embraced low-tax, business-friendly initiatives. Her bold style includes the use of red lipstick, which is part of her recognizable image (G.L., 2023b). The role of the red lipstick as a symbol of expressiveness and rebelliousness was expressed in an article about Dolly Parton (Kučković, 2023).

In texts whose subject is the female body and sexuality, whether it is about exhibitions on that subject or about the body and sexuality in general, red lipstick is used as a textual symbol in the context of emphasizing femininity, resistance and female identity, (Delimar, 2023; Hina, 2023), as a symbol of passion and sensuality (vecernji.hr, 2023l), but also as an homage to the past in the 1970s of the 20th century, when red lipstick was a symbol of protest (Šćavina, 2023). In the analyzed media texts, red lipstick is also used in the context of the performance of the Croatian group Let 3 at Eurosnog 2023. In this context, red lipstick is highlighted as a non-verbal tool of performance, extravagance and daring. Let 3 uses red lipstick to emphasize its provocative stage performance, which is highlighted in the lyrics (G.L., 2023b). The article discusses Let 3's performance at Dora 2023, where they won with their song "Mama ŠČ!" The band's entrance on a tractor, eccentric costumes, and theatrical stage presence, including the use of red lipstick, were highlighted as part of their memorable and provocative performance (Milla, 2023; vecernji.hr, 2023g, h).

The thematic elements commonly highlighted in beauty discourse discussions around red lipstick offer rich insights into societal values, gender norms, and individual identity. Therefore, the analysis included the question of how red lipstick is framed in beauty discourse to uncover recurring themes and narratives that shape the public perception of red lipstick, based on analyzed articles. The analyzed texts contextualize the use of red lipstick within the discourse on beauty that includes sophistication and style and the use of red lipstick to emphasize one's modern and glamorous appearance (Dragaš, 2023; G.L., 2023a; vecernji.hr, 2023o) creativity and individuality such as eccentricity and subversiveness in artistic expression (Dragaš, 2023; vecernji.hr, 2023c), elements of costume parties and expressive style (vecernji.hr, 2023c), self-confidence and attractiveness (G.L., 2023b; Prerad, 2023), glamor and belonging to major events (B.L., 2023a, b; Jurić, 2023; S.A., 2023; vecernji.hr, 2023j), expressiveness and intimacy as elements of femininity (Delimar, 2023), resistance and emphasis on identity (Hina, 2023), a tool of sexuality (Šćavina, 2023).

A contextual analysis of the significance of the red lipstick in media discourse reveals a communication platform for the (self) presentation of the cultural, social and psychological meanings attributed to this cult cosmetics. The analysis points to its contextual meaning in terms of the nuanced ways in which red lipstick is used to convey and strengthen beauty narratives. In the context of dance and carnival performances, red lipstick symbolizes elegance and glamour in the context of joy and spreading emotions (D.J., 2023; vecernji.hr, 2023b). Furthermore, in the context of various official and festive public appearances and social events, red lipstick symbolizes elegance and self-confidence (B.L., 2023a, b; G.L., 2023b, c; Jurić, 2023; S.A., 2023; Zavišić, 2023a). In the context of stage performances, red lipstick can symbolize rebelliousness and extremeness and criticism of social norms, which is, for example, in line with the performative style of Let 3 at the 2023 Eurovision Song Contest (jutarnji.hr, 2023a; vecernji.hr, 2023b). As a means of expressing one's identity within, for example, political campaigns and public appearances as a politician, red lipstick can symbolize self-confidence and determination (G.L., 2023b; Prerad, 2023). In the context of artistic expression, red lipstick can symbolize intense emotions and sensuality (Delimar, 2023). In the context of personal stories and biographies, red lipstick symbolizes resistance to traditional norms and the expression of individuality (Kučković, 2023).

Red lipstick plays a role in creating a festive and optimistic look, symbolizing joy and confidence. In the context of an article on the topic of celebration, red lipstick contributes to the festive atmosphere of the New Year celebration (jutarnji.hr, 2023b). Media representations of red lipstick shape perceptions of beauty and style. The appearance of actresses, singers, and models commented on in the text emphasizing the use of red lipstick emphasizes the status and influence of that person in the light of the event at which she appears, from the perspective of boldness, strikingness, elegance and beauty (M.P., 2023; vecernji.hr, 2023u, v; Zavišić, 2023b). Red lipstick can challenge or reinforce traditional beauty standards through its historical association with femininity and attractiveness (Delimar, 2023), importance of expressiveness and resilience in art (vecernji.hr, 2023), reinforcing woman's defiant and strong persona (G.L., 2023a) about what is usual and acceptable, by enhancing the memorable performance and provocative and unconventional image (vecernji.hr, 2023g, i). In such performative contexts, it emphasized both the glamorous and rebellious aspects of the performance (vecernji.hr, 2023f).

6. Conclusion

The analysis highlights instances where public figures have used red lipstick during significant public appearances to project confidence and assert authority, illustrating its role in non-verbal communication strategies. Also, dynamic platform for the presentation of red lipstick is presented. Media texts frequently explore how celebrities use red lipstick as a tool for assertive self-presentation, enhancing their public image by emphasizing their confidence and allure. Defensive uses of red lipstick may involve celebrities addressing criticisms or controversies by altering their appearance to evoke a sense of sincerity or remorse. Conversely, offensive strategies might involve the use of red lipstick to draw attention away from personal faults and redirect it toward external factors or other individuals. Through thematic analysis, it is evident that beauty discourse discussions around red lipstick frequently intersect with discussions of body positivity and feminist ideals, suggesting its role as a symbol of self-expression and rebellion against traditional beauty standards.

The connection between red lipstick, gender representation, and power dynamics forms a critical axis of analysis in this study. Red lipstick serves as a potent symbol through which notions of femininity, power, and agency are negotiated and expressed in the media. The analysis identifies a recurring theme where red lipstick is used by women as a form of self-assertion and empowerment in male-dominated settings. This usage acts as a counterpoint to traditional gender norms that often dictate more subdued forms of female but also male presentation. Red lipstick in such contexts challenges these norms and is sometimes portrayed as a defiance against patriarchal expectations, and therefore as a communication tool for power connotation. In terms of power dynamics, red lipstick symbolizes a reclaiming of the body and by extension, personal agency. Key findings indicate therefore that red lipstick functions not merely as a cosmetic item but as a powerful communication tool that can signify authority, rebellion, sensuality, and professionalism. In conclusion, the discussion of red lipstick's roles in media contexts opens up broader considerations of how gender and power are constructed, challenged, and maintained in contemporary society. It invites ongoing dialog and research into the ways visual and material culture contribute to the shaping of social identities and power relations.

References

Bartky, S. L. (1990). *Femininity and domination: Studies in the phenomenology of oppression*. Psychology Press.

Baumgardner, J., & Richards, A. (2004). Feminism and femininity: Or how we learned to stop worrying and love the thong. In A. Harris (Ed.), *All about the girl: Culture, power, and identity* (pp. 59–67). Psychology Press.

Benoit, A. (2013). 'From our lips:' Lipstick as consumer technology and the MAC VIVA GLAM advertising campaigns. *Scientia Canadensis*, *36*(1), 111–132.

Benoit, A. (2014). "An advertising world gone completely haywire": MAC VIVA GLAM. *Advertising & Society Review*, *15*(1). https://doi.org/10.1353/asr.2014.0007

Bittar, C. (1998). MAC's Feeney to spread the word. *Brandweek*, *39*(36), 41.

Blackman, C. (2018). How the suffragettes used fashion to further their cause. *Stylist*. https://www.stylist.co.uk/fashion/suffragette-movement-fashion-clothes-what-did-the-suffragettes-wear/188043

Borčić, N. (2023). *Vrag je u detalju. Imidž i diskurs u politici.* TIM Press.
Butler, J. (1990). *Gender trouble: Feminism and the subversion of identity.* Routledge.
Carter, I. C. (2021). *The red menace. How lipstick changed the face of American history.* Prometheus Books.
Chapman, J. (2015). The argument of the broken pane. *Media History, 21*(3), 238–251.
Cohen Ragas, M., & Kozlowski, K. (1998). *Read my lips: A cultural history of lipstick.* Chronicle Books.
Corson, R. (2005). *Fashions in makeup from ancient to modern times* (Revised ed.). Peter Owen Publishers.
Davis, K. (1995). *Reshaping the female body: The dilemma of cosmetic surgery.* Routledge.
Delano, P. D. (2000). Making up for war: Sexuality and citizenship in wartime culture. *Feminist Studies, 26*(1), 33–68.
Dellinger, K., & Williams, C. L. (1997). Makeup at work: Negotiating appearance rules in the workplace. *Gender & Society, 11*(2), 151–177.
Entman, R. M. (1993). Framing: Toward clarification of a fractured paradigm. *Journal of Communication, 43*(4), 51–58.
Friedan, B. (1963). *The feminine mystique.* W.W. Norton & Company.
Geiger Zeman, M., & Zeman, Z. (2015). Potrošački snovi chic djevojaka: Rodno lice konzumerizma. *Revija za Sociologiju, 52*(2), 105–137. https://doi.org/10.15176/vol52no206
Gemius. (2024). Gemius audience report: Najčitaniji portali u Hrvatskoj. https://e-public.gemius.com/hr/rankings/17666/748117
Glovacki-Bernardi, Z. (2008). *Kad student zatrudni... rasprava o rodnoj perspektivi u jeziku.* Alfa.
Gurrieri, L., & Drenten, J. (2019). The feminist politics of choice: Lipstick as a marketplace icon. *Consumption Markets & Culture, 24*(3), 225-240. https://doi.org/10.1080/10253866.2019.1670649
Hall, S. (1980). Encoding/Decoding. In S. Hall, D. Hobson, A. Lowe, & P. Wills (Eds.), *Culture, media, language: Working papers in cultural studies, 1972-79* (pp. 128–138). Routledge.
Harris, A. (2004). *All about the girl: Culture, power, and identity.* Routledge.
Humm, M. (1992). *Feminisms: A reader.* Routledge.
Hurd Clarke, L., & Bundon, A. (2009). From 'the thing to do' to 'defying the ravages of age': Older women reflect on the use of lipstick. *Journal of Women & Aging, 21*(3), 198–212.
Jäger, S. (1999). *Kritische Diskursanalyse: Eine Einführung.* DISS.
Jäger, S., & Zimmermann, J. (2019). *Lexikon Kritische Diskursanalyse.* UNRAST Verlag.
Jones, G. (2010). *Beauty imagined: A history of the global beauty industry.* Oxford University Press.
Jutarnji.hr. (2023a, November 06). Miss Universe Hrvatske javlja se iz El Salvadora: 'Ovo je avantura života!'. *Jutarnji.hr.* https://www.jutarnji.hr/scena/domace-zvijezde/miss-hrvatske-javlja-se-iz-el-salvadora-ovo-je-avantura-zivota-15391606
Kandiyoti, D. (1988). Bargaining with patriarchy. *Gender & Society, 2*(3), 274–290.
Lazar, M. M. (2006). "Discover the power of femininity!" analyzing global "power femininity" in local advertising. *Feminist Media Studies, 6*(4), 505–517.

McQuail, D. (2010). *McQuail's mass communication theory*. SAGE Publications Ltd.

Peiss, K. (2001). *Hope in a jar: The making of America's beauty culture*. University of Pennsylvania Press.

Rüdiger, M., & Schütz, A. (2016). Selbstdarstellung. In H.-W. Bierhoff & D. Frey (Eds.), *Enzyklopädie der Psychologie: Selbst und soziale Kognition, Sozialpsychologie* (pp. 191–211). Hogrefe.

Salih, S. (2002). *Judith Butler*. Routledge.

Schaffer, S. E. (2007). Reading our lips: The history of lipstick regulation in western seats of power. *Food and Drug Law Journal, 1*, 165–226.

Scott, L. M. (2005). *Fresh lipstick: Redressing fashion and feminism*. Palgrave Macmillan.

Thornham, S. (2006). Second wave feminism. In S. Gamble (Ed.), *The Routledge companion to feminism and postfeminism* (pp. 25–35). Routledge Taylor & Francis Group.

Turner, C. (2020). The story of: Madonna and MAC's legendary 'Russian Red' lipstick. *29Secrets*. https://29secrets.com/beauty/the-story-of-madonna-and-macs-legendary-russian-red-lipstick/

Wu, Y.-A., Gong, S.-M., & Lee, W.-Y. (2024). A study on the impressions induced by lipstick colors. *Color Research and Application, 49*(1), 1–10. https://doi.org/10.1002/col.22922

Appendix

Internet Sources of Analyzed Articles

B.L. (2023a, September 26). Ovako seksi je već dugo nismo vidjeli! Victoria Beckham iznenadila izazovnim izdanjem i najavila veliku novost. *Jutarnji.hr*. https://www.jutarnji.hr/scena/strane-zvijezde/ovako-seksi-je-vec-dugo-nismo-vidjeli-victoria-beckham-iznenadila-izazovnim-izdanjem-i-najavila-veliku-novost-15378176

B.L. (2023b, March 22). Selena Gomez iznenadila javnost: Svi su zastali u šoku kad je osvanula na ulici u predivnoj vjenčanici. *Jutarnji.hr*. https://www.jutarnji.hr/scena/strane-zvijezde/selena-gomez-iznenadila-javnost-svi-su-zastali-u-soku-kad-je-osvanula-na-ulici-u-predivnoj-vjencanici-15318230

Brico, P. (2023, July 19). Moglo bi vas iznenaditi: 6 znanstveno dokazanih stvari koje žene čine privlačnijima muškarcima!. *Vecernji.hr*. https://www.vecernji.hr/lifestyle/moglo-bi-vas-iznenaditi-6-znanstveno-dokazanih-stvari-koje-zene-cine-privlacniji ma-muskarcima-1696313

Delimar, V. (2023, April 04). Napravila sam kolaž od 12 fotografija koje pokazuju početak orgazma. *Jutarnji.hr*. https://www.jutarnji.hr/kultura/art/napravila-sam-kolaz-od-12-fotografija-koje-pokazuju-pocetak-orgazma-15322396

D.J. (2023, October 27). Indira Levak zabljesnula u Beogradu: 'Konačno damski i otmjeno, bez perja i kostima'. *Jutarnji.hr*. https://www.jutarnji.hr/scena/domace-zvijezde/indira-levak-zabljesnula-u-beogradu-konacno-damski-i-otmjeno-bez-perja-i-kostima-15388440

Dragaš, A. (2023, February 12). Napokon smo svi skupa imali mu*a. Na Eurosong šaljemo staljinovske brkajlije, ali našminkane crvenim ružem. *Jutarnji.hr*. https://www.jutarnji.hr/scena/domace-zvijezde/napokon-smo-svi-skupa-imali-mu-a-na-eurosong-saljemo-staljinovske-brkajlije-ali-nasminkane-crvenim-ruzem-15305026

G.L. (2023a, March 31). Dvoboj dekoltea bujnih plavuša: Christina i Jennifer u modnom okršaju 'prsa o prsa', koja vam je bolja? *Jutarnji.hr*. https://www.jutarnji.hr/scena/strane-zvijezde/dvoboj-dekoltea-bujnih-plavusa-christina-i-jennifer-u-modnom-okrsaju-prsa-o-prsa-koja-vam-je-bolja-15321248

G.L. (2023b, February 20). Ana Gruica pohvalila se jako seksi izdanjem, 'vatrice' se samo nižu: 'Zvijeri moja zgodna!'. *Jutarnji.hr*. https://www.jutarnji.hr/scena/domace-zvijezde/ana-gruica-pohvalila-se-jako-seksi-izdanjem-vatrice-se-samo-nizu-zvijeri-moja-zgodna-15307748

G.L.. (2023c, March 01). Tetovirala se, 'skinula' privatnog detektiva, objavila rat ljevici i na putu je da učini nešto još neviđeno u Madridu. *Jutarnji.hr*. https://www.jutarnji.hr/vijesti/svijet/tetovirala-se-skinula-privatnog-detektiva-objavila-rat-ljevici-i-na-putu-je-da-ucini-nesto-jos-nevideno-u-madridu-15310815

Hina. (2023, May 16). Moje tijelo je moja kuća: Umjetnošću protiv patrijarhata. *Vecernji.hr*. https://www.vecernji.hr/kultura/moje-tijelo-je-moja-kuca-umjetnoscu-protiv-patrijarhata-1680499

Jurić, D. (2023, March 13). Phoebe zaslijepila dekolteom, Cara prošetala vatrene obline, a svi pričaju o haljini Florence Pugh. *Jutarnji.hr*. https://www.jutarnji.hr/scena/strane-zvijezde/phoebe-zaslijepila-dekolteom-cara-prosetala-vatrene-obline-a-svi-pricaju-o-haljini-florence-pugh-15314912

Jutarnji.hr. (2023b, December 26). Kultni ispraćaj Stare i doček Nove godine u podne u Fužinama. *Jutarnji.hr*. https://zivim.jutarnji.hr/zivim/rastem/kultni-ispracaj-stare-i-docek-nove-godine-u-podne-u-fuzinama-15408977

Kučković, Đ. (2023, October 11). Dolly Parton: 'Moj djed propovjednik tukao me jer sam izgledala kao "lokalna raspuštenica". Nisam se pokolebala'. *Jutarnji.hr*. https://www.jutarnji.hr/scena/strane-zvijezde/dolly-parton-moj-djed-propovjednik-tukao-me-jer-sam-izgledala-kao-lokalna-raspustenica-nisam-se-pokolebala-15383222

Milla, S. (2023, February 12). Članovi Leta 3 objasnili naziv svoje pjesme i otkrili što znači 'ŠČ. *Vecernji.hr*. https://www.vecernji.hr/showbiz/let-3-objasnili-naziv-svoje-pjesme-i-otkrili-sto-znaci-sc-1656498

M.P.. (2023, November 14). Tihana Lazović privlačila poglede na svjetskoj premijeri: Čipkasti grudnjak nije prošao nezamijećeno. *Jutarnji.hr*. https://www.jutarnji.hr/scena/domace-zvijezde/tihana-lazovic-privlacila-poglede-na-svjetskoj-premijeri-cipkasti-grudnjak-nije-prosao-nezamijeceno-15394160

Premec, P. (2023, August 03). Žene otkrile u kojoj dobi najviše uživaju u seksu: 'Tek tada moj je seksualni život bio na vrhuncu…'. *Jutarnji.hr*. https://www.jutarnji.hr/life/seks-i-veze/zene-otkrile-u-kojoj-dobi-najvise-uzivaju-u-seksu-tek-tada-moj-je-seksualni-zivot-bio-na-vrhuncu-15361854

Prerad, D. (2023, December 09). Mutna granica osobnog i javnog života: Sanna Marin u novom ruhu. *Vecernji.hr*. https://www.vecernji.hr/vijesti/mutna-granica-osobnog-i-javnog-zivota-sanna-marin-u-novom-ruhu-1729897

S.A.. (2023, May 15). Svi su se okretali za slavnim parom na crvenom tepihu BAFTA-e: 'On nikad nije bio tako uzrujan!'. *Jutarnji.hr*. https://www.jutarnji.hr/

scena/strane-zvijezde/svi-su-se-okretali-za-slavnim-parom-na-crvenom-tepihu-bafta-e-on-nikad-nije-bio-tako-uzrujan-15335837

Slobodnadalmacija.hr. (2023, February 22). Maju Šuput ove sezone nećemo gledati u 'Plesu sa zvijezdama', zna se i razlog. *Jutarnji.hr*. https://www.jutarnji.hr/scena/domace-zvijezde/maju-suput-ove-sezone-necemo-gledati-u-plesu-sa-zvijezdama-zna-se-i-razlog-15308551

Šćavina, K. (2023, July 04). Usne koje slave žensku energiju i strast. *Jutarnji.hr*. https://www.jutarnji.hr/domidizajn/inspiracije/usne-koje-slave-zensku-energiju-i-strast-15351899

Vecernji.hr. (2023a, January 02). Ivana Knoll pokazala kako se u Miamiju zabavljala u društvu slavnog glumca. *Vecernji.hr*. https://www.vecernji.hr/showbiz/ivana-knoll-pokazala-kako-se-u-miamiju-zabavljala-u-drustvu-slavnog-glumca-1646265

Vecernji.hr. (2023b, February 11). Let 3 se istaknuo svojim dolaskom na Doru u traktoru, ali i scenskim nastupom. *Vecernji.hr*. https://www.vecernji.hr/showbiz/let-3-se-istaknuo-svojim-dolaskom-na-doru-u-traktoru-ali-i-scenskim-nastupom-1656460

Vecernji.hr. (2023c, February 11). Maja Šuput u kostimu junakinje Supergirl nastupila je na otvorenju Samoborskog fašnika. *Vecernji.hr*. https://www.vecernji.hr/showbiz/maja-suput-u-kostimu-junakinje-supergirl-nastupila-je-na-otvorenju-samoborskog-fasnika-1656314

Vecernji.hr. (2023d, February 12). ANKETA Što mislite o pobjedničkoj pjesmi? Nastup Leta 3 nikog nije ostavio ravnodušnim. *Vecernji.hr*. https://www.vecernji.hr/showbiz/anketa-sto-mislite-o-pobjednickoj-pjesmi-nastup-leta-3-nikog-nije-ostavio-ravnodusnim-1656491

Vecernji.hr. (2023e, February 12). Gledatelji imaju podijeljena mišljenja o Letu 3: Dio želi diskvalifikaciju, drugi očekuju pobjedu. *Vecernji.hr*. https://www.vecernji.hr/showbiz/gledatelji-imaju-podijeljena-misljenja-o-pobjedniku-dio-zeli-diskvalifi kaciju-drugi-ocekuju-pobjedu-1656489

Vecernji.hr. (2023f, February 12). Tko je pridruženi član Leta 3: Riječki glazbenik i ranije je surađivao s ovim rock bendom. *Vecernji.hr*. https://www.vecernji.hr/showbiz/tko-je-pridruzeni-clan-leta-3-rijecki-glazbenik-i-ranije-je-suradivao-s-ovim-rock-bendom-1656509

Vecernji.hr. (2023g, February 13). Nastup Leta 3 na Dori na YouTubeu u jednom danu pregledan više od 1,5 milijuna puta. *Vecernji.hr.*. https://www.vecernji.hr/showbiz/nastup-leta-3-na-dori-na-youtubeu-u-jednom-danu-pregledan-vise-od-15-milijuna-puta-1656739

Vecernji.hr. (2023h, February 14). Nakon pobjede na Dori Hrvatska se penje na kladionicama, pomaknuli smo se za 11 mjesta. *Vecernji.hr*. https://www.vecernji.hr/showbiz/nakon-pobjede-na-dori-hrvatska-se-penje-na-kladionicama-pomaknuli-smo-se-za-11-mjesta-1657018

Vecernji.hr. (2023i, February 24). Ukrajina više nije na prvom mjestu na kladionicama, sada je to Švedska. *Vecernji.hr*. https://www.vecernji.hr/showbiz/ukrajina-vise-nije-na-prvom-mjestu-na-kladionicama-sada-je-to-svedska-1659557

Vecernji.hr. (2023j, March 11). Prva predstavnica Jugoslavije na Euroviziji prijavila se slučajno, a tamo je ostala i bez cipela i torbe. *Vecernji.hr*. https://www.vecernji.hr/showbiz/prva-predstavnica-jugoslavije-na-euroviziji-prijavila-se-slucajno-a-tamo-je-ostala-i-bez-cipela-i-torbe-1663390

Vecernji.hr. (2023k, May 12). Naša pjevačica otvorila sezonu kupanja i pokazala bujne obline. 'Pa ŠČa bude'. *Vecernji.hr*. https://www.vecernji.hr/showbiz/nasa-pjevacica-otvorila-sezonu-kupanja-i-pokazala-bujne-obline-pa-sca-bude-1679628

Vecernji.hr. (2023l, June 11). Ivana Knoll u minijaturnoj opravici pratila finale Lige prvaka, a imala je i opasnu konkurenciju. *Vecernji.hr*. https://www.vecernji.hr/showbiz/ivana-knoll-u-minijaturnoj-opravici-pratila-finale-lige-prvaka-a-imala-je-i-opasnu-konkurenciju-1686848

Vecernji.hr. (2023m, August 26). Maja Šuput pokazala haljinu u kojoj je nastupila, pratiteljica: 'Bez ovoga je čisto dovoljno'. *Vecernji.hr*. https://www.vecernji.hr/showbiz/maja-suput-pokazala-haljinu-u-kojoj-je-nastupila-pratiteljica-bez-ovoga-je-cisto-dovoljno-1704892

Vecernji.hr. (2023n, August 29). Maja Šuput podijelila snimku: 'Ovo je san svakog frajera. Bloom živi život'. *Vecernji.hr*. https://www.vecernji.hr/showbiz/maja-suput-podijelila-snimku-ovo-je-san-svakog-frajera-bloom-zivi-zivot-1705512

Vecernji.hr. (2023o, September 01). Maja Šuput pozirala u haljini s dubokim dekolteom: 'Prije povratka u realnost'. *Vecernji.hr*. https://www.vecernji.hr/showbiz/maja-suput-pozirala-u-haljini-s-dubokim-dekolteom-prije-povratka-u-realnost-1706315

Vecernji.hr. (2023p, September 09). Uzvanik na svadbi svojim je potezom Maju Šuput ostavio bez teksta: 'Kad pomislim da sam sve vidjela'. *Vecernji.hr*. https://www.vecernji.hr/showbiz/uzvanik-na-svadbi-svojim-je-potezom-maju-suput-ostavio-bez-teksta-kad-pomislim-da-sam-sve-vidjela-1708169

Vecernji.hr. (2023r, September 10). Šuput pokazala kakva je atmosfera među njezinim članovima benda nakon tri neprospavane noći. *Vecernji.hr*. https://www.vecernji.hr/showbiz/suput-pokazala-kakva-je-atmosfera-medu-njezinim-clanovima-benda-nakon-tri-neprospavane-noci-1708319

Vecernji.hr. (2023s, October 21). Ana Rucner istaknula vitku figuru u topiću, a pozornost privukla i jednom promjenom: 'Predobro ti stoji'. *Vecernji.hr*. https://www.vecernji.hr/showbiz/ana-rucner-istaknula-vitku-figuru-u-topicu-a-pozornost-privukla-i-jednom-promjenom-predobro-ti-stoji-1718242

Vecernji.hr. (2023t, October 27). Indira Levak oduševila damskim outfitom: 'Konačno otmjeno, bez perja i kostima'. *Vecernji.hr*. https://www.vecernji.hr/showbiz/indira-levak-odusevila-damskim-outfitom-konacno-otmjeno-bez-perja-i-kostima-1719820

Vecernji.hr. (2023u, November 30). Zgodna Severina odjenula elegantnu kombinaciju: Chanel mokasinke savršeno joj pristaju. *Vecernji.hr*. https://www.vecernji.hr/showbiz/zgodna-severina-odjenula-elegantnu-kombinaciju-chanel-mokasinke-savrseno-joj-pristaju-1728266

Vecernji.hr. (2023v, December 15). Fani Stipković istaknula liniju u pripijenom odijelu nakon poroda: 'Mama gori'. *Vecernji.hr*. https://www.vecernji.hr/showbiz/fani-stipkovic-istaknula-liniju-u-pripijenom-odijelu-nakon-poroda-mama-gori-1731767

Zavišić, S. (2023a, October 12). Taylor Swift prošetala crvenim tepihom u zapanjujućoj haljini vrijednoj oko 12.000 dolara. *Jutarnji.hr*. https://www.jutarnji.hr/scena/strane-zvijezde/taylor-swift-prosetala-crvenim-tepihom-u-zapanjujucoj-haljini-vrijednoj-oko-12-000-dolara-15383728

Zavišić, S. (2023b, October 20). Taylor Swift pustila ruku Travisa Kelcea kako bi uživala u večeri s curama: Bila je tu i Selena Gomez. *Jutarnji.hr*. https://www.jutarnji.hr/scena/strane-zvijezde/taylor-swift-pustila-ruku-travisa-kelcea-kako-bi-uzivala-u-veceri-s-curama-bila-je-tu-i-selena-gomez-15386114

Chapter 9

'We've Got to Take Our Chances': Make-Up as Subversive Practice in Heteronormative Binary DanceSport

Val Meneau

University of Vienna, Austria

Abstract

In June 2021, after 10 years of active participation in the heteronormative competitive DanceSport scene, I came out as non-binary. Having written my dissertation on the barriers that exclude gender non-conforming people in DanceSport, I was acutely aware of the thin ice I was on and agreed to pass as male for the competition season that followed. In parallel, I was exploring my newly found identity in other dance contexts: raving and (queer) clubbing. In this chapter, I discuss my make-up journey as an essential part of my coming out, and the contrasting experiences I have had through it in the (queer) techno/rave scene and the strictly heteronormative Latin DanceSport. Here I emphasise how my makeup journey highlights its potential as both an affirmative and subversive practice. Makeup is not gendered per se, but it is perceived as such and can therefore be used to disrupt the heteronormative gender binary, whether on a personal or political level. In order to answer this question, I draw on autoethnography to discuss both my experiences within and outside of DanceSport between March 2021 and March 2022. I show the potentials of make-up, its functions, roles and meanings within different scenes. This chapter is informed by the dispositive analysis I conducted for my dissertation. Extending the work of Foucault and Butler, it tells of transgressions and constitutive experiences in different scenes, of resistance and subversion, of exclusion and productive power, of internal conflicts and conflicts between micro and macro levels in the DanceSport scene.

Beauty Industry, 183–202

Published under exclusive licence by Emerald Publishing Limited
doi:10.1108/978-1-83608-940-720251030

Keywords: DanceSport; heteronormative gender binary; make-up; queer feminist theory; autoethnography; subversion; non-binary; clubbing; raving

1. Introduction

This chapter paints my make-up journey as an essential part of my coming out as non-binary, and the conflicting and contrasting experiences I have had because of it in two different scenes, the (queer) techno/raving scene and the strictly heteronormative Latin DanceSport scene. DanceSport is the competitive counterpart to ballroom dancing.[1] As a sport, it is particularly appreciated in Europe and North America, where it is performed in competitions with mostly white, middle-class dancers. The experiences I discuss in this chapter mainly took place in Austria.

Make-up in DanceSport is primarily coded as feminine – although male dancers must learn to use foundation and setting powder.[2] Make-up for female dancers is part of a coordinated beauty concept, a Look, that encompasses all elements of aesthetic labour. The aim is to present the couple as unique, distinctive, beautiful, memorable – in short, to sell the couple's dance (Meneau, 2023, chapter 2).

My use of make-up as a person read as male, in contrast, disturbed the neat gender divisions in DanceSport. In this chapter, I show how my journey with make-up highlights its potential as an affirmative, political and subversive practice.[3] I argue that while make-up is not gendered per se, it is perceived as such and can therefore be used to disrupt the heteronormative gender binary.

To do so, I use autoethnography to focus on my experiences both within and outside of DanceSport between March 2021 and March 2022. I take a chronological approach, describing how my make-up journey has evolved from experimentation to appropriation as an affirmative practice, to subversion and political statement. In doing so, I show the potential of make-up, its functions, roles and meanings within the two different scenes.

1.1 Productive Power and the Gender Order

Although primarily based on autoethnography, the chapter is informed by the dispositive analysis I conducted for my dissertation and Foucault's concept of productive power (1977; see also Jäger, 2001, p. 84). He underlined the ways in which subjects are constituted through the effects of power. Power relations precede us and produce the subjects embedded in them (Oksala, 2016, p. 475). This does not mean that individuals are fully determined, but rather that their

[1]DanceSport has two main disciplines, Latin and Standard (also known as Ballroom). Latin consists of five dances: samba, cha-cha-cha, rumba, paso doble, and jive.

[2]More on those contradictions in future publications.

[3]The first part of the title is inspired by the song 'All that glitters' by Kate Earl (2017) – I explain why in the conclusion.

actions are not entirely voluntary. They are constrained, for example by the gender order (Lloyd, 2013, p. 125).

Foucault asserts that all modes of domination, submission, and subjectivation ultimately revolve around obedience (1976, p. 122), because submission to power is 'the means by which individuals are produced as a subject with a particular identity' (Lloyd, 2013, p. 127). In modern societies, people are governed by their inscription into the historically and geographically specific norm. Power operates in our relationship to the norm by shaping our interests, desires, and capacity for critical reflection (Lloyd, 2013, p. 125; see also Oksala, 2016, p. 485; or Hennessy, 2018, p. 147).

Subjects participate because of the compelling character of the dispositive. Power relations are 'tied to powerful sanctions and rewards' (Oksala, 2016, p. 478). Dancers' ability and willingness to submit to the demands of the heteronormative gender binary in DanceSport affects their access to resources, opportunities, and participation. Their inability to do so leaves them with a pervasive sense of inadequacy and shame. This sense of shame is a function of the internalisation of patriarchal heteronormative norms and the feeling of not being able to measure up to them (Oksala, 2016, p. 478).

However, participating in the microphysics of power can bring important rewards to dancers, such as a socially recognised identity and the right to participate in competitions or the professional sphere (Oksala, 2016, p. 478). Adopting and internalising disciplinary practices is preferable to losing a socially recognised identity and the right to participate that comes with it.

The demands of the heteronormative gender binary in DanceSport require dancers to perform according to one of the two binary genders (Meneau, 2023). The DanceSport world knows only binary genders – male and female – as which dancers must identify to gain the right to register for competitions. Men are expected to lead and women to follow. Dancers can only partner with someone of the opposite sex (World DanceSport Federation, 2021), and they are also expected to show romantic and/or sexual attraction to each other (Meneau, 2023, 2024).

As Judith Butler has shown, gender is based entirely on its constant, consistent, compulsive, repetitive doing (or performing) (Butler, 1999, p. XV). It's not an internal feature of ourselves but one that we produce 'through certain bodily acts' (Butler, 1999). Gender is read on the body, on what the body does. It shows in how the body moves; how it interacts with people; how we dress it; how we stand; how we do things (Butler, 1988, p. 519). These actions refer to a ritualised staging of a set of meanings already socially established, highly regulated practices that continually re-enact norms (Butler, 1988, p. 526). The constant repetition, or citation, of these actions creates the illusion of a stable gender identity – a fiction that is collectively shared as an unspoken agreement (Butler, 1988, p. 522). The 'stylised repetition of acts' primarily produces the gendered materiality of the body, a materiality that bears meaning because it is fundamentally dramatic in that it is *performed* to be received by others (Butler, 1988, p. 521).

We draw these actions from a certain established repertoire, which is not arbitrary but determined by the prevailing historical and temporal conditions within a particular culture. There is (to some extent) a right way of doing gender. The possibilities of performance are constrained by a pre-existing genealogy of bodily practices and stylisations through available historical conventions (Butler, 1988, p. 521). Our ability to do gender is judged by others according to how far we deviate from this established repertoire, which conditions our ability to be part of society.

Power relations, according to Foucault, are strictly relational: '[t]hey can only exist as a function of a multiplicity of points of resistance: these play the role of opponent, target, support, surface for a grip in power relations' (1976, p. 126). Power is constituted through opposition. This implies the omnipresence of abject subjects, practices, thoughts, and actions that are considered illegitimate. The elements rejected by hegemony also constitute it. Abject subjects in DanceSport are characterised by anything that queers the heteronormative gender binary. They are constitutive insofar as the dispositive hunts down every inch of queerness and deploys strategies against it (Meneau, 2023). I am aware that the category of the abject always presupposes a subject, which presupposes a norm and can reify it. I am reclaiming abjection as a political strategy to disrupt binary identities, systems and orders (Phillips, 2014), and to embrace both/and rather than the segregation and separation that norms create through abjection (Nicholas & Clark, 2020).

After I came out as non-binary, I gradually refused to conform to the demands of the heteronormative gender binary in DanceSport. The acts I chose to perform were deliberately distant from the pole of the gender binary assigned to me at birth. I was moving towards the abject, posing a threat to the hegemony of DanceSport.

1.2 Methodology

In order to discuss these complex and nuanced experiences, which reveal the inner workings of the heteronormative gender binary in DanceSport, I rely on autoethnography. Judith Lapadat describes this method as 'an approach to qualitative inquiry in which a researcher recounts a story of their own personal experience, coupled with an ethnographic analysis of the cultural context and implications of that experience' (2017, p. 1). Autoethnography allows scholars to challenge hegemonic paradigms and taken-for-granted knowledge that marginalises, oppresses or exploits marginalised groups, thereby advancing social justice goals (Jones & Harris, 2018, p. 4; Lapadat, 2017). As a queer method, autoethnography offers itself as a 'method of intervention that "disturbs the order of things."' It does so through '"counter–normative" relational and political orientations' that do not take the heteronormative gender binary for granted, but deconstruct it (Jones & Harris, 2018, p. 4).[4]

[4](on queer(ing) autoethnography, see for instance Bochner, 2016; Dauphinee, 2010; Johnson & LeMaster, 2020; Pathak, 2010; Vincent & Erikainen, 2020).

This method allows me to make sense of the way my experiences in the DanceSport community dramatically changed after I came out, illuminating new aspects of the heteronormative gender binary that I hadn't yet understood. It is important to remember that autoethnography combines memory work with writing work. In fact, I used some of my personal diaries to write this autoethnography. Ruth Pearce encourages us to use 'diaries, papers, and meaningful mementos from the researcher's own life [that] can provide rich data on the social and cultural contexts in which they are embedded', while warning us not to take them as truth. Autoethnographies are stories about the past, and stories are made, not found, and they ascribe agency and intentionality to the actions of others (Pearce, 2020, p. 5; see also Bochner, 2016).

I remain ethically committed to doing justice to those about whom I speak (Lapadat, 2017, p. 5). Not only am I aware of the responsibility I have as the sole author of this text but I also want to point out that the purpose of my research is to understand how systems of oppression work in DanceSport. I do not want to point the finger at a few perpetrators and celebrate when they are brought down, while turning my back on the next ones who take their place, because the system still works the same way.

Throughout this chapter I use pseudonyms to protect the confidentiality of those I speak of, with two exceptions: my dance partner, Alex, and my research colleague, Giulia Settomini, both to their knowledge. Our proximity makes them both very easy to find on the internet, and associating them with this research does not put them in a potentially difficult position, as they have both been incredibly supportive and central to my journey of gender discovery.

First, I lay the foundation that led to my coming out and the role that make-up played in it, between March 2021 and June 2022. I then contour how, immediately after my coming out, make-up became an affirming practice for play and experimentation as I experienced discrimination and the power of the heteronormative gender binary within the DanceSport scene. In the third section, I smooth out how these elements led me to wear make-up as an affirming and subversive practice at the National Championships in March 2022.

2. Growing Queer Away From DanceSport's Gaze

2.1 Questioning My Gender Assigned at Birth

From March to June 2021, I was doing my PhD in Dance Studies. I had danced ballroom for 10 years and competed in Austria for seven years. I was very familiar with the DanceSport scene, both on a personal level and on a professionally critical level. In fact, I'd been researching the heteronormative gender binary in competitive ballroom dancing for years. First during my Masters in Gender Studies, and then for my PhD, the working title of which was *The Genealogy of Female Hyper-sexualisation in Latin Competitive Dancing*.

I was 27 years old and had become increasingly uncomfortable with the gender I had been assigned at birth. This cognitive dissonance was particularly difficult because I had spent so much time in the DanceSport scene and was acutely aware of how much it valued the heteronormative gender binary. I was blessed with a wonderful dance partner, Alex, with whom I was dancing for a year. I felt quite comfortable with her and trusted her enough to have many discussions and joke about the ambient sexism of the scene to let off steam. Eventually, the two of us became quite adept at making fun of the gendered mechanics involved in dance.

I had been questioning my gender for months. I had been very vocal about it, worked on it in therapy, and caused many conflicts with people around me who felt attacked, some personally, some for the men around them. I'd read books on radical feminism and asked Google about gender identities, and although I didn't know I was approaching some kind of resolution, I felt the undercurrent moving through me.

It was a time of transition. I was changing, a little more each day, but more importantly, a little more with each experience. I let it wash over me, surrounded by my friends and the safe space they created around me. I felt moved rather than actively moving the process, as though I had no choice but to go through it. But I enjoyed pushing my boundaries more and more, letting myself discover what I had denied myself from feeling for decades.

2.2 Gender-Bending and Subverting Heteronormative DanceSport

In the process of discovering my own queerness, I multiplied the experiences of gender-bending in my life. While I was still trying to reconcile 'I' and 'masculinity' in a single sentence with a somewhat peaceful syntax, I allowed myself to experiment with practices traditionally perceived as feminine. These experiences were not the first in my life, but back then they hadn't meant much to me.

But in the spring of 2021, these experiences felt different, now that I had been studying Gender Studies for so long. I allowed myself to experiment more and more, always starting in the safest environment with my flatmates, using the playfulness that our more or less illegal Corona house parties gave us.[5] Fond of themes and spectacular performances, the parties we organised during the Covid lockdowns were always full of surprizes and pleasurable transgressions.

I remember longing to bring these night-time experiments into the light of day. It started with nail varnish. My flatmates and I had got drunk and I had let them paint my nails. It wasn't the first time, but I'd always taken it off before. This time I wanted to keep it. I wondered how other people would react if they saw it, and I expected negative feedback that never came. So I pushed the boundaries more and more, showing off my snatched nails wherever I went. In the spring of 2021, I bought and wore a lot of nail polish, although I still wiped it off before competitions, expecting the DanceSport scene to be hostile to my queerness.

House parties were also an opportunity for Alex and I to show our progress to my flatmates. We had prepared a short Cha Cha Cha for one of them, but with

[5]We used to call them 'kitchen dance' because we would push the kitchen table to the side and dance there. We had a sticker that said 'This kitchen is for dancing'.

the roles reversed, she as the leader and I as the follower. We had taken a piece of our own choreography and taught each other the steps.

In keeping with the cross-dressing theme, I lent her some of my clothes, perfume and jewellery, and she drew a fake moustache with eyeliner. I went all in with the aesthetic labour 'just to try it out'. I wanted to know what it felt like to have shaved legs.[6] I shaved my beard, wore tights, a dress, jewellery from my flatmates and perfume I had borrowed from Alex. Another friend did my make-up and I put lots of glitter on my arms.

Alex and I danced the Cha-cha piece first with the roles reversed, and then the same piece again with the roles we were used to – me leading and her following. I danced my steps with the masculine styling, leading, cross-dressed as a woman. She danced her steps, with the feminine styling, following, cross-dressed as a man. The joy I felt in showing queer DanceSport in a safe space was rejuvenating, but I was acutely aware that these pleasures were subversive and doomed to be experienced in what felt like an underground setting, an illegal party featuring queer performances.

This was roughly the state I was in before Pride on July 3, 2021. My years of research into the heteronormative gender binary in DanceSport, combined with my discovery that I was not only unable but also not interested in performing the heteronormative masculinity expected of me in the DanceSport world, contributed to a growing anxiety. I had spent the better part of two and a half decades trying my best to conform to the gender I was assigned at birth, like a plant that had been entrusted to me with the requirement to keep it alive. But AMAB (Assigned Male At Birth) just felt like an uncomfortable, outgrown jumper. I'd much rather have been Assigned Mushroom At Birth (at least that would have made Haraway smile). Anyway, all the plants I had ever owned in my life had died.

2.3 Coming-Out

As I grew more confident in my queerness, I asked a friend if she'd give me a make-up 101 lesson a week before the Pride parade. She taught me the basics. I already knew how to use foundation and setting powder because every man had to learn that for competitions. She brought in a rainbow eye shadow palette and some brushes and taught me how to make a wing and blend different colours. I experimented until I could make a rainbow of eye shadow, which I wore to Pride.

I had put together a group to go to the parade with me, consisting of Alex and my flatmates. I didn't know yet how important this event was going to be for me; I subconsciously felt that I really needed these people to be there with me, but without imagining that this would be the moment I fully realised that I was queer. I was in the process of exfoliating the last bits of eggshell from my shimmering queer self.

---

[6]I don't think I've let my hair grow since.

The pride felt incredible. I had gone, 'as an ally', in previous years. But this was the first time it meant something to my own identity. And it felt so warm, with my community and under the early July sun. We followed the techno truck during the parade. We drank a lot of alcohol. We camped out in front of the DJ stage and danced as soon as they started playing, in the middle of the afternoon. Then we went clubbing until the sun came up.

I couldn't believe how it felt to just be myself. To wear the clothes I wanted, to put on nail polish and make-up. It meant so much to me. The day after, I felt overwhelming waves of emotion, alternating between a compulsive need to cry and a manic smile on my face. 'I went to Pride', I kept repeating, glowing alone in my room, in the aftermath.

I had been looking up queer jargon on the internet over the past few months, and I felt most comfortable calling myself 'genderqueer'. It had a political dimension to it that gave me the legitimacy I felt I was lacking. I thought it was OK for me to call myself that, to dress that way, because I was actively trying to disrupt the gender binary.

I came out to my parents and tried to explain the concept to them. It put a bit of a damper on things when my mum found it so hard to understand. But my support system was very strong. I could rely on my flatmates, Alex and therapy to keep me going. Overall, though, it was a very fragile beginning. I was just beginning to blossom, a shy bud under the first rays of the summer sun...

3. The Cognitive Dissonance

In the phase leading up to the National Championship in March 2022, my cognitive dissonance grew, fed both by the experiences with discrimination and with the injunction to pass as a man. In parallel, I grew more optimistic – or delusional – because of my professional engagement with my PhD experts who all advocated for gender-neutral ballroom dancing. I also surrounded myself with a bubble who provided me with the necessary space to be myself. Finally, I wore make-up wherever I could, whenever I could, growing more confident in my skills.

3.1 Cognitive Dissonance and Discrimination

One of the most significant changes for me at this stage was discovering how I wanted to dress. Shopping in the women's section wasn't really an option because of the residual shame and because most of the cuts or sizes didn't fit me. So I asked the tailor who had designed my outfits for the competition if she'd be willing to make clothes for me.

Wearing her first tailored outfits to training led to my first experience of discrimination after coming out. The trainer, Rachel, told me to pass, to conceal my queerness, to dress and behave differently to minimise the risk of discrimination. She confessed the following week that she had reacted so strongly because she was afraid I would want to present like this at competitions. She implied without saying it that this would not be an option and I would need to cleanse my presentation from any queerness.

At the time I was willing to pass for competition or political lessons. I knew I'd have to blend in in clearly queer-hostile spaces I would be discriminated against. But that club had felt like home, like my living room. I was angry at her because she was supposed to be teaching me how to dance and nothing else. And I couldn't help but notice the hypocrisy – a few weeks ago she had taught me how to tweeze my eyebrows to make them look better at competitions.

Eventually she tolerated me dressing the way I wanted, but remained hermetic about who I was. She could no longer understand me, calculate me. I had become unintelligible and illegitimate. She stopped calling me a man after I asked her to, but referred to certain styles as more 'classic', using it as a euphemism for 'masculine', clearly regretting that I had distanced myself from it. I think we both tried for Alex, who had worked with Rachel for 5 years, but I was relieved when our schedules eventually prevented us from going and working with her again.

We took part in a few competitions before the lockdown in November 2021. My passport still said M for male, and I passed (far too easily, in my opinion) as a man, but I had worn nail polish and a bit of eye shadow – both matte, almost invisible. Rachel was so worried that we might have been discriminated against. I thought we had been fairly placed. It could have been better if our preparation had been better, but it wasn't, so it was fair. Her concern was everywhere. I had to convince her that it was unlikely that we had been discriminated against on the basis of my gender performance – a job I would expect my trainers to do for me, I reflected afterwards, rather than the other way around.

These experiences dampened my mood and cast a shadow over my radiant need for self-expression. Throughout those months, despite my best efforts to disrupt people's compulsive association of my body with masculinity, I failed to disrupt the binary enough for them to see me as anything other than a 'weird' man. The most outrageous, daring acts were appropriated or erased within the gender binary. I was fascinated by how powerful people's delusions about gender were, and deeply disturbed that the meaning of my body was being contested. I disrupted the category of masculinity SO MUCH with my neon pink nail polish or my perfectly blended eye shadow, and yet people still assumed I was a man. I didn't present as one, but I was read as one.

I was so upset by all the fuss that I changed my label to non-binary rather than genderqueer and switched to they/them pronouns. I didn't mind being political in spite of myself, which was what I was doing by dressing fabulously. But I didn't really want my gender to be inherently political anymore. I just wanted to dress the way I wanted and couldn't believe how much of a problem it was.

I felt alone in the margins. There was no guidance. I couldn't believe that no one had ever fought for me to be included in the rules. That I was the first, that there had been no one before me.[7] The DanceSport scene seemed at once empty of

[7]The Regulations only recognise the two binary sexes (Meneau, 2023, p. 52).

role models, possibilities, opportunities, and the path to follow was dark and lonely...

I had considered transitioning, but was aware that hormone replacement therapy (HRT) would make me even more of a freak and push me further to the margins of the dance community. What would the scene think of me if I suddenly had breasts? Would I still be allowed to lead? What would that change, for our choreographies? Would I still be allowed to dance with Alex in the first place? Or would I be expected to follow and dance with a male partner instead?[8] With a heavy heart, even though I was not yet sure I wanted to transition, I considered distancing myself from the DanceSport world. What was I going to do, surrounded by heteronormative couples on the floor, the object of ridicule or stares or uncomfortable questions? I did not know.

DanceSport denied me the right to be myself. I had to tone myself down, hide or fear being discriminated against. It was a particularly threatening thought because of the place that DanceSport had held in my life until then. My level of commitment had always been exceptionally high, so the cognitive dissonance hit me all the harder.

I struggled with the injunction to pass and tried hard, but in the end I could not get over it. I felt increasingly uncomfortable with the world of DanceSport, its norms and requirements, and the violence associated with it. The cognitive dissonance was fed by the requirement to pass and my experiences of discrimination – but I was not yet ready to quit.

3.2 The Interview Phase

At the same time, in autumn and winter 2021, I conducted and transcribed 15 interviews for my dissertation, each lasting one hour. I chose the interviewees for their expertise and advocacy against discrimination in DanceSport. In the interviews we talked about how dance can and should be gender neutral. We strobed the inconsistencies and logical fallacies of DanceSport and the gender-based violence that arises from the heteronormative gender binary. During these months of full-time work, I talked to experts on the subject, transcribed and analysed their interviews, listened to and learning from their arguments.

In my dissertation I built a solid case that dancing required only an able body, not a gendered one (see Meneau, 2023, chapter 4). I began to believe that movement quality was more important than gendered performance, not only because my experts said so but also because of the methods I used to triangulate their knowledge. I had become aware through the dissertation that dance could be something other than heteronormative. So, armed with this knowledge, Alex and I prepared for the national championships in the spring of 2022, spraying our dance with queerness.

---

[8]At the time, regulations in Austria required dancers to dance with the opposite sex (Meneau, 2023, p. 52).

3.3 My Allies

But to do that I had to be more radical, for my own self-care. Firstly, I didn't want to dance heteronormative figures anymore, so we needed new routines. And secondly, I needed to be surrounded by people who welcomed my journey. I stayed involved in the DanceSport scene despite the cognitive dissonance, despite the outright hostility and adversity, because I surrounded myself with a bubble.

Alex had always supported me in exploring my gender and expanding my presentation of it. She celebrated small moments and victories with me. I could be myself with her. I didn't have to mask, hide, dress differently for her. She understood that we needed to change our routines, and when Austria went into lockdown again in November 2021, and the competitions stopped, we seized the opportunity.

I also needed trainers who would support me in my development. Rachel was out of the question. S, our main trainer, had never commented on the fact that my outfits got weirder and weirder every time we went to him for private lessons. We continued to work with him. And in the autumn of 2021, I met Giulia Settomini, an Italian trainer and choreographer, with whom I began a research collaboration. Giulia and I shared a deep understanding of the wheels of the heteronormative gender binary in DanceSport. She helped us to queer our dance routines. She also became a dear friend, someone I could be myself with and felt safe with. She had the habit of putting on make-up before leaving the house, so I did the same when we met in London, Berlin, Trieste or Graz.

These people became particularly significant in my gender journey during these months, supporting me in the trajectory I was taking in DanceSport. They were partly responsible for the affects that drove my research and my survival strategies. In the face of this unbearable conflict situation, with Alex's and Giulia's help, I found solace in (queer) clubbing settings.

3.4 (Queer) Clubbing/Raving and Make-Up

I went clubbing, a lot. The first significant time was Halloween 2021, with Giulia. We ended up dancing to Psytrance until dawn. In the following months I immersed myself in the electronic music scene, both queer and straight. Make-up became a central part of my self-discovery that year. I put on make-up every time I went out, whether it was clubbing or just meeting friends for drinks in the evening. I challenged myself to do a different style each time and took party themes very seriously, aiming to perfect my skills and give life with every occasion. I found make-up to be one of the most affirming things I could do for myself.

I felt so electrified by what was possible. I dove into this world of bright colours, bold neons and sparkling crystals. I blossomed in it as my bank balance plummeted. I purchased many top-quality products, mostly advertised by queer or trans make-up artists for queers, Gen Z or ravers. Neon liquid liners, holographic lip gloss, Swarovski rhinestones, Morphe and Urban Decay palettes, pigments that shone in two different colours, all kinds of glitter, pink liquid lipstick and lip gloss...

And I couldn't help but find it all sexy. As I looked at myself in the mirror, I thought my queer self looked incredible. 'It's just so hot. I look so lit. People in the DanceSport scene don't get it – but honestly, I'll never believe I'm the only one who thinks this is hot', I thought to myself. It made it hard to be in the DanceSport scene, to be constantly reminded that I wasn't valid and that I was weird and didn't fit in. But I didn't care. The euphoria I felt when I put on make-up and looked at myself in the mirror was just a reminder that what I was doing was totally okay.

I used those moments as opportunities to be myself and to feel that I could be celebrated for whom I was. I could wear glitter and bright neon colours and people loved it. It was so refreshing and affirming when people commented positively on my make-up at techno parties – mostly because they were all pretty high and the light effects of drugs are dazzling. These experiences helped me to see the world differently, to connect with people in a way I had never experienced before, and to vibrate to the music. I could dance without caring much about anything other than how I felt, a shiny, vibing fur ball of euphoria.

These were moments of re-existence outside of the competitive dance world, where I experienced being who I am without too many problems. Clubbing allowed me such moments, academia others – especially in a queer setting. People understood and validated me, complimented my make-up and outfits. I felt safe and warm and used them as a runway that helped me become more confident. These experiences helped me understand how much I craved diversity in my life. They also showed me that if the DanceSport community was so unwelcoming, it wasn't the case for everyone.

In the lead up to the National Championships in March 2022, I was grieving and slowly understanding that I might have to leave the scene at some point. I had employed several coping mechanisms to carry on in the DanceSport world despite the rampant queer-phobic violence. I had lost myself in the utopian ideas of my dissertation; I had surrounded myself with loyal allies; and I had experienced alternative scenes that showed me that I was okay as I was. At the same time, because of the experiences of discrimination, research, and the euphoria of queer clubbing, I felt a growing need for confrontation and actively resisted assimilation as an act of self-care.

4. The Nationals: Preparation, Placing, Aftermath

4.1 Preparation for the Nationals

By the time the National Championships rolled around, I was still so unsure of where my participation in DanceSport would end up. My commitment was waning and I was becoming increasingly alienated by the heteronormative gender binary. As a result, I became increasingly bold with my make-up and nail polish at competitions. At the same time, our training capacity diminished because Alex had much less time to devote to it. Our results began to deteriorate, making it difficult to determine whether we were being discriminated against or whether the quality of our dancing was simply not good enough.

In the lead up to the National Championships, I spent a lot of time trying to find a loophole in the Dress Regulations that would allow me to create an image that I felt comfortable in – an image that didn't feel like a clown costume. I had found ways of expressing my identity through clothing that gave me a lot of gender euphoria, similar to make-up.

However, I was overly disappointed to find no loophole to exploit for my outfits. I felt so dysphoric, seeing myself in my masculine competition outfit. I felt so restricted by the Dress Regulations and it depressed me so much (see here Meneau, 2023, p. 77). The only loophole I was able to exploit was the mention that make-up was Not Regulated by the Dress Regulations cite (World DanceSport Federation, 2024, p. 142). I could wear as much make-up as I wanted, so I did. I went all out. I wore foundation, primer, setting powder, eyeliner, eye shadow, fake lashes, mascara, glitter, iridescent rhinestones, lip liner, liquid lipstick, lip gloss. I was frustrated about the rest, but my make-up was on fleek!

This was my mental state when I entered the Austrian Championships on 15 March 2022 in Vienna. All in all, we were less prepared than the year before because we had less time to train and were more vulnerable to discrimination, because we had changed our routines to be less heteronormative and because I was wearing make-up.

4.2 The Nationals

At Nationals I felt the power of alienation as never before, watching my competitors warm up as if it were an intimidation strategy. I felt jealous of other couples for whom life was easier. I doubted myself, I bargained, I thought maybe I could just be someone else? I felt so sad at my thoughts of changing myself for them. I felt angry because, in the end, I did not want to leave. But it had been months since I had last enjoyed training without questioning myself...

I was ashamed to be who I was, always illegitimate and weird to everyone in DanceSport. When self-confidence is key on the dance floor, to be constantly told that I was not good enough and that I would never ever be, was a blow to my ability to even feel competitive (regardless of the quality of my dancing). You could say that my mental training should be stronger. But this was just another obstacle to my participation in DanceSport, more labour that I was expected to do as a queer person in order to participate.

I felt so alienated. I ended up wondering why I'm here. I wanted to escape, to go find other people, other practices, where I could be who I am without it being such a f*cking problem... I remember finding the (gendered, sigh!) bathroom to take a break from it all, sitting on the toilets and wondering if my relationship with DanceSport would pass those tests you find on Facebook to see if your relationship is toxic (spoiler: it didn't).[9]

---

[9]I took the test 'Is your relationship healthy?' from www.loveisrespect.org and answered with DanceSport as my partner. According to this test, I am definitely in a toxic relationship with DanceSport.

We passed Rachel in the hall of the competition venue. She looked me over from head to toe and told me she liked my hair. Clearly I had upstaged my eyes and my hair was nothing special. I had grown it out over the last six months and the Dress Regulations forced me, as a 'man', to wear it in a ponytail. But my beat was to capacity, and it was for the Gods! Even Alex didn't wear such beautiful make-up – but Rachel ignored it with all her might.

4.3 The Placing

We placed lower than we had hoped, and lower than the year before. We wondered if we had been discriminated against. Our trainer, S., had been on the judging panel. The week after the competition, he told us that my wearing make-up hadn't been a big issue among the judges. They had rather discussed how uncoordinated I was.

But I wondered. Would they really have spoken out if they hadn't liked the make-up? What would it have gained them, apart from the possibility of being labelled a reactionary? What would have prevented them from thinking of me in disgust and turning to someone else to give them a mark instead, and then telling our trainer something other than how they felt? Nothing. It sounded like a convenient excuse to say I was 'less coordinated' if they didn't like me or my make-up in the first place. I knew they didn't even have to say why they didn't mark me, because judges don't have to justify why they judge the way they do (Meneau, 2023, p. 146).

As for the criticism that I seemed uncoordinated, I couldn't help but wonder if I was being judged by a masculine standard that I was deliberately not trying to meet. Did I have to convince them more now that I was visibly queer compared to when they judged me with the overlay of hegemonic masculinity? If their expectations were gendered, and the coordination the judges wanted to see was masculine, and I was performing more feminine, then of course I would be uncoordinated by their standards.

Overall, I remained sceptical of every attempt to convince me that we had not been discriminated against. It's not that I thought we should have done much better, or that discrimination was the only reason we finished so low. We knew our level had dropped. Compared to other couples, we lacked time, commitment and preparation. Our private lessons had been much more inconsistent and we had worked too much on routines and not enough on technique.

But even if our dancing had improved, I argued, we still wouldn't have placed very high because we didn't meet the judges' heteronormative expectations. And I knew this very well from my research. The competition was so obviously anti-queer. Judges tell couples to be readable to ensure a good place in competitions, and the heteronormative gender binary is THE only readability marker (Meneau, 2023). Queerness would always be unreadable to adjudicators, regardless of the elements we queer (mechanics, routines, make-up, hairstyles), because it disrupts the grammar between the binary genders (Meneau, 2023; Richardson, 2018).

All in all, I had yet to be presented with a convincing counter-narrative to the hypothesis that we had been discriminated against. And that left a bitter taste in my mouth. I knew I had to present in a masculine way to be successful, and I knew I didn't want to.

4.4 The Reactions to My Make-Up

I took to Facebook to rant about the restrictions of the Dress Regulations (see Fig. 9.1):

The reactions I received fall into four categories.

(1) 'Tell me what you need so I can tell you how to do without'
Many people, instead of trying to understand how discriminatory the Dress Regulations are, asked me what I would like to wear. They responded to my descriptions with counter-proposals. I explained: 'I'd wear a crop top, but it's not allowed', and people would reply: 'Well, you could wear a shirt, but transparent' (meaning: it's allowed). I used to get this reaction a lot and it always bothered me. I never really knew what to say. What they were suggesting wasn't the same, it wasn't what I had said, it wasn't what I wanted.

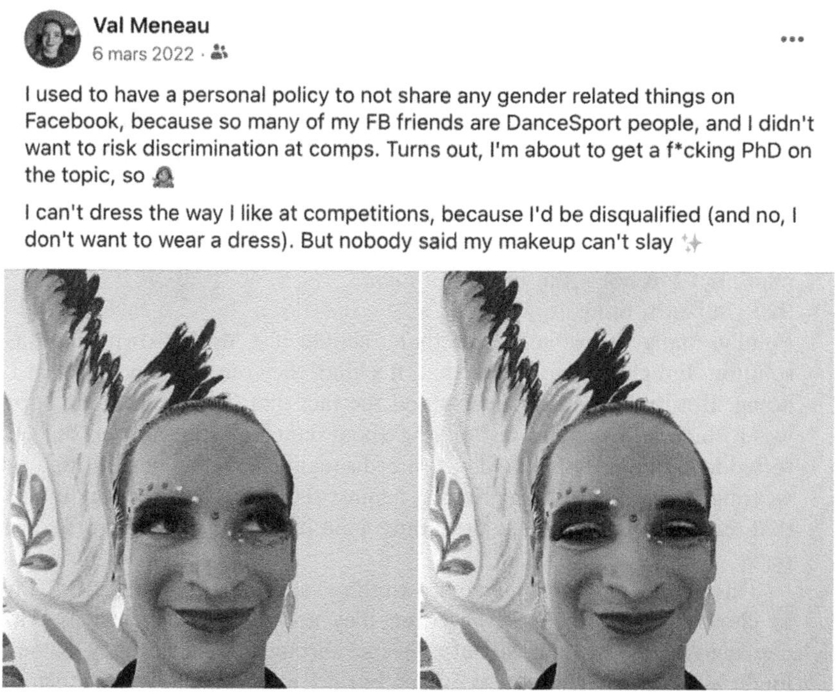

Fig. 9.1 Facebook Post About My Make-Up at the Nationals.

Similarly, when I complained about how I was expected to perform hegemonic masculinity, experts for my dissertation asked me why I didn't try dancing with a man as a follower in same-sex competitions. I hadn't thought about it, but I didn't know why I should. I didn't want to be a follower and dance with a man. It was probably the strangest piece of advice I've ever been given. I felt so unrecognised. I loved dancing with Alex and I'd always wanted to dance with women. I just didn't want to have to do heteronormative dancing to have a real chance at competitions, because it never suited me, and it was only getting worse.

(2) Patronising me while misunderstanding the issue
One interviewee in particular assumed from reading my Facebook post that I didn't understand the goal of the Dress Regulations. During the interview I had with him shortly after the Nationals, he tried to explain them to me even though he didn't understand the problems I was facing – which is a question of privilege. He's never had to deal with them because they've never been a problem for him.

(3) Hostility
I was told that nobody thought a man would want to wear decorative, feminine make-up, so the Dress Regulations had a loophole and did not regulate make-up for people they read as male. I was scolded for daring to exploit this loophole. The argument was that it's not because something isn't forbidden that it's allowed, and that couples increasingly lack the understanding, or simply the knowledge, of conventions, traditions and general rules.

One adjudicator regretted that this had led to an ever-expanding catalogue of prohibitions. He concluded with the reproach that this distracts us all from dancing, which is the only thing we should be concerned with. This is a gaslighting argument. The fact that I am trying to make space for myself to simply exist is seen by him as an unnecessary and disturbing distraction. There's always the assumption that I'm doing something forbidden, 'as a man', but I'm not – I'm just not a man.

(4) 'Do your own thing'
Finally, many people suggested that I should just 'do my own thing' as a solution. I'm glad they told me that, it's kind, they're supportive of what I'm doing. But this advice misunderstood the fact that 'what makes me happy' was forbidden. I was not just talking about dancing as a follower, but plain forbidden things that would get me disqualified from competitions, like wearing a crop top. I was grinding against the power of an entire industry that refused to acknowledge how much pain it was causing the world in this regard.

This argument pits 'doing your own thing' against 'being successful'. I had to choose one or the other because they are mutually exclusive. Was I dancing for my own enjoyment or to get through the proficiency classes? I might not dance as 'manly' as others, but if I was dancing for me, then that should be enough, these people seemed to suggest – except that I didn't know why it should be enough. I don't know why I should be content to be

> tolerated for dancing and regularly told that I'm not good enough.[10] Other people didn't have that problem. It felt like I had to sacrifice myself to get ahead.
>
> Sometimes the request to 'do my own thing' was accompanied by a strong investment in my project. Other people's insistence felt strange. I was being pushed so hard by everyone, but without much concern for my mental health, wellbeing or even the obstacles, adversity and violence I faced in DanceSport. They cared much more about the kind of change I could make by just being in the scene.

These people were very liberal with the word 'pioneer', using it to describe me, my dancing, my research. But those we remember as pioneers of social and political movements are the people who had the strength to stand until the last moment, until their struggle was recognised and someone cared enough to make change happen. They are wounded and broken by the violence they faced up to that point, and carried by the labour of those who preceded them, who fought the same struggle in vain. I didn't want to be a pioneer. I was exhausted. It wasn't worth it. I felt used, like a pawn in the political game.

So, realising that the overwhelming majority of professionals in DanceSport were unable to think outside the heteronormative gender binary and that my options, given my resources, were almost non-existent, I quit. Distancing myself from the scene was an act of self-preservation.[11] It wasn't because of specific people and their personal failings per se, but more because of the communal situation. But it wasn't also mine; it was DanceSport's fault.

5. Conclusion

My make-up journey from March 2021 to March 2022 was an essential part of my self-expression and accompanied my queerness journey. It fulfiled many roles, also depending on the spaces in which I wore make-up. Before coming out, I used it as an experimental practice, a kind of drag, to put on a feminine presentation and performance. Later on, it was as an affirmative practice, wearing make-up whenever and wherever I could, particularly in the queer setting and in safe spaces – but not in DanceSport.

The scene required me to obey to the heteronormative gender binary – to present in a masculine way, to lead, to use my body in a masculine way on the dance floor. Submitting to it would have afforded me a subject position, as a 'man'. But because I was unable and unwilling to comply, I was sanctioned, made to feel inadequate. I experienced policing through violence and discrimination,

---

[10]Not only through the results but also directly, in the private lessons, because each trainer carries the personal project of making me more of a man, despite my own will.

[11]I have received a lot of support from my fellow competitors in these competitions. The younger generations seem much more willing to engage with the issue than the older ones – unfortunately for me, the older generations are the ones who judge and teach.

and saw my access to participation and opportunities restricted. Experiencing the violence of the heteronormative gender binary in DanceSport started a grieving process that took me months to go through. My experiences of discrimination made me angry and the cognitive dissonance made me depressed. Thoughts of passing or questioning whether I was really queer or whether I could not just be cis again felt like bargaining; and believing with all my heart that DanceSport was about gender-neutral quality criteria was a sign of denial.

I refused to pass as a man and appropriated a practice commonly gendered as feminine for my body that others read as masculine. By the standards of the scene, I was performing gender incorrectly. They didn't read me as someone expressing their non-binary identity in the way they chose, but as a man doing something forbidden because I was mixing bodily acts in a fluid way that threatened society's fiction of stable binary gender identities. This pushed me into the realm of the abject in DanceSport, thereby reinforcing the subject position of those who reified the heteronormative gender binary rather than disrupting it.

The support I received from Alex or Giulia or my trainers, coupled with the anger and despair of the grieving process, made me feel more and more confrontational. Eventually I took advantage of the only loophole I could find in the Dress Regulations that allowed me a gender presentation closer to what I envisioned for myself: make-up. There, I wore make-up as a political and subversive practice aimed at disrupting my association with masculinity and the injunction that Alex and I, as a couple on the dance floor, conform to the aesthetics of the heteronormative gender binary.

Wearing make-up was my only chance to stand up for myself in this queerphobic scene. 'We've got to take our chances', sings Kate Earl in 'All that glitters' (2017), and I am reminded me of Foucault's anti-normative governmentality (Dean & Zamora, 2021, p. 127). In the eyes of the patriarchal DanceSport Law, I am a criminal – someone who invested in an action (putting on make-up), expected to gain from it (aligning my presentation with my gender), and accepted the risk of loss (discrimination and abuse). I exploited a loophole, one that allowed me to be seen as I wanted to be seen, to reclaim ownership of my body and to exercise self-determination in a scene that was taking it away from me. In doing so, I optimised risk, loss and the dangers I was willing to tolerate for the gains.

Autoethnography as a queer method allowed me to retrace in this chapter the links between my experiences at the micro level and domination at the macro level. By unravelling the impact of systems of oppression on my personal life, I was able to highlight how they work – what constellation of knowledge/power supports them, through what practices they are (re)enacted. At the same time, my experiences between the scenes highlight that they are not universal but culturally specific, meaning that they are the result of human action and can therefore be reversed in the pursuit of social justice.

Make-up is not gendered per se, but it is perceived as such and can therefore also be used to disrupt the heteronormative gender binary, whether on a personal or political level. In the co-constitution between my non-binary self and the outside world, putting on make-up was an act of negotiation with others – in

DanceSport, even confrontation. It was also about gaining confidence, learning for myself that I could be who I was and standing up for it. In a way, the story of my make-up journey is a story about my relationship with myself and, by extension, my relationship with others.

Make-up can be a queer practice, a joyful one. It can be used as an identity affirming practice, as an element of beauty that has political potential. The meaning it carries depends on the context in which it is worn, and the meaning it has for the people who use it, but also for the people who see it/for the wearer's relationship to the norm. If I hadn't had wonderful experiences wearing make-up in a queer environment, I might not have known that I mattered for whom I am, so when the time came, I knew I had to leave the DanceSport scene.

References

Bochner, A. P. (2016). Notes toward an ethics of memory in autoethnographic inquiry. In N. K. Denzin & M. D. Giardina (Eds.), *Ethical futures in qualitative research: Decolonizing the politics of knowledge* (pp. 197–208). Routledge.

Butler, J. (1988). Performative acts and gender constitution: An essay in phenomenology and feminist theory. *Theatre Journal*, *40*(4), 519–531.

Butler, J. (1999). *Gender trouble*. Routledge.

Dauphinee, E. (2010). The ethics of autoethnography. *Review of International Studies*, *36*, 799–818.

Dean, M., & Zamora, D. (2021). *The last man takes LSD: Foucault and the end of revolution*. Verso.

Earl, K. (2017). *All that glitters [Song]. On tongue tied [Album]*. BMG.

Foucault, M. (1976). *Histoire de la Sexualité* (Vol. 1: La Volonté de Savoir). Gallimard.

Foucault, M. (1977). Préface. In G. Deleuze & F. Guattari (Eds.), *Anti-Oedipus capitalism and schizophrenia*. Viking Press.

Hennessy, R. (2018). *Profit and pleasure: Sexual identities in late capitalism* (2nd ed.). Routledge, Taylor & Francis Group.

Jäger, S. (2001). Diskurs und Wissen. Theoretische und methodische Aspekte einer Kritischen Diskurs- und Dispositivanalyse. In R. Keller, A. Hirseland, W. Schneider, & W. Viehöver (Eds.), *Handbuch Sozialwissenschaftliche Diskursanalyse* (pp. 81–112). VS Verlag für Sozialwissenschaften. https://doi.org/10.1007/978-3-322-99906-1_4

Johnson, A., & LeMaster, B. (2020). *Gender futurity, intersectional autoethnography: Embodied theorizing from the margins*. Routledge.

Jones, S. H., & Harris, A. M. (2018). *Queering autoethnography*. Routledge.

Lapadat, J. C. (2017). Ethics in autoethnography and collaborative autoethnography. *Qualitative Inquiry*, *23*(8), 1–15.

Lloyd, M. (2013). Power, politics, domination, and oppression. In G. Waylen, K. Celis, J. Kantola, & L. Weldon (Eds.), *The Oxford handbook of gender and politics* (pp. 111–134). Oxford University Press. https://doi.org/10.1093/oxfordhb/9780199751457.013.0004

Meneau, V. (2023). *DanceSport's economy of desire – A dispositive analysis of the heteronormative gender binary in Latin american competitive dancing*. PhD Dissertation. University of Salzburg.

Meneau, V. (2024). Queer dancers' experiences in the Dancesport world: Exclusion, invisibilisation, and assimilation. *Equality, Diversity and Inclusion*, *43*(9), 55–70.

Nicholas, L., & Clark, S. (2020). Leave those kids alone: On the uses and abuses and feminist queer potential of non-binary and genderqueer. *INSEP – Journal of the International Network for Sexual Ethics & Politics*, *8*(SI), 7–8.

Oksala, J. (2016). Microphysics of power. In L. J. Disch & M. Hawkesworth (Eds.), *The Oxford handbook of feminist theory*. Oxford University Press.

Pathak, A. A. (2010). Opening my voice, claiming my space: Theorizing the possibilities of Postcolonial approaches to autoethnography. *Journal of Research Practice*, *6*(1), 1–12.

Pearce, R. (2020). A methodology for the marginalised: Surviving oppression and traumatic fieldwork in the neoliberal academy. *Sociology*, *1*(19), 806–824.

Phillips, R. (2014). Abjection. *TSQ: Transgender Studies Quarterly*, *1*(1–2), 19–21. https://doi.org/10.1215/23289252-2399470

Richardson, N. (2018). 'Whether you are gay or straight, I don't like to see effeminate dancing': Effeminophobia in performance-level ballroom dance. *Journal of Gender Studies*, *27*(2), 207–219.

Vincent, B., & Erikainen, S. (2020). Using duoethnographyto research gender and-sexuality minorityexperiences oftransgender relationships. *Sexualities*, *23*(1–2), 28–43.

World DanceSport Federation. (2021). *WDSF competition rules*. (WDSF AGM, Budapest, June 9th, 2019).

World DanceSport Federation. (2024). *WDSF competition rules*. (WDSF AGM, Warsaw, October 27th, 2024).

Chapter 10

'Beauty Secrets' of the 'Cool-Girl': Representation of Beautification as Everyday (Pop)cultural Practice[1]

Marija Geiger Zeman[a], *Mirela Holy*[b] *and Rebeka Mesarić Žabčić*[a]

[a]Institute of Social Sciences Ivo Pilar, Croatia
[b]VERN' University, Croatia

Abstract

Everyday life is an important area of sociological understanding. The paper starts from an idea about inseparable connections between everyday life and popular culture Practices of everyday beautification are part of popular culture. The focus of the analysis are beauty products, consumerism and practices of beautification that indicate interesting dynamic between macro and micro levels. The media have an important role in the (re)production knowledge related to beautification. Vogue's 'Beauty Secrets' is a beauty series which introduces the global audience with beauty regimes and everyday beauty routines of celebrities. The focus of the critical analysis is the beauty video by Kate Moss. As a fashion model icon, Kate Moss acts as an intermediary between production and consumption. She promotes and sells cosmic wellness and perpetuates neoliberal narratives about health, healing, self-care, and new definition of attractive feminine look.

Keywords: Everyday life; popular culture; beauty products; consumerism; beautification; postfeminism; Vogue's 'beauty secrets'; beauty video/tutorial; Kate Moss; 'cosmic wellness'

[1]The first part of the title is inspired by the video title 'Kate Moss's Guide to Cool-Girl Beauty | Beauty Secrets | Vogue' (2022b).

Beauty Industry, 203–221

Published under exclusive licence by Emerald Publishing Limited
doi:10.1108/978-1-83608-940-720251032

1. Introduction: Beauty, Popular Culture and Everyday Life

Everyday life is an underestimated area of life in many ways. From the position of 'ordinary' people, everyday life is the domain of predictability, familiarity, boredom, 'normality' and repetitiveness. From the standpoint of sociology and other scientific disciplines, everyday life and the routines that constitute it have long been considered an uninteresting, marginal and irrelevant topic (Bennett & Watson, 2002). After all, 'larger scale events' could not happen without 'individual people doing little things in local places', and '"micro"-level' practices are shaped and influenced by '"macro"-level patterns' (Scott, 2012, p. 1). Waskul and Vannini (2016) introduce a fresh perspective in the sociological reflection of everyday life, connecting everyday life with popular culture, more precisely defining 'popular culture as everyday life' (2016, p. 1). According to Waskul and Vannini (2016, p. 7), popular culture is 'an assemblage of ideas, practices, experiences, representations, material objects and other "things" and phenomena that comprise mainstream, ordinary ways of life of large groups of people' (italics by Waskul & Vannini). Popular culture permeates people's lives in numerous ways, plunging into the most private and intimate everyday practices and rituals that have multiple and ambivalent meanings, for example, making and sharing selfies (Klein, 2016), shopping (Berry, 2016), 'going to the bathroom' (Waskul, 2016, p. 145), etc. Waskul and Vannini (2016, p. 5) highlight three approaches to popular culture focused on 'the production of commodities, their consumption, and what people do with them'. If these three approaches are conveyed in the sphere of everyday beautification practices, the focus of the analysis is directed on three interconnected topics that indicate an interesting and complex dynamic between the macro and micro levels. These topics are: (1) products of the beauty industry; (2) the purchase of beauty products; and (3) their daily use. In the first part of the paper, the focus is on: (1) beauty products as (pop)cultural artefacts or 'materialities' (Katz, 2019, p. 1) that have been attributed different, often ambivalent and contradictory meanings (Asa Berger, 2009); (2) relationships between everyday beauty practices, beauty products and the culture of consumerism, which encourages conspicuous consumption by using various marketing activities (e.g. engagement of famous people and/or fashion models in the promotion of luxury beauty products) and different channels (media, social networks, etc.), and (3) beautification practices as mundane and repetitive activities that reflect and reproduce power and social life (Scott, 2012). In addition to having a key role in constructing cultural definitions and ideas of beauty, the media play an important role in the re/production of beauty knowledge and beautification skills. This is particularly evident in digital beauty culture and beauty videos/tutorials as popular cultural texts that reproduce power relations and ideologies related to gender, race and class. Beauty series Vogue's 'Beauty Secrets' introduces the audience to everyday beautification practices and beauty regimes of celebrities through its beauty videos/tutorials. The rich and successful modelling and entrepreneurial career of Kate Moss will be briefly recapitulated, and the results and insights of the empirical analysis of the Vogue's 'Beauty Secrets' video/beauty tutorial by Kate Moss will be presented.

2. Complex Meanings of Beauty Products

Beauty products are 'cosmetics and personal care products' of a wide range and different culturally and socially defined functions and purposes ('cleaning, beautifying, promoting attractiveness or changing its appearance') – 'oral care, skin care, sun care, hair care, decorative cosmetics, body care and perfumes' (Cosmetics Europe, n.d.). However, beyond their practical function, cosmetic products are cultural artefacts that 'embody and concretize various cultural values', (Fairchild, 1967, as cited in Asa Berger, 2009, p. 17), as well as complex meanings that are produced, reproduced, understood and questioned in different contexts, different systems and through different optics. From the perspective of everyday life beauty products are 'materialities' (Katz, 2019, p. 1), i.e. cosmetic items/objects/things that are related to the practices of constructing a gendered identity, producing a 'visible self' (see the title of the book by Eicher et al., 2000) and the image that will be presented (and performed) in the social arena. Ogilvie and Kristensen-Bach (2001, p. 5) emphasize the importance of lipstick in daily beautification rituals and state that many consumers consider it 'a necessary addition to their faces in order to feel presentable, comfortable and more confident' Ghoshal (2022, p. 23) from a sociological perspective analyzes lipstick as a makeup item that is simultaneously 'a tool of women's emancipation and beautification as well as a symbol of consumerism' while Gurrieri and Drenten (2019, p. 225) describe the controversial history of lipstick as a beauty product that is 'simultaneously associated with both women's autonomy and oppression'. The history of lipstick is turbulent and contradictory, and it perfectly shows the extent to which everyday artefacts are carriers of different social, cultural, political, religious and economic meanings. Schaffer (2006) states that in the Middle Ages, religious institutions expressed extremely critical attitudes towards lipstick, and Pallingston (1999, as cited in Schaffer, 2006, p. 7) points out that in England, women who applied makeup were considered 'an incarnation of Satan' because these changes on their faces 'challenged God and his workmanship'. At the beginning of the 20th century in the USA, lipstick occupies a 'symbolic and economic' position that it still has today, however, in addition to the old meanings, according to which it is a symbol of femininity, it also acquires new meanings (Schaffer, 2006, pp. 17–18). For suffragettes, wearing red lipstick signified female emancipation and rebellion against male authority, but in the 1970s, rebellions were waged 'both with and against lipstick' (Schaffer, 2006, p. 45). On the one hand, lipsticks – especially purple and black ones – were considered symbols of non-conformity and rebellion against the establishment and were worn by both men and women (Schaffer, 2006, p. 45). On the other hand, second-wave feminists articulated a sharp critique of lipstick as an important part of patriarchal oppression and domination over women (Bartky, 1998; Wolf, 2002). Many feminist authors emphasized the harmfulness and oppressiveness of the practice of beautification (and applying lipstick) as a form of internalizing patriarchal culture and conforming to the mythology of beauty (Wolf, 2002), i.e. male culture that attributes central importance to the physical appearance of women and imposes unrealistic standards of appearance and beauty on women (Gurrieri & Drenten, 2019, p. 226). But in the early 1990s, new (post) feminist positions were articulated regarding beautification practices in general as well as wearing lipstick, emphasizing the emancipatory, creative, ludic, and pleasurable aspects of beautification (Geiger Zeman & Zeman, 2015). Despite the polarized feminist positions related to wearing lipstick and beautification practices in general, the relationship between feminism and lipstick remained complex, contradictory and ambivalent, showing how everyday beautification practices are simultaneously practices of resistance and conformation. Judy Chicago, a famous artist and feminist activist, in an interview for the USA Vogue, stated that most of her life she had 'the standard feminist view' which considered 'fashion, beauty, and makeup' to be 'oppressive to women' (Anbouba, 2023). As a young feminist activist and artist, Chicago 'didn't have a beauty routine', but over time she developed a simple beauty routine consisting of skincare, applying perfume and putting on lipstick. Describing her daily beauty routine, Chicago pointed out: 'Now that I'm old, lipstick is essential, it makes me feel bright' (Anbouba, 2023). Gurrieri and Drenten (2019, p. 225) call lipstick 'a marketplace icon' because every day 'with nearly 7 in 10 women applying makeup to their lips' (Mintel, 2019, as cited in Gurrieri & Drenten, 2019, p. 225) it supports the incredible profitability of the beauty industry.

3. Beauty and Consumerism

Everyday beauty practices that use beauty products in different ways are inseparable from the culture of consumerism, consumerist practices and 'choices available and desirable to consumers' (Hitt, 1996, as cited in Berry, 2016, p. 255). The global beauty industry is a highly competitive and highly profitable market in which various actors operate (from multinational corporations, smaller beauty companies, advertisers, celebrities of various kinds, beauty bloggers, fashion portals and magazines, etc.). The development of digital technology has opened new spaces for the beauty industry. Lupton introduced the term 'digital food cultures' (2020, p. 2). Analogous to 'digital food cultures' (Lupton, 2020), it is possible to talk about the digital culture of beauty and beautification, which refers to all those 'representations and practices' related to beauty and beautification that are produced and reproduced in the online space.

In the context of everyday life and consumerist culture, beauty products are commodities. Fiske (1989, as cited in Paterson, 2010, p. 30) points to the symbolic meanings of buying commodities as well as the permanent construction of meaning and 'maintaining aspects of our identity' through their everyday use. The purchase and consumption of beauty products (for example, makeup products, perfumes, etc.) does not take place in the domain of satisfying primary existential needs but is positioned in the playful and symbolic sphere of hedonism, ludism, and aesthetics, which actualizes the potential for self-expression, reconstructing identity and some forms of self-fulfilment (Geiger Zeman & Zeman, 2015). In that aspect, 'shopping can serve as a site of identity performance' (Miller et al., 1998, as cited in Scott, 2012, p. 141), that is, in Goffman's dramaturgical categories, 'shopping provides us with items of identity equipment, which we use to present versions of ourselves to others' (Scott, 2012, p. 141).

Consumerism and shopping activities have a significant place in postfeminist culture and its media representations (Adriaens & Van Bauwel, 2014; Geiger Zeman & Zeman, 2015; Radner, 2011). Feminist critics point to the advertising exploitation of feminist messages about power, independence and strength with the aim of encouraging the consumption of so-called feminine commodities (which also include beauty products for different purposes) which dissolve the political power of feminism (Radner, 2011). Lazar (2011, p. 37) analyzes advertisements for makeup products and questions the connection between 'postfeminist identity and consumer beauty advertising'. Through new ways of advertising makeup products, 'make-up is construed as light hearted and fun', more precisely 'seriously girly fun' (italics by Lazar, 2017, p. 55), while 'make-up experience' is associated with 'enjoyment and pleasure' (Lazar, 2017, p. 53). In this way, 'the actual feminine labour involved in beauty practices' is recontextualized as 'non-work' and 'pleasurable feminine activity' (Lazar, 2017, p. 55). In the analysis of postfeminism and its implications, Adriaens and Van Bauwel (2014) go beyond the good-bad binarism and position and analyze postfeminist phenomena in the context of neoliberal, consumerist, postmodern and individualistic society. From this perspective, postfeminism is 'a pluralistic and contradictory feminism', which allows women to be simultaneously 'feminine, attractive, and a feminist' (Adriaens & Van Bauwel, 2014, p. 179; see also Geiger Zeman & Zeman, 2015, p. 115).

In consumerist and popular culture, fashion models are represented as the embodiment of cultural ideals of beauty (Soley-Beltran, 2012; see also Geiger Zeman & Zeman, 2021), but this is only one aspect of the modelling profession. Entwistle and Wissinger (2014, p. 1) point out that 'models have been integral to the development of modern consumer culture', that they play a significant role in creating sales of various commodities, and that they are a specific 'barometer of the current state of attitudes towards women, race and consumerism'. Brown (2012, p. 37) defines the modelling profession as 'a form of labour where the models and other cultural brokers transform subjective aspects of modern selfhood – gesture, appearance, presence – into immaterial commodities' which adds 'surplus value to manufactured goods'. Models are simultaneously involved in the processes of commodification and branding with the aim of promoting consumption in such a way that they 'lend their image to sell products' and encourage consumption, therefore they function as '*intermediaries* between production and consumption' (italics by Wissinger, 2009, p. 274; see also Wissinger, 2012, p. 157). According to Brown (2012, p. 37), 'models sell commodities by using their bodies to produce commercialized affect in relationship to specific goods: glamour, elegance, cool'. Models, as well as many other celebrities from different domains during (and after) their modelling careers start entrepreneurial initiatives in other industries. Given that the beauty industry is a highly profitable sector and that the development of digital technology and social networks has created spaces for new ways of promotion and advertising, celebrities are launching their own beauty brands. Social media has enabled celebrities to become influencers and endorsers (Israeli et al., 2024). How much the trend is visible and in the expansion is also shown by the title of the article 'It's Official: Every Celeb Now Has a Beauty Line' by Rubin (2020) for the New York Times. Recent trends point to synergies between the beauty industry and the wellness industry, which open highly profitable market niches for brands that promote sustainability, clean beauty, self care and personalization (NIQ, 2023). More and more beauty brands are turning 'towards health and wellness' and trying to incorporate them 'into their DNA' (Parkkinen, 2022, n.a.). 'Beauty, glow, health and "mighty cosmic flow"' (Living Wholly, 2019, as cited in Conor, 2021, p. 2) are key features of the phenomenon that Conor (2021) calls 'cosmic wellness' (p. 1). Conor (2021, p. 2) defines cosmic wellness as a 'broad constellation of materials, foods, imagery and discourse' that is sold, promoted and consumed by privileged white women. According to Conor (2021), cosmic wellness is a response to the unstable and uncertain conditions of life in a class-polarized neoliberal late modern society. One of the key imperatives for individuals in such a context is optimization through 'susceptibility and enhancement' (Rose, 2006, as cited in Conor, 2021, p. 4). Cosmic wellness is focussed on a holistic idea of health that encompasses body, mind, and spirit. One of the fundamental ideas of the cosmic wellness industry is the optimization of health and happiness through self-care practices (e.g. detoxification, meditation, practicing yoga, etc.) and the purchase of products that are attributed spiritual values (Conor, 2021, p. 5), although, in fact, some products and practices of cosmic wellness are 'unhealthy and dangerous' (Conor, 2021, p. 2). Conor understands cosmic wellness as 'the newest example of narcissistic self-absorption' (2021, p. 2) and a 'postfeminist phenomenon' (2021, p. 7).

In addition to promoting their own beauty brands, celebrities use their 'superior status' to gain 'attention' which in return maintains their privileged position (Kurzman et al., 2007, p. 356). The audience's attention is drawn to 'the most mundane experiences of celebrities', and by sharing their everyday experiences with the public, celebrities become 'intimate strangers' (Schickel, 1985, as cited in Kurzman et al., 2007, p. 356), inspiration and role models with whom fans identify, compare, copy, etc., which, among other things, encourages 'imitative consumption' (Kurzman et al., 2007, p. 357) (e.g. buying cosmetic products advertised and praised by a celebrity, etc.). Before the Internet and social networks, traditional media offered information about beauty routines, fashion styles, exercise, and diet of celebrities, and today this information is created and disseminated by celebrities through their profiles on social networks. Everyday beauty regimens are based on specific expert and lay knowledge and techniques (e.g. how to use an eyelash curler, how to apply eye shadow to achieve a cat-like look, etc.). Celebrities in this domain also assume the role of authority (Kurzman et al., 2007, p. 358) by sharing advice on beauty and beautification practices either through formal media channels or through their profiles on social networks.

4. Beautification Practices in Everyday Life

Everyday life is a 'mundane' and 'familiar' domain permeated with seemingly 'routine, repetitive and rhythmic' activities that reflect social patterns (Wright Mills, 1959, as cited in Scott, 2012, p. 2), 'power, politics' (Martin, 2003, as cited in Scott, 2012, p. 2) and 'reproduces social life' (Scott, 2012, p. 2). Beautification practices are part of the daily habits and routines of many people around the world. In the most general sense, they can be defined as the application of beauty products to the 'whole face, lips, eyebrows, eyelashes, nose, cheeks, hair, and nails' (Ambarwati, 2018, p. 88) with the aim of 'cleansing, beautifying, promoting attractiveness, or altering the appearance without affecting the body's structure or its functions (www.fda.gov, 2016)' (as cited in Ambarwati, 2018, p. 88).

Everyday practices of beautification take place in certain temporal and spatial contexts. In order to understand everyday life and the series of popular cultural activities that shape it, the inclusion of the temporal dimension is crucial. Scott (2012, p. 69) highlights the repetitive cyclicity of activities and practices that form the experience of the everyday. Our daily schedules are repetitive and predictable, and the practices of beautification and carrying out the beauty regimen take their place in them, repeating most often in the morning and evening rhythms. As part of the daily routine, personal and private beautification practices are also interesting from a gender perspective because they indicate gender differences in the temporal investment/time duration of beautification activities. Beautification practices are spatially situated, where bathrooms are socially and culturally marked as 'the primary location' for engagement with personal appearance and the practice of grooming (doing of beauty) (hair, face, make up, etc.) (Waskul, 2016, p. 152).

Beautification as a feminine disciplinary practice (Bartky, 1998) in the context of everyday life can also be observed in the categories of habit and routine (Arlinghaus & Johnston, 2018; Giovagnoli, 2018) which is also indicated by widespread expressions such as 'skin care habits', 'beauty routine', 'skin care routines', etc. Everyday beautification practices are imbued with layers of meaning and 'with social and cultural implications' (Pruit, 2016, p. 155) that can be observed and analyzed through different theoretical lenses. For Plante (2016, p. 165) 'putting on makeup is creative, indulgent, mostly gendered, possibly political, often engrossing act that is ritual and a chore'. In this inspiring definition of the practice of applying makeup products to the face, the ambivalences and contradictory meanings attributed to this practice are not exhausted – whether it is a matter of confirming (gender) conformity or an act of individual creativity, an internalized gendered societal expectation or a matter of personal choice, the legitimation of the gender order or its transgression, camouflaging or glorifying one's face, coercion or entertainment? Practicing beautification can be conformist in the sense of adopting and respecting norms that reproduce traditional femininity, but it can also be a transgressive, creative and subversive practice that transcends and criticizes gender expectations and conventional feminine aesthetics (Scott, 2012). Using the example of women's experiences with hair, Weitz (2001) shows how resistance and conformity are simultaneously present in women's everyday bodily experiences (see also Sault, 1994).

Within feminism, there are many debates and opposing viewpoints about the political, social, cultural, psychological meanings and consequences of beautifying and applying makeup as a daily grooming activity, i.e. an important aspect of daily aesthetic work, the ultimate goal of which (for most people who practice it) is 'looking good' (Elias et al., 2017, p. 4), but also achieving a certain type of normative feminine appearance (Bartky, 1998) that will be publicly presented in the social arena (Plante, 2016). Elias et al. (2017, p. 5) open a discussion about gender, femininity, beauty and beautification practices in the context of late modern capitalism and inaugurate new topics that position beauty in the context of neoliberalism and an ideology that glorifies 'active, entrepreneurial, self-optimizing subjects'. Everyday beauty work (Lazar, 2011, 2017) is a type of 'affective', 'emotional', and 'glamour' labour (Wissinger, 2015, as cited in Elias et al., 2017, p. 5) engaged in self-presentation that transcends the boundaries of the fashion or modelling industry (because in neoliberalism everyone is 'aesthetic entrepreneurs') (Elias et al., 2017, p. 5).

5. Methodology

Rituals and routines related to self-representation (or everyday beautification) is a popular cultural practice situated in everyday schedules and specific locations and (no matter how banal it may seem at first glance) is imbued in every aspect with different meanings, power, and ideologies. The media have a significant influence in the production, maintenance and representation of beauty and its cultural meanings (Engeln-Maddox, 2006; Henriques & Patnaik, 2021; Wolf, 2002). At the same time, the media play an important role in the production and reproduction of knowledge, techniques and advice related to beautification practices and beauty regimes. Video beauty tutorials are important elements of digital beauty culture. These are popular culture texts produced and consumed in specific contexts.

The digital beauty culture and practices of beautification is present in different (visual and written) ways on the portal of the famous fashion magazine Vogue (USA edition). Celebrities are represented in the media as the embodiment of normative ideas about beauty, and this discourse is also taken over by Vogue, calling celebrities 'the ultimate beauty muses' who 'deliver endless inspiration across skin, hair, makeup, and even fragrance' (The Beauty Secrets Shop: All-Star Products As Seen in the Series, n.d.). In 2016, Vogue started with a beauty series or 'intimate show' called Vogue's 'Beauty Secrets', which introduces the audience to 'the routines and regiments of well-known and beloved beauty, fashion, and pop culture figures' (Beauty Secrets, n.d.). Every week on Vogue's web portal and YouTube channel, audiences have the opportunity to see which beauty routines celebrities practice on a daily basis. Celebrities record their videos in private and intimate bathroom space, showing not only their intimate 'beauty secrets', beauty tips and tricks they learnt from beauty professionals they worked with, but also endorsing/promoting/advertising/cosmetic products of well-known beauty brands (or their own beauty brand). Vogue's 'Beauty Secrets' series functions as both a shopping guide and a virtual shopwindow for the promotion of luxury beauty products. Below each video is a transcript and a list of all the beauty products and 'tactical tools' (The Beauty Secrets Shop: All-Star Products As Seen in the Series, n.d.) that a particular celebrity used in their beauty routine. A separate website also highlights products used by celebrities from favourite episodes (The Beauty Secrets Shop: All-Star Products As Seen in the Series, n.d.). In addition to the emphasized consumer aspect of Vogue's 'Beauty Secrets', celebrities are assigned the role of beauty authorities from whom the audience acquires beauty knowledge.

The focus of the analysis is the video/beauty tutorial 'Kate Moss's Guide to Restorative Wellness and Feel-Good Beauty' (Vogue, 2022a)/'Kate Moss's Guide to Cool-Girl Beauty' (YouTube, 2022b) published on the website of the fashion magazine Vogue (USA) as part of the Beauty Secrets series. The video lasts 6 minutes and 11 seconds, it was transferred from the official Vogue USA website to the Vogue YouTube channel. The YouTube video had 2,650,980 views and 1,905 comments (as of May 13, 2024). The analysis is based on the following research questions: How is the daily beauty routine of models with iconic status organized and performed? Which beauty products were used during the public representation of the daily practice of beautification? How are everyday beautification practices presented and performed in the beauty video? How are the beauty products applied? What connections are made between the everyday beauty regime and consumerism? How beauty products and represented beauty practices are linked to 'power, politics' and wider socio-cultural meanings (Martin, 2003, as cited in Scott, 2012, p. 2), including gender, race and class. In addition to the beauty video, additional relevant materials were collected (website of the beauty and wellness brand *Cosmoss* by Kate Moss; materials related to the career and meaning of Kate Moss as a fashion model and entrepreneur). As specific texts, beauty video and beauty brand are understood and analyzed in: (1) the context of modelling career and entrepreneurial achievements of Kate Moss and (2) and in a wider social, cultural and economic context, focussing on 'power relations of meaning making; for example, in reproducing ideologies about postfeminism, neoliberalism, capitalism, gender, race and class' (Swan, 2017, as cited in Conor, 2021, p. 11). The analysis is based on: (1) the 'modes of multimodal visual analysis' (Kress & Van Leeuwen, 2001, as cited in Conor, 2021, p. 11); (2) elements of textual analysis developed by Lacey (2009) (for example, facial expression, gaze, gestures, posture clothes, appearance, etc.), (3) semiological analysis by Dyer (1982, as cited in Rose, 2010, pp. 81–82) (for example, representations of body, manners, activities, props, settings) and (4) critical discourse analysis by Fairclough (1989, 1995), based on a three-dimensional model that includes: (a) 'text analysis (description)'; (b) 'processing analysis (interpretation)'; (c) 'social analysis (explanation)' (Janks, 1997, p. 329).

6. Kate Moss: The Icon and the Brand

Kate Moss undoubtedly occupies a special status in the fashion and modelling industry. Her modelling career began with a chance encounter with Sarah Doukas, the founder of the Storm model agency, at JFK airport in 1988 (Berrington, 2014). During the 1990s, her career made excellent progress and Moss became a well-known public person. Berrington (2014) points out that 'as a model Kate Moss defies categorization'. Although she is the undisputed holder of the prestigious title of supermodel during the 1990s, Moss was also called an 'anti-supermodel' (Phillips, 2023). Unlike the famous supermodels of that era whose appearance was characterized by hyperfeminization and glamour, Moss with her thin figure, relatively modest height (5 foot 7 inches), street style and her natural appearance did not fit the conventional glamorized supermodel standard of the 1990s (Britannica, last updated 2024). Entwistle (as cited in Hess, 2018) points out that the iconic status of Kate Moss was created 'on a foundation of ordinariness' and accessible appeal that suggests relaxation, laughter, fun and sociability. Mears points to coolness as a characteristic attributed to Moss – 'She invokes cool in everything she does. Even her mishaps are understood as cool' (as cited in Hess, 2018). From the beginning of her rich and successful career, Moss provoked public debates and controversies, where her professional engagements and private life, which was followed by the tabloid and sensationalist media, were intertwined in complex and contradictory ways. During the 1990s, Moss was publicly called out and criticized for embodying and promoting the so-called heroin chic (Helmore, 2019). Moss successfully overcame all the scandals that filled the pages of tabloids and sensationalist portals and while other celebrities during major scandals would give a public response and try to repair the damaged public image, 'Moss maintained a dignified silence' (Hess, 2018).

Despite the moral panics, the ridicule from the tabloids and the scandals she faced, Kate Moss maintained and confirmed the status of a pop cultural and fashion icon, which was described in fashion magazines without exception in superlatives – 'Not just a model, she's the girl every young girl wants to dress like, she's the celebrity no one can resist reading about, and she's someone whose antics fascinate. She's a style icon for a generation' (Berrington, 2014). In a highly competitive and extremely volatile market, Kate Moss has managed to maintain her position of power and relevance for decades. The reasons for the longevity of Moss's career are a combination of several factors that are not exclusively related to her appearance. Mears (as cited in Hess, 2018) emphasizes 'strategic alliances with the right brands and collaborations and friends', also her 'character, social circle and lifestyle, which are, ironically, aspects of her identity she has aimed for many decades to conceal from the public eye'.

Kate Moss can also be thought of in brand categories (Entwistle & Slater, 2012). The perspective 'models as a brand' is developed by Entwistle and Slater (2012, p. 15) and they emphasize 'the model brand is enacted in and through specific objects, actions and signs, but is always a kind of moving assemblage of all of them, something they all both perform and are performed by' (2012, p. 17). In the context of the analysis of the model as a brand, Entwistle and Slater (2012, pp. 16–17) introduce the idea of 'the look', which they differentiate from 'images' and 'representations', and it is defined as 'an object of calculation, something continuously worked upon, moulded, contested, performed, something that is identifiable out there in the world' (Entwistle & Slater, 2012, p. 17). The look is changeable and in a state of permanent change and transformation into new forms. The model embodies a certain look, however, the look is not something that is intrinsic to the model (Entwistle & Slater, 2012, p. 30). From this position, models are understood as 'complex objects whose meanings are actively constituted in multiple locations' (Entwistle & Slater, 2012, p. 17) (e.g. fashion magazine, model agency, tabloids, campaigns, etc.) (Entwistle & Slater, 2012, p. 18). Complex relations between production and consumption are established through the look and with the help of the look, and everything the model does, buys, consumes and performs has an impact on her/his/their look (Entwistle & Slater, 2012, p. 27).

On the threshold of her 50s, Moss is still relevant in the fashion and modelling industry, but as Mears points out, 'the most radical chapter' in her career still lies ahead of her (as cited in Hess, 2018). Given her status, influence and respectable heritage in the modelling industry, Moss has the ability to redefine established definitions of beauty as a privilege of youth and thus destabilize and change the ageist 'barrier in our repertoire of beauty that is almost rarely broken' (Mears as cited in Hess, 2018).

Kate Moss developed not only her modelling but also a successful entrepreneurial career, which in recent decades and years has been established in several business locations – from successful and long-term collaborations with numerous brands from the world of fashion and beauty industry (e.g. Topshop, Longchamp, Rimmel, etc.), through creating her own perfume line and founding a talent management agency (Segran, 2016) to launching her own cosmetics brand *Cosmoss* (Cosmoss by Kate Moss, n.d.). Moss is 'one of the richest women in Britain' (Marks, 2016, n.a.). At the end of August 2022, after two and a half years of work on new products, Kate Moss presented her new cosmetic brand, whose name *Cosmoss* combines two words – 'cosmos' and the surname Moss, which semantically defines the brand and positions it in the domain of 'cosmic wellness' (Conor, 2021). It is a business in which Moss has gained rich experience through her modelling career, as well as acquaintances from the world of the beauty industry. Given her iconic status, all leading fashion portals participated in the presentation of the *Cosmoss* brand. Fashion media described this business initiative as a transition from 'fashion's favourite party girl' to 'glow-getting entrepreneur' (Young, 2023), i.e. the entry of the 'queen of Glastonbury' festival into the 'wellness establishment' (Elwick-Bates, 2022). In the branding categories, it is rearranging the specific Kate Moss look into new forms, whereby the constant meanings of *cool*, naturalness and authenticity are transferred to new lucrative locations. Moss presented her new entrepreneurial initiative with the self-care–balance–inner peace narrative (Young, 2023), connecting it to personal wellness experiences, thus commodifying a part of her own privacy, intimacy and everyday life. In an interview with Harper's Bazaar, Moss described the brand *Cosmoss* 'as a "genuine reflection"' of her 'own personal wellness journey' (Young, 2023). Neglected self-care in the earlier stages of her life Kate Moss has now replaced with daily holistic practice of a healthy life – with positive psychology, self-care spirituality, detoxification, yoga, gong baths, homoeopathy, meditation… But unlike cosmic wellness queen Gwyneth Paltrow (Conor, 2021), Moss in her own *cool* way lives and practices a new lifestyle by combining it with Diet Coke and cigarettes (Young, 2023).

7. 'Beauty Secrets' of the 'Cool-Girl'

In the foreground of the Vogue's 'Beauty Secrets' video (2022a, b) is the face of Kate Moss (2022a, 00:05; see also 2022b). Her blonde hair is slightly tossed back, and her face is seemingly make-up free – her skin is clean, shiny, slightly sun-kissed, fresh, toned, wrinkles are only occasionally visible under her eyes while Moss slightly turns her head to the side. The glow of the skin emphasized on the upper part of the face highlights the shine of her eyes, which gives the whole face a youthful and somewhat ageless look. Moss is dressed in a simple white T-shirt, has discreet earrings on her ears, and as she tilts her head back in the last frames of the video, it is visible that she is wearing gold and silver bracelets on her hands (Beauty Secrets, 2022a, 05:56–05:59; see also 2022b). Moss looks straight into the camera, her facial expressions are always controlled, and she radiates calmness and confidence as she focuses on her daily beauty routine. Her facial expressions change as she talks about her youthful modelling days – she tilts her head, smiles, widens her eyes, thus performing expressions of conventional femininity (Bartky, 1998). Moss's glowing face is an extension of lived well-being and Self transformed by cosmic wellness. As 'white, slim and blonde' Moss, like Paltrow and the models on Goop Glow promotional Instagram posts, embodies the '"ideal" subject of cosmic wellness' which is 'gendered, raced and sexualized' (Conor, 2021, p. 14).

The minimalist aesthetic of Kate Moss contrasts with the interior where the video was shot. It is a private and intimate space in a luxurious bathroom decorated in vintage style. The bathroom is a combination of a conventional bathroom, as indicated by the sink with beauty products, a mirror above the sink, and two dressing gowns in gender-neutral white and feminine dusty pink. Cloaks are hung on the door of the room. On the opposite side, there is a sofa covered with velvet, also in dusty pink colour, and as a contrast to the pink colour, there is a black cushion with a white pattern. At one end of the sofa there is a cabinet with a retro-looking table lamp, and at the other is an indoor plant whose leaves gently fall towards the middle of the room. The sofa suggests leisure and enjoyment in a space that, in addition to maintaining hygiene, is intended for rest and leisure activities. Behind Kate Moss is a white chest of drawers and a mirror with a carved silver frame, which connects the classic bathroom part of the space with the part intended for resting and enjoying beautification or self-care practices. The walls are painted in white and light grey stripes, and on the leisure side of the room there are pictures and a gramophone record. White, grey, dusty pink, green and black details are the colour palettes that dominate the space and suggest a feminine and luxurious space intended for leisure, domestic wellness and self-care.

Kate Moss 'daily beauty routine is presented as a self-care ceremony that begins with drinking tea (*Cosmoss* product) from an elegant white porcelain cup and lighting a rose quartz candle (Beauty Secrets, 2022a, 00:13, 00:27; see also 2022b). After that, Moss uses a number of products from luxury brands intended for skin care (cleanser, rose water, moisturizer/*Cosmoss* product, "magic tool"' Gua Sha (Beauty Secrets, 2022a, 02:09; see also 2022b), sunscreen, sleep musk used as lip musk, CBD oil/*Cosmoss* product); health care (dietary supplement/ supplementation – CBD oil/*Cosmoss* product); make up routine (concealers, bronzer, blush, eyelash curler, brow gel, lip tint, cosmetic tools – sponge, eyelash curler brush); hair styling (Sam McKnight's Cool Girl hair mist) and applying fragrance (Sacred Mist/*Cosmoss* product) (Beauty Secrets, 2022a, 01:05–06:05; see also 2022b).

The meanings that Moss attributes to *Cosmoss* beauty and wellness products imply her involvement and engagement in the production and reproduction of the cosmic wellness discourse. Kate Moss's beauty video is not only a representation of her daily beauty routine but also a promotion of her new brand, which is an extension and reflection of her new lifestyle focused on self-care and trying new things that bring grounding and balance as a reward (Beauty Secrets, 2022a, 00: 43–01:00; see also 2022b). Personal experiences are commodified in her new beauty and wellness brand, and *Cosmoss* products embody these new values and experiences. Moss occupies a position of wellness and health authority partly by appropriating the manner of Goop discourse. For each *Cosmoss* product consumed, its health value is emphasized, whereby the explanation combines scientific-medical and spiritual argumentation, which confirms the 'magic' and 'healing' effects of her brand's products. For example, Moss starts her day with Dawn tea, and she explains her choice by highlighting the delicious taste and the alleged health benefits of the product, which is an alternative to the popular lemon water and its alleged negative effects on the teeth (Beauty Secrets, 2022a, 00: 13–00:25; see also 2022b). Moss highlights the naturalness of its products and their grounding, balancing and calming effects (for example *Cosmoss* moisturizer, CBD oil Golden nectar for external and oral use) (Beauty Secrets, 2022a, 01: 47–02:07, 02:55–03:31; see also 2022b). The discourse of spirituality is evident in the highlighting of the words sacred, magic, magical, which are associated with certain products or objects Using the gua sha stone as a 'magic tool' (Beauty Secrets, 2022a, 02:10; see also 2022b) and declaring its beneficial health effects ('It's good for the lymphatic drainage') (Beauty Secrets, 2022a, 02:15; see also 2022b) is connected with cultural appropriation and the use of untested and scientifically unproven arguments.

Moss presents her daily skin care and beauty routine as a self-care and domestic wellness ritual. Looking at the website of the *Cosmoss* brand, we see that Moss performs a daily morning/Dawn ritual in the video, which consists of three steps (see Cosmoss by Kate Moss Shop, n.d.): drinking a cup of tea; skin care and fragrance application. The result of this ritual and the effect of the consumed products are gentle awakening, protection from 'stress, pollution, toxins', removal of impurities from the skin, stimulation of natural collagen, younger looking skin, grounding, emotional balance and peace (*Cosmoss* by Kate Moss Shop). After facial care, Moss applies make-up products to the face to create a fresh, natural and glowing look (Beauty Secrets, 2022a, 03:33–05-40; see also 2022b). Although Moss identifies herself as 'not very high maintenance' in doing makeup (Beauty Secrets, 2022a, 03:47; see also 2022b) but she declares herself as a make-up lover (Beauty Secrets, 2022a, 04:08; see also 2022b) and makes a distinction between her recent daytime make-up, which is basic and discreet, and her more creative and intense night-time make-up, in which she emphasizes the eyes (Beauty Secrets, 2022a, 03:53–03:59; see also 2022b). In addition to the distinction between day and night, Moss also introduces a temporal component, creating in her beauty-self-care narrative the distinction between then and now. Moss compares the recent make-up style with her younger version of grunge modelling (Beauty Secrets, 2022a, 04:10–04:26; see also 2022b) and in general earlier practices of models intervening in the work of make-up artists on their faces, which is a prohibited and sanctioned practice today (Beauty Secrets, 2022a, 04:35–05:07; see also 2022b). Performing a daily beauty routine and sharing beauty secrets is at the same time-sharing memories from the modelling past as well as sharing private experiences of the intergenerational transfer of beauty knowledge and beautification techniques from daughter to mother. Moss attributes the role of authority to her daughter, who advises and educates her about beauty products and care practices (Beauty Secrets, 2022a, 02:32–02:38, 02:42, 02:47–02:53; see also 2022b). Although she is awarded the status of a fashion and modelling icon, Moss assigns the iconic status to her colleague Christy Turlington, implying a definition of beauty that is not only related to physical appearance but also to inner qualities. According to Moss, Turlington is the embodiment of this ideal of beauty (Beauty Secrets, 2022a, 05:17–05:23; see also 2022b).

There is an evident consumerist component and an incentive for conspicuous consumption reserved for white and well-off women. In the video, Moss uses other brands' products in an semi-anonymizing way predominantly without naming the manufacturer or the brand (eg the name of the brand can be seen on the used products), but for each *Cosmoss* product, she clearly declares that it is her brand (Beauty Secrets, 2022a, 00:14, 01:05, 01:46, 02:56, 06:03; see also 2022b). The one exception is Sam McKnight's Cool Girl hair product (Beauty Secrets, 2022a, 05:46; see also 2022b), which was inspired by Moss because of her 'a little bit shabby looking' hair (Beauty Secrets, 2022a, 05:52; see also 2022b). Highlighting herself as a muse for hair products, Moss confirms her iconic status and signals excellent connections and acquaintances in the world of the beauty industry. On the Vogue website and on the Vogue YouTube channel, all the products Moss used in her demonstration of her daily beauty routine are listed for viewers to purchase. Namely, the practice of Kate Moss' self-care and beauty routine requires the investment of significant financial resources (about US$823), which points to the importance of class and the maintenance of class differentiation.

8. Conclusion

In Vogue's 'Beauty Secrets' video Kate Moss acts as an 'intermediarie' between production and consumption (Wissinger, 2012, p. 157). In addition to selling products of hers own and other brands, guaranteeing their quality, Moss sells and promotes a specific lifestyle by appealing to specific consumerist choices legitimized by neoliberal wellness ideology and the logic of post-feminism. Using the language, imagery and aesthetics of cosmic wellness also promoted by Gwyneth Paltrow on the Goop platform, Moss perpetuates neoliberal narratives about health, healing, self-care and personal development. In doing so, she commodifies her own life experience and uses her own recognition and privileged position in the fashion industry and the media. In the case of *Cosmoss*, it is evident that it is a postfeminist gendered phenomenon in which a white and privileged woman consumes and sells luxury products that promise personal peace, physical health, emotional stability and balance in an insecure and variously divided world (Conor, 2021). Moss presents daily beauty rituals as a daily practice of spirituality. Her beauty rituals are represented as self-care ceremonies, the primary goal of which is the restoration of balance and health. The analyzed video as a text of digital beauty culture shows how everyday beautification regimes are popular cultural practices that connect micro and macro levels in interesting ways and establish layered relationships between beauty products, beautification practices and consumerist culture (see Waskul & Vannini, 2016). In this way, power relations and ideologies related to race, gender and class in the neoliberal context and postfeminist culture are reflected and reproduced through mundane activities.

Acknowledgements

This chapter is partially based on the presentation 'Balancing Body and Soul: Kate Moss, Rejuvenation Narratives, and Postfeminist Aging' (by Marija Geiger Zeman and Zdenko Zeman) for the *Talking Bodies 2023 conference, University of Chester* (June 12–16, 2023). We thank Dr Zdenko Zeman for reading and commenting on the manuscript and for translation.

References

Adriaens, F., & Van Bauwel, S. (2014). Sex and the city. A postfeminist point of view? Or how culture functions as a channel for feminist discourse. *The Journal of Popular Culture*, *47*(1), 174–195.

Ambarwati, N. T. (2018). Beauty class and the practice of beautification among lower middle-class young women. *Digital Press Social Sciences and Humanities*, *1*, 87–94.

Anbouba, M. (2023, October 15). Feminist icon Judy Chicago on aging, makeup, and "Gratuitous Beauty". *Vogue*. https://www.vogue.com/article/judy-chicago-beauty-interview

Arlinghaus, K. R., & Johnston, C. A. (2018). Importance of creating habits and routine. *American Journal of Lifestyle Medicine*, *13*(2), 142–144. https://doi/org/10.1177/1559827618818044

Asa Berger, A. (2009). *What objects mean. An introduction to material culture*. Left Coast Press, Inc.
Bartky, S. L. (1998). Foucault, femininity, and the modernization of patriarchal power. In R. Weitz (Ed.), *The politics of women's bodies. Sexuality, appearance and behavior* (pp. 25–45). Oxford University Press.
Beauty Secrets. (2022a, August 29). Kate Moss's guide to restorative wellness and feel-good beauty. *Vogue*. https://www.vogue.com/video/watch/beauty-secrets-kate-moss
Beauty Secrets. (2022b, August 31). Kate Moss's guide to cool-girl beauty | Beauty Secrets | Vogue. *YouTube*. https://www.youtube.com/watch?v=VQGvii7XSkc
Beauty Secrets. (n.d.). Beauty secrets: Watch the best celebrity beauty secrets videos. *Vogue*. https://www.vogue.com/tag/misc/beauty-secrets. Accessed on April 15, 2024.
Bennett, T., & Watson, D. (2002). Understanding everyday life: Introduction. In T. Bennett & D. Watson (Eds.), *Understanding everyday life* (pp. ix–xxiv). Blackwell.
Berrington, K. (2014, February 11). Kate Moss. *Vogue*. https://www.vogue.co.uk/article/kate-moss-biography
Berry, K. (2016). Shopping. In D. D. Waskul & P. Vannini (Eds.), *Popular culture as everyday life* (pp. 255–263). Routledge.
Britannica. (2024, May 19). Kate Moss. https://www.britannica.com/biography/Kate-Moss#ref1205585
Brown, E. H. (2012). From artist's model to the 'Natural Girl': Containing sexuality in early-twentieth-century modelling. In J. Entwistle & E. Wissinger (Eds.), *Fashioning models. Image, text and industry* (pp. 37–55). Berg.
Conor, B. (2021). 'How Goopy are you?' Women, Goop and cosmic wellness. *European Journal of Cultural Studies*, *24*(6), 1–21. https://doi.org/10.1177/13675494211055735
Cosmetics Europe. (n.d.). Cosmetic products. https://cosmeticseurope.eu/cosmetic-products. Accessed on April 15, 2024.
Cosmoss by Kate Moss. (n.d.). https://www.cosmossbykatemoss.com/en/. Accessed on April 15, 2024.
Cosmoss by Kate Moss Shop. (n.d.). https://www.cosmossbykatemoss.com/en/shop/rituals/#products. Accessed on April 15, 2024.
Eicher, J. B., Evenson, S. L., & Lutz, H. A. (2000). *The visible self. Global perspectives on dress, culture, and society*. Fairchild Publications.
Elias, A., Gill, R., & Scharff, C. (2017). Aesthetic labour: Beauty politics in neoliberalism. In A. S. Elias, R. Gill, & C. Scharff (Eds.), *Aesthetic labour: Rethinking beauty politics in neoliberalism* (pp. 3–49). Palgrave Macmillan.
Elwick-Bates, E. (2022, August 31). Kate Moss opens up about her new wellness brand and the concept of compassionate self care. *Vogue*. https://www.vogue.com/article/kate-moss-wellness-cosmoss
Engeln-Maddox, R. (2006). Buying a beauty standard or dreaming of a new life? Expectations associated with media ideals. *Psychology of Women Quarterly*, *30*(3), 258–266.
Entwistle, J., & Slater, D. (2012). Models as brands: Critical thinking about bodies and images. In J. Entwistle & E. Wissinger (Eds.), *Fashioning models. Image, text and industry* (pp. 15–33). Berg.

Entwistle, J., & Wissinger, E. (2014). Introduction. In J. Entwistle & E. Wissinger (Eds.), *Fashioning models. Image, text and industry* (pp. 1–14). Berg.

Fairclough, N. (1989). *Language and power*. Longman.

Fairclough, N. (1995). *Critical discourse analysis*. Longman.

Geiger Zeman, M., & Zeman, Z. (2015). Potrošački snovi chic djevojaka: rodno lice konzumerizma. *Narodna Umjetnost*, *52*(2), 105–137. https://doi.org/10.15176/vol52no206

Geiger Zeman, M., & Zeman, Z. (2021). Ageing like a supermodel: Negotiating body in the celebrity 'self-life writing'. *Northern Lights: Film & Media Studies Yearbook*, *19*, 101–115. https://doi.org/10.1386/nl_00025_1

Ghoshal, R. (2022). Lipstick in the time of Corona: A sociological musing. *Social Trends, Journal of the Department of Sociology of North Bengal University*, *9*(31), 23–37.

Giovagnoli, R. (2018). From habits to rituals: Rituals as social habits. *Open Information Science*, *2*, 181–188. https://doi.org/10.1515/opis-2018-0014

Gurrieri, L., & Drenten, J. M. (2019). The feminist politics of choice. Lipstick as a marketplace icon. *Consumption Markets & Culture*, *24*(3), 225–240. https://doi.org/10.1080/10253866.2019.1670649

Helmore, E. (2019, May 23). 'Heroin chic' and the tangled legacy of photographer Davide Sorrenti. *The Guardian*. https://www.theguardian.com/fashion/2019/may/23/heroin-chic-and-the-tangled-legacy-of-photographer-davide-sorrenti

Henriques, M., & Patnaik, D. (2021). Social media and its effects on beauty. *IntechOpen*. https://doi/org/10.5772/intechopen.93322. https://www.intechopen.com/chapters/73271

Hess, L. (2018, September 26). Kate Moss: What makes a muse? *Dazed Digital*. https://www.dazeddigital.com/beauty/article/41548/1/kate-moss-what-makes-a-muse

Israeli, A., Avery, J., Schlesinger, L. A., & Higgins, M. (2024, May–June). What makes a successful celebrity brand. *Harvard Business Review*. https://hbr.org/2024/05/what-makes-a-successful-celebrity-brand

Janks, H. (1997). Critical discourse analysis as a research tool. *Discourse: Studies in the Cultural Politics of Education*, *18*(3), 329–342. https://doi.org/10.1080/0159630970180302

Katz, S. (2019). Introduction. In S. Katz (Ed.), *Ageing in everyday life. Materialities and embodiments* (pp. 1–21). Policy Press.

Klein, U. (2016). Sharing selfies. In D. D. Waskul & P. Vannini (Eds.), *Popular culture as everyday life* (pp. 85–94). Routledge.

Kurzman, C., Anderson, C., Key, C., Lee, Y. O., Moloney, M., Silver, A., & Van Ryn, M. W. (2007). Celebrity status. *Sociological Theory*, *25*(4), 347–367.

Lacey, N. (2009). *Image and representation. Key concepts in media studies*. Palgrave Macmillan.

Lazar, M. M. (2011). The right to be beautiful: Postfeminist identity and consumer beauty advertising. In R. Gill & C. Scharff (Eds.), *New femininities. Postfeminism, Neoliberalism and subjectivity* (pp. 37–51). Palgrave Macmillan.

Lazar, M. M. (2017). 'Seriously Girly Fun!': Recontextualising aesthetic labour as fun and play in cosmetics advertising. In A. S. Elias, R. Gill, & C. Scharff (Eds.), *Aesthetic labour: Rethinking beauty politics in neoliberalism* (pp. 51–66). Palgrave Macmillan.

Lupton, D. (2020). Understanding digital food cultures. In D. Lupton & Z. Feldman (Eds.), *Digital food cultures* (pp. 1–16). Routledge.

Marks, G. (2016, September 21). Why this start-up founded by the world's most famous model just might succeed. *The Washington Post*. https://www.washingtonpost.com/news/on-small-business/wp/2016/09/21/gene-marks-will-this-start-up-founded-by-the-worlds-most-famous-model-succeed/

NIQ. (2023, July 18). 4 wellness trends that are changing the beauty industry. https://nielseniq.com/global/en/insights/education/2023/4-wellness-trends-beauty/

Ogilvie, M., & Kristensen-Bach, P. (2001). Why women wear lipstick: Preliminary findings. In *Proceedings of the 2001 ANZMAC: Bridging Marketing Theory and Practice*, Massey University. https://www.researchgate.net/publication/49282703_Why_women_wear_lipstick_preliminary_findings. Accessed on April 12, 2024.

Parkkinen, S. (2022, July 25). How the convergence of beauty, health and wellness is impacting commerce. *Forbes*. https://www.forbes.com/sites/forbestechcouncil/2022/07/25/how-the-convergence-of-beauty-health-and-wellness-is-impacting-commerce/

Paterson, M. (2010). *Consumption and everyday life*. Routledge.

Phillips, H. (2023, September 21). These are the '90s supermodels who weren't featured in "The Super Models"—But should have been. *People*. https://people.com/90s-supermodels-not-featured-in-the-super-models-docuseries-7972297

Plante, R. F. (2016). Putting on makeup. In D. D. Waskul & P. Vannini (Eds.), *Popular culture as everyday life* (pp. 165–174). Routledge.

Pruit, J. C. (2016). Getting dressed. In D. D. Waskul & P. Vannini (Eds.), *Popular culture as everyday life* (pp. 155–163). Routledge.

Radner, H. (2011). *Neo-feminist cinema. Girly films, chick flicks and consumer culture*. Routledge & Taylor & Francis Group.

Rose, G. (2010). *Visual methodologies. An introduction to the interpretation of visual materials*. Sage.

Rubin, C. (2020, November 19). It's official: Every celeb now has a beauty line. *New York Times*. https://www.nytimes.com/2020/11/19/style/celebrities-its-official-every-celeb-now-has-a-beauty-line.html

Sault, N. (1994). The human mirror. In N. Sault (Ed.), *Many mirrors. Body image and social relations* (pp. 1–31). Rutgers University Press.

Schaffer, S. (2006). Reading our lips: The history of lipstick regulation in western seats of power [2006 third year paper]. *Digital Access to Scholarship at Harvard (DASH)*. https://dash.harvard.edu/handle/1/10018966

Scott, S. (2012). *Making sense of everyday life*. Polity.

Segran, E. (2016, September 19). *Kate moss is launching her own talent agency*. Fast Company. https://www.fastcompany.com/4019514/kate-moss-is-launching-her-own-talent-agency

Soley-Beltran, P. (2012). Performing dreams: A counter-history of models as glamour's embodiment. In J. Entwistle & E. Wissinger (Eds.), *Fashioning models. Image, text and industry* (pp. 97–115). Berg.

The Beauty Secrets Shop: All-Star Products As Seen in the Series. (n.d.). *Vogue*. https://www.vogue.com/beauty-secrets. Accessed on April 15, 2024.

Waskul, D. D. (2016). Going to the bathroom. In D. D. Waskul & P. Vannini (Eds.), *Popular culture as everyday life* (pp. 145–154). Routledge.

Waskul, D. D., & Vannini, P. (2016). Introduction: Popular culture as everyday life. In D. D. Waskul & P. Vannini (Eds.), *Popular culture as everyday life* (pp. 1–18). Routledge.

Weitz, R. (2001). Women and their hair: Seeking Power through resistance and accommodation. *Gender & Society*, *15*(5), 667–686. https://doi.org/10.1177/089124301015005003

Wissinger, E. (2009). Modelling consumption: Fashion modelling work in contemporary society. *Journal of Consumer Culture*, *9*(2), 273–296.

Wissinger, E. (2012). Modelling consumption: Fashion modelling work in contemporary society. In J. Entwistle & E. Wissinger (Eds.), *Fashioning models. Image, text and industry* (pp. 157–173). Berg.

Wolf, N. (2002). *The beauty myth: How images of beauty are used against women*. Perennial. An Imprint of Harper Collins Publishers.

Young, K. (2023, June 12). *Following Kate Moss: From model to wellness guru and entrepreneur*. Harper's Bazaar India. https://www.harpersbazaar.in/beauty/story/following-kate-moss-from-model-to-wellness-guru-and-entrepreneur-574769-2023-06-12

Index

Printed and bound by CPI Group (UK) Ltd, Croydon, CR0 4YY
15/09/2026
14962483-0006